Normative Theory and Business Ethics

New Perspectives in Business Ethics

A new series which explores both foundational and cutting-edge issues in business ethics

Series Editor

Denis G. Arnold, Surtman Distinguished Professor in Business Ethics, University of North Carolina at Charlotte

Description

Rowman & Littlefield's engaging new series, *New Perspectives in Business Ethics*, has one core rationale: to find leading experts as well as rising stars in business ethics studies to bring their new, fresh perspectives on topics and issues which include both foundational questions as well as cutting-edge problems which require ethical analysis and evaluation. Under the general editorship of Denis Arnold, the titles in this series encompass a broad range of topics with appropriate attention to both theoretical and practical dimensions.

Titles

Jeffery Smith, *Normative Theory and Business Ethics* (2009)

Chris MacDonald, *Business Ethics in Biotechnology: Theoretical Foundations and Practical Problems* (2010)

Normative Theory and Business Ethics

Edited by Jeffery Smith

ROWMAN & LITTLEFIELD PUBLISHERS, INC.
Lanham • Boulder • New York • Toronto • Plymouth, UK

ROWMAN & LITTLEFIELD PUBLISHERS, INC.

Published in the United States of America
by Rowman & Littlefield Publishers, Inc.
A wholly owned subsidiary of The Rowman & Littlefield Publishing Group, Inc.
4501 Forbes Boulevard, Suite 200, Lanham, Maryland 20706
www.rowmanlittlefield.com

Estover Road
Plymouth PL6 7PY
United Kingdom

British Library Cataloguing in Publication Information Available

Library of Congress Cataloging-in-Publication Data:
Normative theory and business ethics / edited by Jeffery D. Smith.
    p. cm. — (New perspectives in business ethics)
  Includes bibliographical references and index.
  ISBN-13: 978-0-7425-4842-8 (cloth : alk. paper)
  ISBN-10: 0-7425-4842-2 (cloth : alk. paper)
  ISBN-13: 978-0-7425-4841-1 (pbk. : alk. paper)
  ISBN-10: 0-7425-4841-4 (pbk. : alk. paper)
  eISBN-13: 978-0-7425-6468-6
  eISBN-10: 0-7425-6468-1
  1. Business ethics. 2. Normativity (Ethics) I. Smith, Jeffery D., 1971-
HF5387.N67 2009
174'.4--dc22   2008021875

Printed in the United States of America

∞™ The paper used in this publication meets the minimum requirements of American
National Standard for Information Sciences—Permanence of Paper for Printed Library
Materials, ANSI/NISO Z39.48-1992.

Contents

Foreword

Far too many essays in business ethics begin with an extended attack on the use of traditional normative theory as applied to problems in business ethics. I confess that I find such attacks extremely off-putting. My annoyance is intensified when the author is a philosopher or other humanist scholar rather than a person doing empirical research. I understand an empirical researcher who does not appreciate the contribution that normative disciplines make to the complete understanding of our complex world. That person needs to be more broadly educated. But I cannot understand those philosophers or other humanist scholars who denigrate theory. After all, if traditional moral and political philosophy cannot be fruitfully applied to problems in business, arguably the most influential institution in contemporary society, then normative ethics is in a crisis. The wisdom of the ages no longer applies. That seems counterintuitive on its face.

However, this skepticism about the utility of applying traditional moral and political theory to business problems is so widespread that relatively few normative business ethics articles have a normative theory as their theoretical base. There are of course some exceptions here. Tom Donaldson and Tom Dunfee have created integrated social contracts theory, the only "new" ethical theory to come out of theorizing about business ethics. The late Robert Solomon theorized from an Aristotelian perspective, although Bob never felt obliged to apply Aristotelian ethics completely or systematically. As a contrarian I have consistently and I believe fruitfully applied Kantian ethics to problems in business ethics.

The publication of *Normative Theory and Business Ethics* is a truly important event, because Jeffery Smith has skillfully and comprehensively edited a volume that makes normative theory front and center. He has put together a set of articles that does an outstanding job of showing the important logical and insightful role that moral and political theory can play in business ethics. This volume should rejuvenate the interest in and discussion of normative theory in business ethics writing. It should also encourage others to contribute to the development and application of theory in business ethics. Indeed several of the authors will, I am sure, make additional contributions to the development of a specific theory in future research. I am genuinely excited by the publication of this volume. Such a volume is long overdue and we are in Jefferey Smith's debt for publishing it.

THE APPLICATION OF ETHICAL THEORIES IN BUSINESS ETHICS

In this foreword I cannot comment in depth on each individual article, but I would like to say a few words about every article and comment on some articles in greater depth. It is interesting that several authors show the applicability of contemporary statements of traditional normative theorists to business ethics rather than simply apply the original theory. I generally applaud that move since it enables the traditional theories to be applied in all their richness. One example of this strategy is provided by Geoff Moore, who defends the Aristotelian position. What makes his essay unique is his attempt to show how MacIntyre's version of Aristotelianism can be applied to business. Moore shows how MacIntyre's concept of a practice and an institution can provide us with a better understanding of a virtuous business organization. Another example is Denis Arnold's use of Kant to ground a rights-based approach to business ethics. In his essay Arnold shows how a Kantian rights approach can help resolve ethical issues in international business ethics, where he uses Kantian rights theory to provide a list of minimum moral duties for any multinational corporation.

No volume on normative theory and business would be complete without a discussion of social contract theory, or contractarianism. Smith has included two articles with very different perspectives on the topic. The article by Ben Wempe critiques Donaldson and Dunfee's integrated social contracts theory (ISCT). Wempe proposes four design criteria for any contractarian business ethics and argues that traditional social contract theory does a better job of meeting those criteria than does integrated social contracts theory. Integrated social contracts theory has certainly come in for its share of criticism, but since it is the only original normative theory in contemporary business ethics, I would have liked to see an article that emphasized the contributions that the theory has made to the study of business ethics.

Although Donaldson and Dunfee's ISCT is the leading social contract theory in contemporary business ethics, the leading social contract theorist in the twentieth century was John Rawls. Nien-hê Hsieh shows how Rawls's theory can be fruitfully applied to business ethics. Hsieh's work is particularly important because Rawls's statement that his theory only applies to the basic structure of society has, I believe, impeded the use of Rawls as a theoretical foundation for certain normative conclusions in business ethics. Hsieh points out that other scholars have tried to circumvent the limitation of Rawls's theory to the basic structure of society. Although Hsieh is sympathetic to these approaches, his own work shows how Rawls can be meaningfully applied "in a manner keeping with Rawls's focus on the basic structure of society." Hsieh believes that the concepts of non-ideal theory, natural duties, as well as an understanding of the appropriate relationship between business and the legal and political institutions of society, will provide support for a number of important normative conclusions in business ethics. In addition to a cursory mention of how these features can be applied to several issues in business ethics, there is an extended discussion of the implication of these aspects of Rawls's theory on compensation as well as worker participation. Hsieh's article gives a good overview of the work of scholars using Rawls, as well as a good understanding of his own Rawlsian approach. Of course, the features of Rawls's theory that Hsieh uses are not those most related to the contractarian portion of Rawls's theory, so my discussion of Hsieh's Rawls with contractarianism may be a bit off the mark.

Rawls is surely in the contractarian tradition, but he was also heavily influenced by Kant. The continental philosopher Jürgen Habermas is often overlooked by business ethicists, even by those who are strongly influenced by other continental philosophers. Readers will immediately notice that Habermas is also influenced by Kant and features of his normative theory are comparable to those of Rawls's theory of justice. Editor Jeffery Smith provides an excellent overview of Habermas's normative theory, which has two focal points—a theory of communication action that provides universal norms for cooperative behavior and a theory of discourse for achieving agreement on such norms or for rediscovering them when they break down. Smith then applies Habermas's normative theory to business ethics at two levels. At the institutional level, Smith points out that when business organizations are embedded within a democratically organized political society they have responsibilities to respect and uphold the universal norms necessary for the process of democratic law formation. At the organizational level, managerial discretion needs to be legitimized. Smith describes how this is to be done. Readers familiar with traditional stakeholder theory and Kantian approaches to the firm will see many similarities between a Habermasian approach and stakeholder or Kantian theories.

NONTHEORETICAL OR ANTITHEORETICAL APPROACHES

Five of the authors in this volume have argued for the application of an ethical theory as traditionally understood to business. However, many useful normative discussions in business ethics take place without the application of theory. For some writers, theory has a limited use or no use at all. This volume contains a number of articles that limit or deemphasize theory in certain ways. This provides a useful balance to the articles that show how traditional ethical theories can be applied to issues in business ethics.

Jeffrey Moriarty focuses on the concept of desert and its application to business ethics. Moriarty recognizes a role for traditional theory, since he gives both a Kantian and a consequentialist justification for desert. However, he chooses to emphasize desert rather than one of the moral theories when making normative judgments about two important issues in business ethics. In this insightful article Moriarty operates from a certain conceptual understanding of desert and then asks whether the arguments against desert in political philosophy apply with equal force against the use of desert in business ethics, specifically with respect to jobs and wages. He argues that these arguments against the use of desert in business ethics are not decisive. Moriarty concludes by showing that if desert were taken as the main criterion in hiring and firing as well as in wage determination, we might depart far from current practice in these areas. For example, there might need to be extensive preferential hiring for those who had disadvantageous backgrounds over which they had no control.

Mitchell Haney argues that "business ethicists should continue their trend away from modern ethical theory and toward various proposals endorsed by the antitheorists in ethics." Haney points out that doubts about ethical theory go back at least a half century. Haney builds his argument by setting out the conditions that an ethical theory is supposed to meet—conditions he refers to collectively as "generalism." I am not terribly surprised that traditional theories like deontology or utilitarianism do not meet Haney's rather stringent tests. To show how stringent the tests are, Haney argues that no form of pluralism meets the tests either. The evidence that the use of traditional and pluralistic theories in business ethics does not meet the tests rests on one very unconvincing counterexample—the shift in American values from saving to a credit mentality caused by comedies and advertising on the then-1950s new medium of television. As one who was alive in the 1950s, I can tell you that Haney vastly overestimates the extent and power of television in that time. In addition, his claim that advertising is coercive is a controversial view that has been much discussed in business ethics. However, these are minor points. He also claims that a change in values would not be possible under the goal of generalism and thus traditional theory cannot succeed. But surely that is false. If the facts about the world change, our ethical theories must adapt. The birth control pill changed traditional theoretical arguments regarding sexual morality in the 1960s. Surely traditional ethical theories could accommodate the changes required by post–World War II economic conditions.

Moreover, traditional ethical theories like Kantianism or virtue ethics need to carry with them an interpretation of central moral notions like desert, fairness, and conflict of interest. Traditional theories function at a very abstract level. They get additional power when they are integrated with central moral concepts like desert, fairness, and transparency. When enriched in this way, they are most useful in addressing issues in business ethics, as can be seen both by several of the articles in this volume and in the scholarly literature of business ethics over the past thirty-plus years. But what if we grant Haney his point? If neither the traditional theories nor the pluralistic theories help us in business ethics, than how are we to make decisions that require moral choice or justify the choices that we make? Haney leaves us adrift here, and ironically the failure of his antitheoretical argument helps us see why theory when integrated with other ethical concepts is useful in business ethics and can remain important in showing us a way to make ethical decisions.

Another way to limit the scope of theory is to limit the scope of business. This is the strategy of Alexei Marcoux, who argues that we should understand business as an "exchange-transaction-executing practice." Understood in this way, Marcoux focuses on ethical issues that arise in business so characterized, and these are important questions indeed. However, I am less convinced that business need be characterized in this limited way; I would allow for a much larger number of legitimate questions and thus an expanded role for theory as this larger range of questions is addressed.

Finally, Christopher Michaelson points out that in addition to moral values or ethical values, there are also aesthetic values and, using two vivid examples, these aesthetic values are both important in business and can limit the applicability of ethical values. By implication, if Michaelson is correct, aesthetic theory could limit the applicability of a traditional ethical theory in the analysis of an issue in business ethics.

Of course, no volume covers everything. We are missing a good analysis of the application of utilitarian moral theory, a strong pragmatist approach, and as previously mentioned, an article documenting the useful application of integrated social contracts theory. Also I think it important to note that Smith is correct not to include stakeholder theory as one of the normative ethical theories. Contrary to Haney, the stakeholder theory is not an ethical theory but rather a theory of management—a theory of management that can be justified by a multitude of ethical theories or can be expressed by a number of narratives, as Freeman and many of his students now frame the theory. We have many good articles and books on applying a stakeholder theory of management. I am delighted that we have a volume that focuses on the application of ethical theories to the making of normative judgments about ethical issues in business. However, this volume should be just the start of a continuing line of research. Traditional ethical theory still has much to offer both scholars of business ethics and managers of business organizations.

Norman E. Bowie
University of Minnesota

Acknowledgments

During the last two years there have been a number of people and institutions that have enabled the completion of this collection. I owe the University of Redlands School of Business and the Banta Center for Business, Ethics and Society a debt of gratitude for offering consistent financial support. These resources provided ample opportunity to complete the research, writing, and editing associated with each chapter. I also need to recognize the support offered by the Banta Center's administrative specialist, Joanie James, and her assistants, Susan Griffin and Sharon Audelo, for their work directly and indirectly related to the completion of this volume. Their efforts were always appreciated.

In 2008 I was visiting professor in the Department of Philosophy at the Universiteit van Tilburg in the Netherlands. During this time I put the finishing touches on this collection, in the midst of my day-to-day activities. The business ethics faculty there, including Wim Dubbink, Bert van de Ven, and Johan Graafland, need to be thanked for their collegiality and support during this time. The financial and administrative support offered in Tilburg was also instrumental in the timely completion of this book.

It goes without saying that this collection would not be possible but for the diligent work of each of the contributors. Each of them has invested a substantial amount of time in making this volume what it is today. They each deserve recognition. It was a pleasure to be able to work with such a distinguished group of young scholars.

Finally, on a personal note, there were inevitably countless moments in which the support of my wife, Rita, was important in providing not simply extra time in front of the computer, but also motivation. As always, I thank her for her encouragement.

Introduction

Past and Present: The Role of Normative Theory in Business

Jeffery Smith, University of Redlands

Over the last twenty-five years, philosophers have applied a broad range of normative moral and political theories to analyze ethical problems in business life. The following contributions have a relatively simple goal: to reflect upon and critically examine the relevance of this past work and engage the reader with new theoretical insights. This simple goal, however, belies the complexity involved in each individual exploration. The philosophical terrain covered here is subtle and diverse. It represents a rich and growing field of inquiry, motivated by underlying philosophical interests and the practical realities of business as the dominant social institution of our time.

These philosophical interests are not limited only to the substantive intellectual traditions discussed in this volume's essays. Although the contributors give due consideration to those traditions, including Aristotelian, Kantian, contractarian, and Rawlsian, there are important insights gained from the methodological comparisons that naturally follow from a survey of the work assembled within the following pages. It is tempting to think of these insights as metatheoretical in nature, but I will not venture into using such terminology. It is sufficient to simply say that there are new lessons to be learned from the very *process* of developing normative theory for business.

It is also important to note that normative theory in business has not remained static over the past three decades. Indeed, it cannot remain static. Like developments in moral and political theory, as well as those in management and organizational studies, normative theory in the field of business ethics has grown more diverse. This diversity is represented here. This volume includes discussions that feature explorations of normative economics, critical social theory, pragmatism, aesthetic theory, and even so-called anti-theory. This design was intentional. It represents the extent to which the discipline of business

1

ethics has strengthened its presence within the academy and has the potential to be an exemplar of an interdisciplinary field grounded in philosophical inquiry.

Before turning my attention toward the particular contributions of each of the following essays, I will tackle two important issues related to the state of normative theorizing in business ethics. First, it is important to understand what is distinct about normative moral and political theory and its relation to business. Business studies in general and business ethics in particular have greatly benefited from the methodological insights of various disciplines grounded in the social sciences; however, while complementary in many respects, normative theory and social science have distinct agendas. I aim to clarify these agendas without calling into question the interdisciplinary nature of business ethics. Second, normative theory is, first and foremost, an endeavor with limitations—some of which are explicit and others implicit. I will clarify these limitations with an eye toward forestalling objections regarding the applicability of normative theory to questions in business ethics.

1. NORMATIVE AND EMPIRICAL QUESTIONS IN BUSINESS ETHICS

It is extremely fashionable today to extol the virtues of interdisciplinary inquiry. On the one hand, it is easy to understand why this is the case. Complex intellectual problems can be analyzed using methods from an array of disciplines. The fullest account of these problems would naturally be uncovered through an inclusion of many disciplinary perspectives. On the other hand, disciplinary differences often lead to practical methodological problems. The purposes, questions, and techniques of different disciplines make it difficult to communicate across disciplinary boundaries. Worse yet, it is not always clear that academics across disciplines are willing (or able) to invest the time necessary to integrate the significance of the work of their colleagues.

These two considerations remain relevant to the field of business ethics. Normative business ethicists ask questions and construct theories that focus our attention on *ideals* that inform *prescriptions* for how business ought to be organized. How can the ends of justice be served by the operation of businesses in the free market? How should business managers make operational decisions? For whom is the business firm to be managed? Can the rights of shareholders be adequately protected under the prevailing forms of corporate governance in the United States? These questions stand in contrast to the efforts of business disciplines that focus on describing the contours of organizational life in business so as to *explain* and *predict* activities within and between firms. Is employee morale enhanced through improved benefits packages? How will customers respond to the implementation of new labor standards within the supply chain? How do executive stock options impact share prices over the long term? Research within business ethics remains divided between academics who seek to conceptualize how businesses ought to be managed and governed, and those who seek to understand the nuances of why businesses operate the way they do.

An example will serve to illustrate this basic point. Within the last ten years there has been a push, by both practitioners and academics, to think more systematically about the relationship between the social and environmental performance of a company and its financial strength. This focus on the so-called triple bottom line has proved to be one of the most significant trends in business management within recent memory. Analyses of the connection between social, environmental, and economic performance abound, including meta-analytical work that has attempted to find generalizable connections between corporate social performance and corporate financial performance.[1] It strongly suggests that managerial practices emphasizing transparency, honesty, community involvement, environmental awareness, and other "socially responsible" activities tend to reap additional financial benefits.

Complexities of this research aside, the social scientific interest in the connection between social and financial performance is one case where the interests of normative and descriptive business ethics are distinct. Research that establishes a positive relationship between social and financial performance remains agnostic on a number of related normative questions. Are so-called social responsibilities actually responsibilities and, if so, what are the grounds for this inference? Do business firms have an obligation to minimize environmental impact even when it is not legally required? If not, why? More directly, do financial motives for socially responsible management practices diminish the moral worth of these practices? It would obviously be unfair to expect that all research, in all domains, should shoulder the burden of addressing the entire range of issues related to (in this case) corporate social responsibility; however, it is also important to recognize the normative limitations of descriptive research. The significance of descriptive research is often connected to certain normative assumptions about the purposes, roles, and responsibilities of business. Many of these assumptions are addressed systematically through normative inquiry that asks how we ground these claims in the first place.

At the same time, descriptive research in the field of business ethics remains an important source of information for normative theorists to consider. This is what keeps normative theory in business squarely anchored in the methods of *applied* ethics. It would be problematic, for instance, for a normative theory that aims to justify workplace democracy to ignore empirical research that employees have a strong preference to voluntarily give up rights to participation. Similarly, theoretical calls to conceive of business organizations as purposive, moral communities (as some authors do in this volume) need to take account of social scientific research that indicates that individuals conceive of business relationships in largely strategic or instrumental terms. So while we should be careful not to blur the lines between normative and social scientific methodologies, normative theorists would be foolish not to recognize the countless ways in which normative theories rely upon claims about the nature of business practice itself. This is no more evident than in the development of so-called stakeholder theory. Advocates of this approach have recognized that the justification of the normative foundation of stakeholder theory—i.e., the idea that business organizations ought to be managed for *all* corporate constituencies and not simply equity investors—is something that can be strengthened or weakened with evidence regarding the plausibility, effectiveness, and acceptability of actual stakeholder management practices.[2]

The challenge, then, is to walk a fine line between the interdisciplinary methods of business ethics and the basic recognition that normative theory construction in business is inquiry informed by practice. We must protect the philosophical home of normative theory without losing sight of the practical realities of how businesses operate within the market, how their participants understand their roles and identities, how business activities succeed in generating wealth, and most importantly, what it takes for business managers to implement the principles prescribed by normative theory. This idea will naturally be thought of as a call to keep normative business ethics practically useful to those who regulate or manage actual business firms. This is indeed one important aspect of my message; however, lest business practitioners and management academics lose sight of the significance of philosophical inquiry, I want to also underscore that normative theories cannot be evaluated simply on the basis of whether they can be useful in guiding managerial practice. There are moments when practices need adjustment in light of new philosophical insights. The fit of theory and practice can and should be measured in each direction.

2. DISTINCTIVE FEATURES OF NORMATIVE THEORY IN BUSINESS ETHICS

Normative ethics deals with substantive issues regarding moral values, principles, notions of well-being, and character.[3] There are schools of thought that approach each of these issues in distinct ways. Virtue ethicists take questions related to human well-being as basic and move to identify forms of conduct that reflect the qualities of a good life. Contemporary consequentialists arguably take a different route; although they are also interested in identifying some basic feature that defines human welfare, their emphasis is on the boundaries of action rather than (primarily) character. So-called deontological theories share many things in common with both virtue ethicists and consequentialists. At the same time, however, it is fair to say that deontologists share a core interest in identifying notions of what is right for human conduct independently of substantive conceptions of the good life.

Drawing these generalizations is notoriously dangerous. Business ethics texts are replete with characterizations of these and other theoretical approaches that do a great disservice to the intellectual traditions from which they originate. Contrary to popular thought, for instance, supposedly deontological Kantian moral theorists have discussed at great length the importance of virtues, conceptions of the good, and most notably, the role of judgment in the application of principles.[4] Some virtue theorists, while undeniably concerned with questions of well-being, argue that they need not be resistant to generalizable action-guiding principles, similar to those offered by deontological theorists. Consequentialists of various stripes have dealt systematically with the objection that there appear to be a plurality of different moral values that are "incommensurable" and hence resistant to some general assessment of what is the greatest good for the greatest number.[5] It should therefore not be surprising that normative theorizing in the field of business ethics has drawn heavily upon each of these three broad approaches to normative ethical theory.

Work in political philosophy, like normative ethics, has also proved important to the development of normative theory in business. Stakeholder theorists such as Edward Freeman and William Evan have developed principles for the management of stakeholder interests through an application of the political theory of John Rawls.[6] In this work, there is a parallel drawn between the maintenance of just social cooperation at the level of the "basic structure of society" and the maintenance of cooperation within business organizations. Principles designed by Rawls to preserve fairness at the level of society's basic political and economic institutions find analogues at the level of the organization for Freeman and Evan. The social contract tradition is another interesting case of political philosophy's influence on normative business ethics. Within the history of modern Western thought, the social contract has been used to justify not only the authority of the state, but proper forms of government that exercise such authority. Business ethicists interested in thinking along similar lines have developed two ways of applying the social contract argument to business: one that conceives of business organizations as having operational legitimacy in virtue of following norms specified in idealized contracts between stakeholder groups and one that conceives of the institution of business as something having entitlements and responsibilities based upon norms set forth in contracts formed between citizens and the state.

Whether they are built from the emergent traditions of normative ethics or political philosophy, the use of normative theories in business is as diverse as the philosophical traditions upon which they are built. There are, however, some common features that normative theories in business share in virtue of focusing on business as a common object of concern. It is worth pausing for a moment to review these features.

First, normative theory in business has had to come to grips with the morally ambiguous nature of the free market. Businesses and their agents act within a (historically) unique sphere in life where the norms of the market have been socially endorsed. At the same time, however, the norms of the market often conflict with norms that govern our lives as citizens, family members, or participants in other nonmarket associations. Markets operate by commodifying certain goods that are, in principle, interchangeable with other goods through pricing and the exchange of money. Markets assume egoistic, mutually disinterested motives on the part of individual actors. They place emphasis on the ability of actors to freely exit from nonpreferential transactions in order to pursue other, more preferable ones. Markets also presuppose a system of private property rights whereby one person's possession of a good is rival and therefore excludes possession by others.[7] Competition between individuals for the exchange of goods and services is thought to result in superior levels of preference satisfaction and wealth among communities that adopt markets for production and distribution. All of these norms present distinctive challenges.

Businesses are the organizational manifestation of these norms; they coordinate the activities of many individuals for the sake of producing goods and services that can be exchanged so as to produce wealth and satisfy preferences. Normative theory in business thus needs to be built around the norms of the market, because the market is the institutional home of business. This means that normative theory in business is essentially involved in the interpretation of the meaning, significance, and appropriate limits (if any) of markets and the ways in which businesses can balance the norms of the market with other nonmarket expectations.

Second, normative theory in business (either explicitly or implicitly) addresses a very basic issue: Is business ethics an organizational endeavor, focusing on the internal development of principles for management, or is it an institutional endeavor, focusing on how political and economic institutions should be arranged so as to produce more just outcomes in the operation of the market? A cursory examination of the themes addressed in this volume will show that the view of normative business ethicists is not uniform. Some clearly opt for one approach over the other, while others take the stand that business ethics is properly conceived of as both an organizational and institutional effort. Those business ethicists who argue for greater separation between the markets, the state, and other associations in civil society tend to be the same theorists who opt for an organizational focus; business ethicists focusing on institutional design resist the temptation to draw comparable divisions. Many of these differences will come to light in the chapters that follow.

A third and final feature of normative theory in business is its degree of removal from the day-to-day realities of business practice. It is reasonable to expect normative theory to offer principles and frameworks that can reasonably be internalized and used by business managers and regulators, given the presumptive importance of free markets. The challenge for normative theory in this regard is relatively straightforward: Normative theories are necessarily *abstracted* from many features of actual business practice.[8] This challenge plays out on many fronts. The motives and attitudes of individuals in business (including investors, managers, and employees) are not oriented toward the ends that normative theory deems important. There are inevitable costs associated with behavior prescribed by normative theories. Standards of success in business often conflict with standards of morality and justice.[9] Normative theory is in the uncomfortable position of having to take account of such realities while prescribing organizational and institutional solutions that may conflict with the ways in which business is practiced.

The fact that normative theory is abstract may therefore seem like an immediate problem. I take an alternative view. Abstracting ourselves from the conventional norms of business practice is exactly the sort of endeavor that helps us question whether what is done in business ought to be changed. Bracketing the assumptions behind the operation of business also has the helpful effect of eliminating bias and prejudice in the moral assessment of it. It would indeed be a misguided task to think systematically about the moral boundaries of business with the attitudes of those who benefit from, or have a vested interest in, the current constitution of the market. There is a very fine line between assuring that normative theory has relevance to actual practice and deferring to the conventions of practice without good reason. This is precisely the reason why normative theory should strive to suspend popularly held convictions about the role of management, the overall purpose of business, or the social benefits of profit-seeking, in order to reconstruct such convictions with philosophically credible arguments. Only then will normative theory have the hope of being well grounded as well as practically relevant.

The process of abstracting ourselves from business practice involves setting aside assumptions and conventional norms in order to reduce bias. It also
involves setting aside information that is less pertinent to developing broad-
based principles and frameworks for business. Some have referred to this as
idealization or the use of *ideal* assumptions in normative theory. Consider a
point taken up by Nien-hê Hsieh in chapter 5. There he notes that John
Rawls's theory of justice is designed to apply to a "well-ordered" society—
i.e., a society where each citizen understands what justice entails and has a
developed set of convictions to support just social arrangements. Obviously,
this assumption has little connection to actual societies, where motives are
imperfect and there is disagreement over what justice entails. The purpose of
this assumption, however, is to focus our attention on the content of justice
rather than on its effective implementation in the non-ideal world. Implementing justice is, to be sure, an important task; however, this is an issue well
left to separate consideration. Similarly, in the case of business, readers will
get the distinct sense that the authors assembled in this volume have made an
array of idealizing assumptions regarding the motives of individuals, the relationships between business constituencies within civil society, and the economic realities of the market. Although these assumptions certainly require
attention when academics begin to build bridges between normative theory
and business practice, they are not inherently problematic. They simply aid
the process of uncovering the normative core of our beliefs regarding the just
operation of business.

These three features of normative theory in business—its perspective on
the market, its organizational and institutional foci, and its abstraction from
actual business practice—manifest themselves in different ways in the following essays. It is therefore fitting to preview the diversity assembled in this
volume with an eye toward how each author builds upon theoretical work of
the recent past.

3. NORMATIVE THEORY: PAST AND PRESENT

This volume begins in chapter 1 with an essay designed to limit the very application of normative theory in business. In "Business-Focused Business
Ethics," Alexei Marcoux deliberately positions himself in opposition to the
dominant trends in normative business ethics. Drawing upon work in other areas of applied ethics—in particular, medical and legal ethics—Marcoux argues that business ethics should be properly understood as a "practice-based"
effort that requires an intimate understanding of the defining features of business. The feature that Marcoux draws our attention to is the transactional na-

ture of business; specifically, business is defined by *self-sustaining transactions* between individuals or organizations. Profit seeking is the natural mechanism through which transactions become self sustaining. Marcoux draws the conclusion that business ethics should be narrowly conceived of as a discipline that examines the ethical requirements of profit-seeking transactions between individuals and organizations.

The limited space that Marcoux affords normative inquiry in business will be much too confining for some theorists. He explicitly contrasts his methodological recommendations with some dominant lines of thinking within the field. He is particularly critical of approaches that have appropriated political philosophy for use in business ethics. He singles out the work of stakeholder theory and, more recently, the arguments of Jeffrey Moriarty as examples of authors who have mistakenly conceived of business ethics as an effort to reduce ethical responsibilities in business to responsibilities of distributive justice—i.e., responsibilities for carrying out decisions, developing governance strategies, and adopting operational policies that justly balance the entitlements of an array of individuals and groups. He interprets this "firm-state analogy" as problematic because it neglects that fact that business ethics is centrally about the *activity* of business, not the *venue* of business. Businesses are voluntary associations predicated on individual contracting; they are not trustees of the welfare of a citizenry.

Marcoux's discussion is informative on a number of levels, the most important of which is that business ethics is thought to be exclusively transactional in nature. The scope of ethical inquiry in business, thus, is necessarily limited to questions of pricing, contract negotiation, and settlement. Marcoux's discussion also complicates the distinction I raise above between organizational and institutional foci in business ethics. On the one hand, focusing on the activity of business suggests an organizational focus. Business ethicists should concentrate their attention on the nature of transactions within and between organizations. On the other hand, there is nothing in Marcoux's discussion that would rule out institutional responses to unethical transacting. Indeed, we might naturally expect that large-scale economic and legal institutions are ideally suited to set the terms (and limits) of profit-seeking transactions. The recommendations made by Marcoux in the closing pages of his essay suggest that institutions external to business firms should play a strong role in managing problems related to price discrimination, fraud, and competition.

In the end, Marcoux's thought-provoking discussion challenges business ethicists who regard the ethical management of business firms as an effort to incorporate a broad range of ethical considerations, not simply those related to pricing and information disclosure. Geoff Moore's contribution in chapter

2, "Virtue Ethics and Business Organizations," begins to map out a more complicated arrangement of business as both an organization, situated within communities and between individuals, and an institution, projecting the broad-based values that integrate activities of business and nonbusiness life. In contrast to Marcoux, Moore stresses that while business is indeed a practice, it is a practice that remains embedded within a diverse range of expectations that are not exclusive to business life. This picture is developed largely within an Aristotelian framework that receives inspiration from the work of contemporary virtue ethicist Alasdair MacIntyre.

Moore's chapter is valuable in two important ways. First, his efforts to situate his work within recent literature provides a nice set of comparisons with the seminal work of Robert Solomon and Daryl Koehn, two scholars that have paved the way for a serious consideration of virtue ethics in business.[10] Although his comments are certainly friendly in spirit, Moore's position displays a certain level of sophistication that builds upon the foundation built by Solomon and Koehn. Second, Moore distinctively notes that it is unclear how the psychological tensions between the attitudes of participants within business and the attitudes of a virtuous person can be resolved within the framework of virtue ethics. His resolution to this tension is found in a novel contrast between business as a practice and business as an institution. In his words, institutions "house" practices; in the case of business, business practice demarcates "internal" goods related to the excellences of the craft or enterprise in which a business is engaged. Business, however, is also partly an institution, in that it is oriented toward "external" goods that promote the operation of the practice. While such external goods—e.g., wealth, power, and status—are instrumentally necessary to sustain business, they generate motives and attitudes that conflict with the distinctive virtues of business practice. The challenge thus is to reorient business as an institution to balance external goods with the internal goods of business as a practice. Moore provides a number of comments designed to explain how this balance can be found.

Denis Arnold's essay in chapter 3, "The Human Rights Obligations of Multinational Corporations," also draws our attention to the need to build upon important scholarship within the field of business ethics. In this case, Arnold develops a neo-Kantian approach to human rights and tests these theoretical insights against the backdrop of problems within international business. Immanuel Kant famously wrote that individuals ought not treat others merely as a means to our private ends, but that we should strive to treat others as ends in themselves, beyond price and having incomparable worth in virtue of their rational capacities.[11] Arnold leverages this starting point to justify not only the existence of basic moral entitlements to freedom, but also of other entitlements that form the basis of human dignity. Multinational corporations (MNCs) bear special responsibilities to protect these entitlements, both from direct infringement and from indirect infringements that occur through cooperative activities with suppliers and foreign governments. Arnold concludes with a topical section exploring the extent to which individual claims to human rights are a distinctively Western notion. This essay serves as a nice illustration of the ways in which normative theorizing in business can remain abstracted from the actual world of multinational business while still providing practical direction to ethically inclined management.

The next four chapters deal with the role of political philosophy in business ethics, broadly construed. Ben Wempe argues in chapter 4, "Contractarian Business Ethics Today," that the social contract in political theory has been used in controversial ways by business ethicists. In response, he outlines what he takes to be the central features of any future contractarian business ethics (CBE) that understands both the nature of business as well as the normative core of the social contract tradition.

The main target of Wempe's criticism is the integrative social contracts theory (ISCT) put forth by Thomas Donaldson and Thomas Dunfee.[12] Donaldson and Dunfee have diligently argued that managerial responsibilities in business stem not only from actual "micro" social contracts between local communities and the firms that they host, but also hypothetical "macro" social contracts between citizens of would-be societies with business actors. In most cases, Donaldson and Dunfee seem comfortable to allow that micro social contracts establish suitable norms for management that regulate and guide operational decisions. They are aware, however, that micro social contracts may conflict with one another or violate more general moral principles that govern social relationships no matter what the particular micro social contract a business has entered into. This prompts them to posit the existence of principles that result from the procedural, structural, and substantive norms that structure the macro social contract. Donaldson and Dunfee refer to these principles as *hypernorms*. Wempe's concern is that this effort fails to provide the practical guidance that Donaldson and Dunfee promise; more seriously, their work runs afoul of some key methodological constraints for CBE. Wempe's constraints are worth serious consideration, especially those that focus our attention on the historical aims of social contract theory. I will leave it to the reader to judge whether Wempe's demands are reasonable or not, given the history behind the social contract and the practical aims of business ethicists.

In chapter 5, Nien-hê Hsieh builds upon Wempe's discussion by examining the extent to which the political theory of John Rawls provides avenues of application to business beyond his use of the social contract. Hsieh's essay, "The Normative Study of Business Organizations: A Rawlsian Approach," begins with a modest concession: namely, that it is indeed problematic to automatically apply Rawls's theory of justice to life within business firms because he is very clear that his theory is intended to order the "basic structure of society."[13] Hsieh is cautious and offers a reasonable reply to this problem. Contrary to Marcoux, as well as to other critics of the use of political philosophy in business ethics, Hsieh maintains that there is precedent within Rawls's own thinking to apply features of his theory of justice to the management of business firms.[14] This is true even without thinking, per Marcoux, that the application of political philosophy to business necessarily involves a close analogy between business firms and states.

There are four ways in which Hsieh approaches the application of Rawls. First, drawing upon work in the *Law of Peoples*, he maintains that Rawls's theory of justice provides avenues for businesses to serve as agents of justice when we recognize that not all societies are well ordered.[15] When businesses operate within "burdened societies," for example, Hsieh maintains that MNCs have a responsibility to render assistance, as a condition of their operation. This requires neither the assumption that firms are analogous to states, nor the assumption that principles of justice apply to anything other than the basic structure of society. Second, Hsieh argues that it is perfectly compatible with Rawlsian theory to maintain that businesses have natural duties "to further justice," apart from obligations that may result from the ordering of society's basic economic and political institutions. Third, Hsieh ventures from received interpretations of Rawls to argue that standards of justice apply not simply to how society's dominant institutions are organized, but also to the "choices that individuals make within the basic structure." This opens the door for an examination of firm-level responsibilities that follow from the demands of justice. Finally, Hsieh incorporates literature from democratic theory to argue that it is empirically plausible, and theoretically justified, to maintain that Rawls's principles of justice may require consideration of how productive property is owned and controlled. This suggestion, again, underscores Hsieh's basic view that justice with regard to broad-based political and economic arrangements is not easily separable from the responsibilities of businesses and their agents. Normative theory in business, thus, is not purely an institutional or organizational endeavor. It remains both.

In chapter 6, "Deserving Jobs, Deserving Wages," Jeffrey Moriarty creatively extends Hsieh's discussion of distributive justice within business to address a concept that has received virtually no attention by normative business ethicists: desert. Since Rawls's *A Theory of Justice*, desert, or deservingness, has had little influence on normative moral and political theory. Moriarty believes that this is unfortunate. First, many of the standard objections related to the use and application of desert can be reasonably dealt with by clarifying the basis upon which individuals deserve goods derived from social cooperation. Second, there are important problems in business ethics, most notably problems related to hiring and compensation (what Moriarty refers to job and wage justice, respectively) that can be effectively addressed once a suitable concept of desert has been offered. Moriarty's discussion is subtle and complicated in places; it is a fine example of the extent to which normative conceptual analysis can cast rehearsed problems in a new light. It also serves as another case in which the methods of political philosophy are extended beyond the normative analysis of institutions to include a normative analysis of commercial relationships within business firms.

In chapter 7, I try to further the role of normative political theory in business by examining the implications of Jürgen Habermas's critical social theory. This essay, titled "Institutions and Organizations: Communicative Ethics and Business," begins with an examination of communicative (or discourse) ethics and its relation to Habermas's broader theory of democracy. Like Rawls, Habermas begins with the notion that principles of justice governing the arrangement and organization of society's basic institutions ought to reflect a kind of consensus. Unlike Rawls, however, Habermas maintains that it is not the role of the normative theorist to identify the substantive content of these principles; rather, such principles should reflect the considered judgments of individuals engaged in institutionalized discourse. This restores what Habermas refers to as *communicative action*, or social action oriented toward mutual understanding. In modern, pluralist societies, communicative action is essential to maintain ongoing forms of cooperation between individuals with different conceptions of the good life.

Discourse is something that can occur in multiple locations and at multiple times within the formal political institutions of society. I extend Habermas's line of thinking to argue that discourse is also something that can occur within the informal associations of civil society, including those within the economy. Businesses play an important role in this regard. They have responsibilities to support discursive interactions within society's formal political institutions because, like Hsieh, I maintain that businesses have duties to support just social arrangements.

I also argue that managers and directors have responsibilities to foster discourse *within* business organizations, for two reasons. First, businesses organizations are explicitly designed under the law to exercise discretion on matters related to the production and distribution of public goods. Since such discretion presupposes the exercise of authority, it stands to reason that managerial authority stands in need of legitimation, from the moral point of view. To preserve the greatest level of managerial discretion possible, I argue that the legitimate exercise of managerial authority should be largely procedural in nature, calling for management to implement practices that encourage the ongoing consideration and review of the interests of each stakeholder group. The moral responsibilities of managers are therefore tied to promoting critical dialogue and discursive interaction with affected stakeholder groups. Second, the social activity of business is integral to fostering effective communicative action throughout modern society, both in other informal associations and within formal political institutions. Stakeholder interactions create opportunities for individual citizens to problematize laws and policies as well as to gain additional intellectual insight into the reasons that support existing political and economic arrangements. Critical dialogic interactions between stakeholders, in short, are instrumental in promoting the development of a well-informed citizenry that can examine the terms of social cooperation at all levels of society.

This volume concludes with two contributions that are truly unique in the business ethics literature, in part because they resist the received methods of normative theory and its application. Chapter 8, titled "On the Need for Theory in Business Ethics" and written by Mitchell Haney, maintains that the project of normative theory in business suffers from a basic problem; specifically, he argues that normative theory's efforts to prescribe generalizable principles is theoretically objectionable and deliberatively misguided. On the one hand, marshalling lines of argument from so-called moral particularists, Haney maintains that the moral reasons supporting proposed principles do not function as consistent constraints on behavior.[16] Moral reasons function differently in different decision contexts and, as such, principles function as blunt rules of thumb, rather than generalizations that can be prima facie valid. On the other hand, even if we concede that principles may be generally true, Haney argues that principles do little, if any, work in helping us deliberate about what we ought to do in particular, complicated circumstances. His line of criticism here receives inspiration from a number of sources, including Aristotle and recent pragmatism. Indeed, there are parallels to be drawn with the remarks made by Moore at the beginning of chapter 2.

Chapter 9 also represents a perspective that is normally left out of discussions within business ethics. Christopher Michaelson's "Values and Capitalism" explores the extent to which aesthetic values impact our moral assessment of business life. It is not always clear that our objections to business activities, or business actors, are always exclusively ethical in nature. Businesses perpetuate economic measures of success that crowd out considerations of the good life. The latter are, for Michaelson, matters that sometimes pertain to style and beauty, rather than merely moral obligation. He profiles two interesting cases to illustrate his point: the construction and environmental impact of the Three Gorges Dam in China and the life of Paul Gauguin and the sale of his art. Each of these cases is designed to exemplify how there is an appropriate place for questions of beauty and *forms* of living that purely ethical or economic measures of value fail to capture. This is not to say that aesthetic and ethical value are not related in interesting ways. It is also not to say that ethical valuations do not rely on economic assessments in certain spheres of life. Rather, Michaelson argues for a modest, yet important, point: How we value commercial activity and its effects on the world around us cannot be separated from aesthetic considerations.

This preview should give the reader a sense of the diversity assembled within this volume. It is an attempt to bring together a number of perspectives on one theme. Each contribution provides unique insight into the process of theorizing about business and how (if at all) philosophers can link moral and political theory with scholarship in business.

NOTES

1. Marc Orlitzky, Frank Schmidt, and Sara Rynes, "Corporate Social and Financial Performance: A Meta-analysis," *Organization Studies* 24, no. 3 (2003): 403–41.

2. John Boatright, "What's Wrong—and What's Right—with Stakeholder Theory," *Journal of Private Enterprise* 21, no. 2 (2006): 106–30. For a discussion of the link between the theoretical and practical commitments of stakeholder theory, see Thomas Jones and Andrew Wicks, "Convergent Stakeholder Theory," *Academy of Management Review* 24, no. 2 (1999): 206–21, and Thomas Jones, "Instrumental Stakeholder Theory: A Synthesis of Ethics and Economics," *Academy of Management Review* 20, no. 2 (1995): 404–37. A detailed overview of the state of stakeholder managerial practice can be found in Jorg Andriof, Sandra Waddock, Bryan Husted, and Sutherland Rahman, eds., *Unfolding Stakeholder Thinking*, vol. 2, *Relationships, Communication, Reporting, and Performance* (Sheffield, UK: Greenleaf, 2003).

3. Shelly Kagan, *Normative Ethics* (Boulder, Colo.: Westview, 1997).

4. Onora O'Neill, *Towards Justice and Virtue: A Constructive Account of Practical Reasoning* (New York: Cambridge University Press, 1996). See also Barbara Herman, *The Practice of Moral Judgment* (Cambridge, Mass.: Harvard University Press, 1996), esp. chap. 7.

5. See Elizabeth Anderson, *Value in Ethics and Economics* (Cambridge, Mass.: Harvard University Press, 1993), chap. 2 and 3, and Daniel Hausman and Michael McPherson, *Economic Analysis, Moral Philosophy, and Public Policy*, 2nd ed. (New York: Cambridge University Press, 2006), chap. 7 and 8.

6. R. Edward Freeman and William Evan, "Corporate Governance: A Stakeholder Interpretation," *Journal of Behavioral Economics* 19, no. 4 (1990): 337–59.

7. I take these norms from Elizabeth Anderson's discussion in *Value in Ethics and Economics*, 145.

8. My understanding of abstraction and idealization in moral theory is drawn heavily from Sarah Holtman, "Three Strategies for Theorizing about Justice," *American Philosophical Quarterly* 40 (2003): 77–90.

9. For a more detailed discussion of these tensions see Tom Sorell, *Moral Theory and Anomaly* (Malden, Mass.: Blackwell, 2000), 65–90.

10. Robert Solomon, *Ethics and Excellence: Cooperation and Integrity in Business* (New York: Oxford University Press, 1992). Daryl Koehn, "A Role for Virtue Ethics in the Analysis of Business Practice," *Business Ethics Quarterly* 5, no. 3 (1995): 531–39.

11. Thomas Hill, *Dignity and Practical Reason in Kant's Moral Theory* (Ithaca, N.Y.: Cornell University Press, 1992).

12. Thomas Donaldson and Thomas Dunfee, *Ties That Bind: A Social Contracts Approach to Business Ethics* (Cambridge, Mass.: Harvard Business School Press, 1999).

13. John Rawls, *A Theory of Justice* (Cambridge, Mass.: Harvard University Press, 1971), 54–55.

14. Robert Phillips and Joshua Margolis, "Toward an Ethics of Organizations," *Business Ethics Quarterly* 9, no. 4 (1999): 619–38.

15. John Rawls, *The Law of Peoples* (Cambridge, Mass.: Harvard University Press, 2001).

16. See Brad Hooker and Margaret Little, eds., *Moral Particularism* (New York: Oxford University Press, 2001).

Chapter One

Business-Focused Business Ethics

Alexei Marcoux, Loyola University Chicago

Business ethics is a form of applied ethics. Some applied ethics forms are *venue*-focused. A good example is environmental ethics. That an activity *occurs in* or *has effects on* the nonhuman environment makes it the subject of evaluation in terms of the theories, principles, and considerations theorized about and developed in the environmental ethics literature. There, the nonhuman environment is conceived of as a place. Human activity altering that place's character triggers analysis and argument in terms of environmental ethics. Other applied ethics forms are *practice*-focused. Good examples are medical ethics and legal ethics. These are concerned principally not with what occurs in or has effects on the hospital or the law office, but instead with articulating what physicians ought to do or avoid when treating patients, and what attorneys ought to do or avoid when protecting or advancing clients' legal interests. This way of dividing the conceptual space is not intended to deny that there are practice-oriented considerations that bear on environmental ethics or that there are venue-oriented considerations that bear on medical or legal ethics. It is intended, however, to assert that one kind of consideration plays a primary or focal role in shaping the inquiry in each, whereas the other kind of consideration plays a secondary or derivative role. This raises an important question about business ethics: Is business ethics better understood as a venue-focused form of applied ethics or as a practice-focused form?

We use the word "business" predominantly in two senses. One sense refers to an *entity* ("a business," "businesses"), the business firm. The other sense refers to an *activity* ("doing business"), business practice. This raises another important question, related to the first: Which is more basic to the subject matter of business ethics—the (business) entity or the (business) activity?

1. ACADEMIC BUSINESS ETHICS

One way to approach answering the two questions raised above is to consider how academic business ethicists conceive of their field and its subject matter. Although it is rare for academic business ethicists to address these questions explicitly (at least, as I have posed them), it may be possible to discern how academic business ethicists conceive of their field and its subject matter implicitly, by considering the cluster of questions that attracts their attention.

A dizzying array of projects is pursued under the rubric of business ethics. Programs of legal compliance, empirical studies into the beliefs and attitudes of business people, arguments for mandatory worker participation in management, a panoply of best-practices claims (in the name of both their moral merit and their contribution to business success), and attempts at applying theories of justice to firms or to the functional areas of business are all advanced as contributions to business ethics—even and especially in its academic literature. These projects vary considerably. They often seem to have little in common other than the conviction, held by their authors, that whatever each is propounding *is* business ethics.

Beneath the apparent, almost kaleidic diversity, however, recurrent themes emerge. Academic business ethicists are centrally concerned with *organizational life*, in general, and organizational life within the *corporation*, in particular.[1] Moreover, it is the *manager's* role in shaping the contours of this organizational life that is crucial to the corporate drama. In short, the academic business ethics literature is focused on organizational ethics, and the organizational ethics pursued is managerial ethics.[2]

This focus on the organization and its management is evident in what is widely regarded among business ethicists as the most significant theoretical construct in their field, *stakeholder theory*. Originating in the work of R. Edward Freeman,[3] stakeholder theory is the view that a business firm ought to be managed in a way that achieves balance among the interests of all who bear a substantial relationship to the firm—its stakeholders. In Freeman's account, the very purpose of the firm is coordination of and joint service to its stakeholders.

My characterization is vague, but deliberately so. For the stakeholder-focused literature in business ethics consists mainly in theorizing over the questions this characterization leaves unanswered: *Who* counts, i.e., *who* are the stakeholders? *What interests*, held by those who count, count? What is *balance*, why is it valuable, and how is one to know when it has been achieved or what activities promote it? *How* are the ends, values, or practices commended by stakeholder theory incompatible with directors and officers extending fiduciary care to shareholders, such that stakeholder theory stands as a *rival* to the so-called shareholder theory? Whatever the success of stakeholder theorists in answering these questions coherently and convincingly, there can be little doubt that stakeholder theory and its mode of analysis (identifying stakeholders and their interests; asking how these interests ought to be accommodated, served, subordinated, or traded off in directing the firm's activities) are the tools for which academic business ethicists reach most readily in considering the moral controversies they address.[4]

If the first point to note about stakeholder theory is its focus on the business organization *qua* organization,[5] the second is that it conceives of the managerial role in essentially *adjudicative* terms. Writing with William M. Evan, Freeman characterizes managing corporations as a challenge calling for Solomonic wisdom.[6] Recall that Solomon's wisdom is demonstrated, in the biblical account, by his skillful adjudication of competing claims of motherhood. For Evan and Freeman, the business manager's fundamental task (at least insofar as ethics bears on it) is to weigh and balance the competing claims of shareholders, employees, customers, suppliers, and the communities in which the firm does business, in order to achieve some joint satisfaction of claims that is appropriately balanced.[7]

The manager-as-adjudicator conception informs business ethics deeply, and not merely among those subscribing to or promoting actively a stakeholder-theoretic vision of the firm. The social scientific organizational justice literature appeals at least implicitly to this understanding of the managerial role. Business ethicist and management scholar Dennis Moberg makes the manager-as-adjudicator the explicit topic of his paper "Management as Judges in Employee Disputes: An Occasion for Moral Imagination."[8]

From the adjudicative focus of managerial ethics, it is but a short step to the view that there is a telling, analogical relationship between business organizations and political states.[9] Call this the *firm-state analogy*. Largely implicit in works appealing to Rawlsian constructs to undergird stakeholder theory,[10] or other, non-stakeholder-theoretic claims about how firms ought to be governed,[11] the firm-state analogy is made explicit by Jeffrey Moriarty,[12] who captures at the outset of a recent article the animating spirit of the business ethics literature:

> The central problems of political philosophy mirror the central problems of business ethics. Political philosophers offer theories of state legitimacy. This leads them to discussions about the best kind of government and about the extent of citizens' political obligations. Business ethicists offer theories of corporate legitimacy. This leads them to discussions about the best kind of corporate governance and about the extent of workers' obligations to their firms. Political philosophers try to determine how to distribute justly the state's benefits and burdens. Business ethicists try to determine how to distribute justly the firm's benefits and burdens.

The similarity between these two sets of problems may lead business ethicists to ask: should political theories be applied to problems in business ethics? This is not the question of whether business ethicists can make use of the concepts common to all branches of moral philosophy: virtue, duty, utility, and so on. It is clear they can. It is the question of whether business ethicists would be justified in applying, in whole or in part, theories of the state directly to the workplace. If a version of egalitarianism is the correct theory of justice for states, for example, does it follow that it is the correct theory of justice for businesses? If states should be democratically governed by their citizens, should businesses be democratically managed by their employees? If the principles of justice for states should be derived from John Rawls's "original position," should the principles of justice for businesses be derived from this position also?[13]

As a description of the questions animating academic business ethics, Moriarty's is without peer. He tells his reader that the business ethics literature is more applied political philosophy than applied ethics and, given the preoccupations of academic business ethicists, perhaps ought to be more so still. The interesting challenge, however, is not characterizing the *degree* to which the firm-state analogy is apt (a question over which organization-focused business ethicists differ—at least by degree[14]). It is determining *whether* the organizational features of firms inform (as Moriarty explicitly, and others by their choice of questions implicitly, claim) "the central problems of business ethics."[15]

2. ACADEMIC BUSINESS ETHICS: VENUE AND ENTITY

In sum, the academic business ethics literature is dominated by concerns about organizational ethics. It takes business ethics to be centrally concerned with ethical issues arising within the organization, in general, and the corporation, in particular. That is, academic business ethics is principally *venue*-focused. That human action occurs in or has effects on the organization ("corporation," "firm") makes it the subject of evaluation in terms of the theories, principles, and considerations ruminated upon and developed in the academic business ethics literature. That academic business ethics is predominantly organization-focused shows also that the business entity informs the academic business ethicist's efforts more so than does business activity. Again, this is not to deny that there are both venue and practice, and both entity and activity, aspects to academic business ethics. It is to assert that in academic business ethics venue considerations and entity considerations tend to frame the discussion.

Imagine that the above-quoted passage from Moriarty were written not about business ethics, but *medical* ethics. If one substituted "medical" for the adjectival "business," "hospital" for "business" ("firm," "corporation") in the noun form, and "health care personnel" for "workers" ("employees"), it would be a *fanciful* description of medical ethics' central problems. It would describe a medical ethics in which the justice of hospital governance is focal—a drama in which the hospital administrator plays the leading role and the physician treating patients the supporting role. Similarly for legal ethics: If one made the appropriate substitutions, Moriarty's would be a fanciful description of legal ethics in which the justice of law firm governance is focal and the moral implications of the attorney's efforts to serve clients are peripheral.

A hospital-focused medical ethics is fanciful because medicine is a *practice* and the moral contours of the practice, not the organizational features of that practice's venue, are focal to medical ethics. Indeed, one would be hard pressed to conceive of a hospital as a *hospital* without its connection to medical practice. This is not to deny that there are moral issues surrounding hospital administration or that these issues may at times be of importance to medical ethics. It *is* to deny that these issues are focal. If they are important to medical ethics, it is because they bear on medical practice—and they are not important to medical ethics if they do not.

A law firm–focused legal ethics is fanciful for the same reasons. Legal practice makes a law firm a *law* firm and not a firm of another kind. This is not to deny that there are moral issues surrounding law office management or that these issues may at times be of importance to legal ethics. It *is* to deny that they are focal. If they are important to legal ethics, it is because they bear on legal practice—and they are not important to legal ethics if they do not.

Of course, Moriarty's is *not* a characterization of medical or of legal ethics, so one may legitimately ask what these observations have to do with Moriarty's account of business ethics' central problems. It is a fair question, for unlike medicine and law, business is not a profession. Professions are defined by particular expertise and technical regularities of practice of a kind largely absent in business. Thus, to conceive of business ethics as a species of professional ethics would be a significant mistake. But although it is not a profession, like medicine and law business is a *practice*. We have an intuitive grasp of what it is to *do* business and it is engaging in that activity that makes the entities engaging in it *business* entities rather than entities of another kind.

Business firms differ from other kinds of organizations not principally in their organizational features, but in what they are organized to do—business. There is a world of difference between Google Inc. and the California Franchise Tax Board, but they are not nearly so different organizationally as they are in the diverging practices each is intended to support.

Business is essentially a practice, not an organizational form, for two main reasons. First, there are organizations that *don't do* business. The Upper Sandusky Ladies Bridge Club is undoubtedly an organization (presumably of bridge-playing ladies in the greater Upper Sandusky area), but it is such even if it does no business — as it may if, for example, its officers do no more than schedule and publicize to members the next game, and its members do no more than play in the appointed place and at the appointed time, taking tea and sandwiches during the break.

Second, there are business-doers who are not organizations. The sole entrepreneur who markets his or her services, performs them, accepts the payment for them, pays his or her costs out of the proceeds, and collects what (if anything) is left over (like the house cleaner I regularly hire) is undoubtedly doing business, but he or she is not an organization and doesn't have recourse to one in order to do business.[16] Together, these two observations underwrite the conclusion that whatever business is, it is not essentially organizational in character. Like the concept of a hospital with respect to medical practice or a law firm with respect to legal practice, the concept of a business organization (entity) is *parasitic* on that of business practice (activity).

The business ethics literature's shareholder-stakeholder debate, interesting though it is, is a debate between those who see the firm principally as a nexus of contracts and those who see it principally as a community or polity. Whichever camp has the better of it, the debate is largely peripheral to the moral contours of doing business. For it is a debate not over how business ought to be done, but over the organizational character of some of the entities who do it. It is a debate over the support structure, rather than over the practice it supports. This is not to say that the shareholder-stakeholder debate is irrelevant to business ethics, but rather that it is derivative. One has to have some idea of what it would mean to do business ethically, in whatever form, before one can say something meaningful about the moral contours governing business firms appearing in the publicly traded corporate form.

Some may think the organizational focus reasonable for business ethics because, after all, the great bulk of businesspeople are not like my sole entrepreneur house cleaner; they work in organizations. But the same can be said of physicians with respect to hospitals (health maintenance organizations, physician practice groups) or lawyers with respect to law offices. Yet, as we have seen, it gets the focus wrong to say that medical ethics is about hospital administration or legal ethics is about law office management.

A skeptical interlocutor may aver that the focus is wrong in medical or legal ethics, but not in business ethics, because medicine and law are *professions*, whereas business is not. The force of this point is not clear. In his *Ethics in Finance*, John Boatright observes that professions typically possess three features: (1) a specialized body of knowledge, (2) a high degree of organization and self-regulation, and (3) a commitment to public service.[17] Medicine and law are indeed recognized as professions, possessed of specialized bodies of knowledge and organized into self-regulating professional societies, whose defining practices are in the first instance committed to public service. The same cannot be said of business practice. That much is clear. But how does this difference underwrite a principal and near-exclusive focus in business ethics on business entities rather than on business activities? To observe that business is not a profession is to observe that when people are doing business they are *not* (1) exercising professional expertise, (2) engaged in a professionally organized and self-regulated activity, or (3) committed to public service. I would be hard-pressed to identify three considerations that better articulate reasons why business *practice* ought to be at the center of an intellectual inquiry advertising itself as business ethics. Remaining unclear is why those three considerations make business *entities*, and especially the governance of large, publicly traded corporations, central to business ethics. Because the moral contours of ethical business practice are not obvious and because the business entity is such because it engages in business activity, business ethics needs a new focal conception of business.

3. BUSINESS PRACTICE

If business is a practice, like medicine or law, then business ethics is a form of practice ethics, like medical ethics or legal ethics. Just as medical ethics and legal ethics focus on the moral contours of their defining practices, business ethics focuses on the moral contours of its defining practice. What is the defining practice of business ethics? What does it mean to *do* business?

Characterizing business practice is not easy, but working from clear cases an account begins to emerge. People do business when they *trade*. One engages in trade by relinquishing some property rights and acquiring other property rights by means of exchange. That is, one engages in trade by executing *exchange transactions*. Business is, at least in part, an *exchange-transaction-executing* practice.

But one does not do business only when executing exchange transactions. Transactional opportunities do not always present themselves immediately or transparently. Often, we have to seek them out. It may be as simple as locating a convenient vendor who sells the commodity one seeks or as complex as identifying potential customers for a product yet unmade. Finding transactional opportunities requires alertness to them and imagination about how best to exploit them. Another way to say this is that business is an *entrepreneurial* practice.[18] Because alertness is critical to executing exchange transactions, business is not just a transaction-executing, but also a *transaction-seeking*, practice.

Exchange transactions are sought and executed typically not for their own sake, but in pursuit of some end. Not all ends one seeks through exchange transactions are business ends. The free medical clinic that transacts with medical suppliers, buying their wares with donations from concerned citizens, is transaction-seeking and transaction-executing, but we are rightly reluctant to characterize its transactional activities as business. The clear or pure case is where the transactor seeks to make her transactional activity *self-sustaining*.[19] One engages in business by seeking to identify and implement *profitable* sets of exchange transactions—aiming to yield something of value that one did not possess before the transactions were initiated. Nothing in this account depends upon the view that people (or even businesspeople) are motivated exclusively, or even primarily, by profit. It says only that people pursue their aims (whatever those aims are) through *business*, rather than through other means, when they attempt to transact in a profit-generating way. Business, then, is a(n intentionally) self-sustaining, transaction-seeking, and transaction-executing practice.

One of the virtues of this account is that it accords well with widely held intuitions about which sorts of entities are business doers and which are not. It is not my purpose here to advance a conclusive standard for identification of business doers—indeed, in many cases the difference may be one of degree (more business doer–like, less business doer–like) rather than kind—but some remarks are worth making.

Garden-variety for-profit firms are undoubtedly business doers on this account. They seek to make the sum of their exchange transactions self-sustaining and, indeed, self-advancing. The aforementioned free medical clinic is considerably less like a business doer, on this account, because its exchange transactions are not intended to be self-sustaining. The free medical clinic seeks monetary or in-kind gifts from some to buy what it needs to give other in-kind gifts to others. The sum of its activities may be self-sustaining (and must be, if it is to continue its activities), but its *exchange transactions* (e.g., purchasing medical supplies) are not. Some social entrepreneurs may be pure business doers on this account, others may not. If the social entrepreneur seeks to make his or her exchange transactions profitable (again, whatever he or she intends to do with those profits), then the social entrepreneur is a business doer. Alternatively, if the viability of the venture depends intentionally upon gifts or donations, then the social entrepreneur is less like a business doer.

Some households are business doers. Those containing members who intend their transactions (e.g., selling their labor, purchasing goods and services) to be self-sustaining are; those containing members who intentionally depend upon monetary or in-kind gifts to sustain the household by supplementing or supplanting transactions are not.

The viewer-supported public television station offers a more interesting case. On the one hand, like the free medical clinic, it seems to rely intentionally on monetary gifts to sustain itself and so is not a business doer, on this account. Indeed, public television donors are often called *sustaining members*—suggesting that it is not the transactional activities of the public television station that are intended to sustain it. On the other hand, these sustaining pledges are not always straightforward gifts. When a pledge of $100 nets the viewer a *Best of Peter, Paul and Mary* CD, this seems at first blush more like a sale—an exchange transaction—than a gift. But upon careful consideration these pledges are better interpreted as involving *two* interactions between donor and public television station where at first there appears to be only one. One interaction is an exchange transaction—sale of the *Best of Peter, Paul and Mary* CD. But note that the donor likely would not pay *just anyone* $100 for the CD. If the donor's local Virgin Megastore sought $100 for the CD, which commands less than $20 on Amazon, the donor likely would be uninterested in paying the extra $80 to Virgin. If $20 is indeed the prevailing market price for the CD, then the donor is more reasonably interpreted as engaging in (1) a $20 exchange transaction for the purchase of the *Best of Peter, Paul and Mary* CD and (2) an $80 *gift* to support the public television station.[20] The public television station is not a business doer, on this account, because its *exchange transactions* are not and are not intended to be self-sustaining.

It may be illuminating to compare business practice, on this account, with other practices one could engage in. Consider a hobby. A hobby may entail much transaction-seeking and transaction-executing activity (as, for example, in the hobby of vintage fountain pen collecting, which entails much buying, selling, and bartering of pens and parts), but it is not business, on this understanding, because the transaction-seeking and transaction-executing behavior is not intended to pay for itself. Indeed, the hobbyist frequently and intentionally raises money from other sources (e.g., his job) to support his continued participation in the hobby. Were the hobbyist to attempt intentionally to make his hobby's exchange transactions self-sustaining, then engaging in the hobby would become business.

Compare also the organizational entity we refer to as a *charity*. A charity may seek and engage in many exchange transactions, but it is considerably less like a business doer, on this account, because the transaction-seeking and transaction-executing behavior is not intended to pay for itself. Conventional charities solicit gifts (which are not exchange transactions) and make gifts.

Although the sum of their activities may be self-sustaining, the sum of their *exchange transactions* is not intended to be self-sustaining, and so they do not engage in business.[21] Business doers (or entrepreneurs) are people who see (or think they see) profitable sets of exchange transactions. Business is the activity or practice of pursuing those transactions with the aim of making them, in sum, self-sustaining. A business organization is a structure intended to support the pursuit and execution of business transactions. The organization may itself be constitutive of a substantial part of the transactions that inform an entrepreneurial vision, for economies in the transactions creating that structure may be essential to realizing the profits that inform the entrepreneurial vision.[22] Nonetheless, managing an organization is not doing business. It is supporting the doing of business (if the organization is a business organization).

If this is correct, then business ethics ought to be done from the transaction *outward*. That is, the transaction ought to be the basic unit of analysis and the ethics of transaction-making ought to form the solid center of business ethics—much as price theory forms the solid center of economics, according to the Chicago School.[23] The non-transactional aspects of business are interesting to this transaction-focused business ethics to the extent that they bear on the making and executing of exchange transactions, and they are not interesting (*qua* business ethics) to the extent that they do not.

On the account sketched here, business is a practice focused on exchange transactions, engaged in by persons seeking self-sustenance from a sum of them. Business ethics, conceived as an account of the moral contours of business practice, is, or should be understood in the first instance as, a transaction-focused, rather than an organization-focused, intellectual enterprise. What questions should a business-focused business ethics address?

4. BUSINESS-FOCUSED BUSINESS ETHICS

Business-focused business ethics takes as *given* a regime of institutions over which normative political philosophers, and business ethicists who view their discipline as applied political philosophy, contend. Because one cannot do business without a regime of private property rights relinquishable and acquirable through bargaining and exchange in markets, business-focused business ethics takes these institutions as given. It asks not which are, all things considered, the best business institutions (which, properly, is a question of normative political philosophy), but what we ought to do when doing business.[24] Again, the analogy to medical ethics is instructive. Medical ethics is not centrally concerned with whether medicine ought to be socialized or private. It takes as given that physicians may treat patients (whatever the institutional context in which they do it) and asks what are the moral contours of that practice.[25]

Business-focused business ethics takes the exchange transaction as its basic unit of analysis. It is concerned with the moral features of transaction-seeking and transaction-executing. It addresses questions like:

- What is a just price? Is it any price agreed to by buyer and seller, absent force or fraud, or are there some substantive pricing norms to which buyers and sellers must adhere, as well?
- Is price discrimination morally wrongful? Does justice demand a unitary price—the same price afforded to one buyer and all?
- In bargaining and negotiation, does the Anglo-American commercial law's distinction between material (i.e., legally wrongful) and immaterial (i.e., legally innocuous) misrepresentations capture also the distinction between morally wrongful and morally innocuous misrepresentations?
- Is the ubiquitous practice in negotiation of deception about one's settlement preferences, or the availability to one of alternatives to a negotiated agreement, morally wrongful or morally innocuous?

It may be contended, correctly, that these are *old* questions. St. Thomas, for example, addresses the just price in the *Summa Theologica*. But although questions about the just price are old, they are not *settled*. More importantly, they are *vital* unsettled questions. Contemporary controversies over the pricing of life-saving drugs[26] or the moral permissibility of abrogating patent rights in them[27] are new manifestations of these admittedly old but nonetheless live questions. The fate of millions, both living and yet unborn, turn on how we answer them.

Like the just price, questions about the morality of price discrimination may be more pressing than ever. The advancing technology of e-commerce raises the specter that an array of goods and services will in the future be priced the way only airline tickets once were.[28] One-size-fits-all, take-it-or-leave-it retail pricing may become the exception rather than the rule. The widespread, visceral dislike of price discrimination threatens to make it an important issue in business. Clear thinking about the ethics of price discrimination will be useful in addressing it.

Bargaining and negotiation are ubiquitous business activities, and they are not confined to those who make a living doing business. Life in a commercial culture ensures that at least as consumers almost all of us will have frequent recourse to bargaining and negotiation in order to acquire the goods and services we seek.

In sum, these admittedly old questions are increasingly vital ones. Business-focused business ethics is connected to a long and increasingly relevant tradition of moral reflection about commerce. In fairness, it must be said that the questions animating business-focused business ethics *are* addressed to some degree in the extant business ethics literature. Issues in advertising and marketing ethics, for example, are informed by concerns about representations made by sellers that are related to the ethics of bargaining and negotiation.[29] (Indeed, one way to construe advertising is as an opening volley, an overture to negotiation.) However, the speed with which discussions of advertising and marketing ethics abandon the transactional context for analysis of aggregate social impact, implications for public policy toward business, or claims about corporate social responsibility is indicative of the thrall in which normative political philosophy–informed organizational ethics holds academic business ethics even when it turns its attention to matters closer to the heart of business practice.

A skeptical interlocutor may aver that, surely, business ethics can be about both transaction-focused business practice and the political philosophy–informed, organizationally focused issues that inform the discussion in academic business ethics. Consequently, one is given cause to ask what is at stake here.

My answer is threefold. First, conceptually speaking, business ethics *can* be about both. Business-focused business ethics is, among other things, a way to tether the political philosophy–informed organizational ethics discussion to the practice business organizations presuppose. Practically speaking, however, the problem is that academic business ethics is *not* about both. Political philosophy–informed organizational ethics sucks all the oxygen from the room. The late Robert Solomon's conception of business ethics is illustrative.[30] He seeks to distinguish three levels of business ethics analysis or argument, which he calls the *micro*, the *macro*, and the *molar*. The micro level concerns "the rules for fair exchange between two individuals." The macro level concerns "the institutional or cultural rules of commerce for an entire society ('the business world')." The molar level ("molar" from the Latin *moles*, meaning "mass") concerns "the basic unit of commerce today—the corporation."[31]

Solomon's micro levels sounds like what I have characterized above as business-focused business ethics. His macro level too, at first blush, sounds like what I have characterized as business-focused business ethics. For what, exactly, would "institutional or cultural rules of commerce" be if not "rules of fair exchange"? To ask that question, however, is to raise another: If the micro and macro levels are fundamentally the same, why distinguish them? The answer is that, for Solomon, they are not the same. His characterization of the macro level emphasizes the institutional and the notion that the rules of commerce of which he writes are *for the whole society*. Solomon's macro level business ethics addresses the relationship between political society and economic activity. It "becomes part and parcel of those large questions about justice, legitimacy, and the nature of society that constitute social and political philosophy."[32] He identifies as archetypal inquiries of macro-level business ethics such questions as these:

> What is the purpose of the "free market"—or is it in some sense a good of its own, with its own *telos*? Are private property rights primary, in some sense preceding social convention (as John Locke and more recently Robert Nozick have argued), or is the market too to be conceived as a complex social practice in which rights are but one ingredient? Is the free market system "fair"? Is it the most efficient way to distribute goods and services throughout society? Does it pay enough attention to cases of desperate need (where a "fair exchange" is not part of the question)? Does it pay enough attention to merit, where it is by no means guaranteed that virtue will be in sufficient demand so as to be rewarded? What are the legitimate (and illegitimate) roles of government in business life, and what is the role of government regulation?[33]

These *are* important questions—of social and political philosophy. However, it is not clear why one would conceive of them as part of business ethics. Engaging in business practice *presupposes* that most of those questions are answered, and in a particular way (or range of ways). If business ethics is to offer something useful—something that is not subsumed by what are, after all, foundational questions of normative political philosophy—it should tell us what we ought to do when engaging in business practice (or articulate principles useful in reasoning about what we ought to do when engaging in business practice).

There are gains to be had from an intellectual division of labor between normative political philosophy and business ethics. Macro-level business ethics, as conceived by Solomon, denies the division and transforms business ethics journals and textbooks into *another* venue for doing normative political philosophy. Macro-level business ethics is more about what most academic business ethicists really want to talk about—their visions of the just political society—than it is about the ethics of engaging in business practice. It is, in other words, more applied political philosophy than applied ethics.

This point is emphasized further by Solomon's conception of the molar level of business ethics, which sees the corporation as "the basic unit of commerce today." Only if one is moved by the view that questions about the justice of the free market or the proper role of public policy toward business are fundamental to business ethics could one claim that the corporation is the

"definitive 'molar' unit of modern business" and that "the central questions
of business ethics tend to be unabashedly aimed at the directors and employees of those few thousand or so companies that rule so much of commercial
life around the world."[34] One suspects that those companies "rule" commercial life in the same way that a firm whose product enjoys 30 percent market
share is said to "command" or to "control" 30 percent of the market. It is a
metaphorical usage that depends upon a *literal* interpretation for its rhetori-
cal bite.

Whatever the merits of Solomon's tripartite division of business ethics
analysis and argument, his own exposition illustrates the problem business-
focused business ethics is intended to overcome. For Solomon's is a detailed
discussion and characterization of the macro and molar issues in business
ethics. Of the micro the reader learns only that it embraces "the rules for fair
exchange between two individuals."[35] What those rules are, or what questions
might animate discussion among academic business ethicists about them, is
nowhere addressed. As it is for Solomon, so too largely for academic business
ethics as a whole.

This brings me to my second response. The justification most often advanced for including business ethics in the business school curriculum is that
instruction in business ethics will make students more ethically aware. It is almost always implied, and sometimes stated, that this will aid them in being
ethical businesspeople. To the curriculum committees who bless the courses
and to the philanthropists who endow business ethics chairs and programs,
this means that students will be aided in acting ethically within the prevailing
institutions of business. Business ethics pedagogy, however, is informed
largely by business ethics research.[36] That research has little to say about what
it would be to do business ethically within the institutional structures in which
businesspeople find themselves, and much to say about the institutions preferred by academics who have scant contact with business. If "the central
questions of business ethics tend to be unabashedly aimed at the directors and
employees of those few thousand or so companies that rule so much of commercial life around the world"[37] and the great bulk of business students will
be neither directors nor employees of those companies (about which more below), then the justification for teaching the content of the business ethics
Solomon so aptly describes is not at all clear. It has little to do with doing
business ethically.

Finally, as I write, the U.S. economy is in the midst of an entrepreneurial
renaissance, begun at the end of the twentieth century and manifest most
prominently (but not primarily) by the 1990s technology boom, that is transforming the business environment in exciting ways. The great bulk of the
American workforce is found in firms of 500 employees or fewer. Job growth

and surging economic productivity are accounted for mainly by firms of 20 employees or fewer. Unprecedented numbers of Americans are abandoning employment entirely—starting their own firms and living on their profits, rather than on a paycheck. Established members of the economic oligarchy of which so many academic business ethicists write, like General Motors and Ford, "rule" no marketplace and find themselves on the verge of collapse. They are replaced not by new oligarchs but by no oligarchs. Young, nimble entrepreneurial firms like Google and Facebook are at the forefront of business—a forefront easy to miss through myopic focus on the ossified corporate entities that make up the Fortune 500.

Business-focused business ethics invites the business ethicist to talk about *business*, the way the medical ethicist talks about medicine and the legal ethicist talks about law. It entertains organizational ethics to the extent that organizational issues bear on self-sustaining, transaction-seeking, and transaction-executing activities, but it distinguishes sharply the focal and the peripheral. Business-focused business ethics leaves little room to entertain the ideological commitments pervading academic business ethics in its current form. But it provides ample room for doing what a business ethics that is not a wholly owned subsidiary of normative political philosophy ought to do: reflect upon the nature of commercial practice.

NOTES

1. See, for example, Tom Donaldson, *Corporations and Morality* (Englewood Cliffs, N.J.: Prentice Hall, 1982) for a comparatively early work in academic business ethics that sees the corporation as the central focus of business ethics.

2. Lest this be thought an unfair characterization, examine the leading business ethics journal. In a recent issue of *Business Ethics Quarterly* I perused for research purposes (vol. 15, no. 3, July 2005), the journal of the Society for Business Ethics included papers bearing titles like "Distributive Justice and the Rules of the Corporation: Partial versus General Equilibrium Analysis" (John H. Beck), "Spirituality and Archetype in Organizational Life" (David W. Hart and F. Neil Brady), and "Can Corporations Be Citizens? Corporate Citizenship as a Metaphor for Business Participation in Society" (Jeremy Moon, Andrew Crane, and Dirk Matten) among the seven regular articles appearing in that issue. By an admittedly informal and unscientific count, 34 of 85 articles (40 percent) appearing in the twelve issues of *Business Ethics Quarterly* preceding and including that issue are devoted explicitly to organizational ethics as I have conceived it here. That is, if anything, an understatement of the degree to which organizational ethics dominates the pages of *Business Ethics Quarterly*—for those twelve issues include three special issues devoted to topics that do not lend themselves as readily to an organizational ethics–focused treatment: "Business

Ethics in a Global Economy" (vol. 14, no. 4), "Accounting Ethics" (vol. 14, no. 3), and "Finance" (vol. 13, no. 3). Had the special issues been regular ones instead, it is a fair conjecture that the share of organizational ethics–focused articles would be at least as high as the 40 percent figure that is diluted by the special issues.

3. William M. Evan and R. Edward Freeman, "A Stakeholder Theory of the Modern Corporation: Kantian Capitalism," in *Ethical Theory and Business*, 4th ed. Tom L. Beauchamp and Norman E. Bowie (Upper Saddle River, N.J.: Prentice Hall, 1993), 97–106.

4. Whether they ought to reach first for those tools is another matter. For a compelling critique of the stakeholder interest–centered conception of business ethics, see Joseph Heath, "Business Ethics without Stakeholders," *Business Ethics Quarterly* 16, no. 4 (2006): 533–57.

5. I say this because *any* organization—whether or not it is a *business* organization—has stakeholders, whose interests are affected by the organization's activities and can be balanced.

6. Evan and Freeman, "Stakeholder Theory."

7. Of course, the disanalogy to Solomonic wisdom is clear: Solomon proposed splitting the baby not as a way to satisfy jointly the competing claims to motherhood, but as an indirect means of determining whose claims were genuine and whose were false.

8. Dennis Moberg, "Management as Judges in Employee Disputes: An Occasion for Moral Imagination," *Business Ethics Quarterly* 13, no. 4 (2003): 454–77. Of course, the manager-as-adjudicator conception does not inform business ethics univocally. For a skeptical view, see John R. Boatright, "Does Business Ethics Rest on a Mistake?" 1998 Presidential Address to the Annual Meeting of the Society for Business Ethics, *Business Ethics Quarterly* 9, no. 4 (1999): 583–91.

9. The step is short because much democratic political theory is informed at least implicitly by an adjudicative conception of legislative action. Legislators in a democratic polity are charged with the task of serving a common good that can be discerned in or constructed out of the many competing interests of the citizenry. An account that sees the promotion and achievement of a preferred conception of distributive justice as the principal aim of state action, like Rawls's in *A Theory of Justice* (New York, Oxford University Press, 1971), will for that reason cast the legislator in an adjudicative role, weighing and balancing competing ends in terms of their promotion of that conception.

10. R. Edward Freeman and William M. Evan, "Corporate Governance: A Stakeholder Interpretation," *Journal of Behavioral Economics* 19, no. 4 (1990): 337–59.

11. Edwin M. Hartman, *Organizational Ethics and the Good Life* (New York: Oxford University Press, 1996).

12. Jeffrey Moriarty, "On the Relevance of Political Philosophy to Business Ethics," *Business Ethics Quarterly* 15, no. 3 (2005): 453–71.

13. Moriarty, "Relevance of Political Philosophy."

14. See, for example, Joshua D. Margolis and Robert A. Phillips, "Toward an Ethics of Organizations," *Business Ethics Quarterly* 9, no. 4 (1999): 619–38, who advance something akin to an ethics of scale in which (ordinary) ethics is addressed to

individual persons, normative political philosophy is addressed to whole societies, and organizational ethics (which they understand business ethics to be) occupies a distinct, intermediate position addressed to subsocietal collections of persons.

15. Moriarty, "Relevance of Political Philosophy."

16. The sole entrepreneur is the crucial case. If we say that the sole entrepreneur too is an organization, then that is a *reductio ad absurdum* on the concept of an organization—not because nothing is organizational but because everything is.

17. John R. Boatright, *Ethics in Finance* (Malden, Mass.: Blackwell, 1999).

18. The alertness-focused account of entrepreneurship is due to Israel Kirzner, *Competition and Entrepreneurship* (Chicago: University of Chicago Press, 1973).

19. "Self" refers to the activity. That is, the aim is to make transactional activities such that they can be continued through the proceeds they generate.

20. This analysis leaves untouched the terms under which the public television station acquired the *Best of Peter, Paul and Mary* CDs. They may have been gifts from the record distributor or, if sold below cost to the public television station, a partial gift/partial exchange transaction like the one between the public television station and the donor.

21. A charity with a large endowment, managed for returns sufficient to support in full its philanthropy, is engaged in business, on this account. The sum of its financial transactions is intended to be self-sustaining—and must be, if it is to continue with its philanthropy. Therefore, the charity that seeks no donations would be engaged in business, on this account.

22. This is what I take Ronald Coase to mean when he says that the firm is a consequence of the fact that there is a cost associated with using the market mechanism. See, for example, Ronald Coase, "The Nature of the Firm," *Economica* 4 (1937): 386–405. On this understanding the firm is a transaction (or set of transactions) engaged in so as to avoid some of the costs of employing the market mechanism that the entrepreneur would otherwise face. The entrepreneur negotiates an employment contract with the employee in part to avoid the costs of purchasing labor anew daily (as, for examples, many building contractors do). The entrepreneur enters into a long-term contract with a supplier in order to avoid the vicissitudes of more frequent purchases in the spot market. Thus, the firm is not so much an alternative to market transactions as it is a transaction (or set of transactions) intended to displace a still larger or more costly set of transactions. Outsourcing is just the reverse of this process, engaged in when the spot market is less costly than employment or other long-term contracts.

23. See, for example, M. W. Reder, "Chicago School," in *The New Palgrave Dictionary of Political Economy*, ed. John Eatwell, Peter Newman, and Murray Milgate (London: Macmillan, 1987), vol. 1, 413–18.

24. In "Two Concepts of Rules," Rawls distinguishes between justifying an action or rule under an institutional arrangement and justifying the institution itself. In the canonical example, justifying the institution of criminal punishment itself calls for a different kind of justification than justifying criminally punishing a particular person under the institution of criminal punishment. On the account sketched here, business-focused business ethics occupies the "justifying an action or rule under an institutional arrangement" side of the distinction, whereas arguments about the moral

permissibility of capitalist economic institutions occupy the "justifying the institution itself" side. My criticism of organization-focused business ethics can be understood as the claim that it occupies the "justifying the institution itself" side of the distinction, and that's the wrong side for a practice ethics like medical, legal, or business ethics. On the distinction, see John Rawls, "Two Concepts of Rules," *Philosophical Review* 64, no. 1 (1955): 3–32.

25. Of course, medical ethics is not unconcerned with this question, either. To the extent that medicine being socialized or private bears on physicians' efforts to treat patients it is relevant, and to the extent that it does not it is not. But whether it is or is not relevant, it is certainly not focal to medical ethics.

26. See, for example, Ian Maitland, "Priceless Goods: How Should Life-Saving Drugs Be Priced?" *Business Ethics Quarterly* 12, no. 4 (2002): 451–80.

27. See, for example, Alexander Rosenberg, "On the Priority of Intellectual Property Rights, Especially in Biotechnology," *Politics, Philosophy & Economics* 3, no. 1 (2004): 77–95.

28. Then again, that same technology has made airlines less able to secure widely differing prices for airplane seats because it has facilitated the emergence of last-minute travel sites.

29. See, for example, George G. Brenkert, "Marketing to Inner City Blacks: PowerMaster and Moral Responsibility," *Business Ethics Quarterly* 8, no. 1 (1998): 1–18.

30. Robert Solomon, "Business Ethics," in *A Companion to Ethics*, ed. Peter Singer (Malden, Mass.: Blackwell, 1991), 354–65.

31. Solomon, "Business Ethics," 359.

32. Solomon, "Business Ethics."

33. Solomon, "Business Ethics."

34. Solomon, "Business Ethics."

35. Solomon, "Business Ethics."

36. Indeed, unlike other, more established fields, research in business ethics is frequently disseminated through textbooks. Important, oft-cited works of business ethics have appeared initially, and sometimes only, as readings in textbooks. Even as publication in academic journals has become the norm in business ethics, the degree to which and the direct way in which business ethics research informs what is taught is striking when taken against other disciplines.

37. Solomon, "Business Ethics."

Chapter Two

Virtue Ethics and Business Organizations

Geoff Moore, Durham Business School

The reemergence of virtue ethics as a mainstream branch of moral philosophy[1] has been quickly followed by attempts to apply virtue ethics to business organizations—the work of DesJardins and Solomon being early examples.[2] There have, however, been two somewhat different ways of approaching this application of virtue ethics to business organizations. In this chapter, once the basic elements of virtue ethics have been outlined, and one particular criticism of virtue ethics in general dealt with, I will contrast what I term an Aristotelian account with an approach based on the work of the moral philosopher Alasdair MacIntyre. MacIntyre's approach, I will argue, best enables the general concepts of virtue ethics to be applied to the particular case of organizational ethics and thence to business ethics.

It is possible to view the reemergence of virtue ethics as growing out of a general dissatisfaction with what DesJardins and Horvath[3] both call the principle-based ethics (PBE) of the Enlightenment. DesJardins, for example, arguing from the perspective of one teaching business ethics, describes the situation in the following way:

> [W]e should take seriously the fact that in practice, ethical principles seldom give any unambiguous practical advice. Adopting a principle-based approach in business ethics leads to numerous practical difficulties. A seemingly endless series of problems arises when one attempts to derive from such principles as the categorical imperative or the principle of utility, solutions to ethical problems faced by business people. Hopeless ambiguity in application, apparent counterexamples, ad hoc rebuttals, counterintuitive conclusions, and apparently contradictory prescriptions create an overwhelming morass in the discussion of particular moral situations.[4]

Horvath, also writing from a business ethics perspective (though with a similar level of generality in his critique), identifies four recurring problems with PBE: It fails to address the issue of ethical motivation (the "Why should I be good or do right?" question); by its very nature it involves generality rather than specificity to particular cases; the two main formulations of PBE (formalism derived from Kant and utilitarianism) are mutually incompatible despite their individual claims to irrefutable logic; and finally, while business ethics tends to be predominantly utilitarian, it represents a corrupt form of pure utilitarianism, regressing instead to a Machiavellian calculation in which given ends justify the means.[5] As such, Horvath argues, since PBE can produce such conflicting answers to the same problem, there is a danger of a drift into ethical relativism where the correctness of any moral judgment is viewed as being "relative to the individual (or group) making that judgment, and therefore one person cannot impose moral demands upon another."[6] MacIntyre offers a similar critique in *After Virtue*—particularly his discussion of the interminable nature of contemporary moral debates, and his characterization of modernity's ethic of emotivism in which "all moral judgments are *nothing but* expressions of preference, expressions of attitude or feeling," such that "[o]thers are always means, never ends."[7]

Solomon[8] is characteristically more forthright in his criticism of PBE: The Kantian approach "shifts critical focus from oneself as a full-blooded person occupying a significant role in a productive organization to an abstract role-transcendent morality that necessarily finds itself empty-handed when it comes to most of the matters and many of the motives that we hear so much about in any corporate setting."[9] And further, "I just want to point out that utilitarianism shares with Kant that special appeal to anal compulsives in its doting over principles and rationalization (in crass calculation) and its neglect of individual responsibility and the cultivation of character."[10]

Horvath, citing Koehn,[11] goes so far as to suggest that PBE may have a role *within* virtue ethics—that, in relation to business for example, "PBE can help to instruct a virtuous manager decide a given case, but PBE cannot work as it should for the non-virtuous manager. PBE can be a subset of virtue ethics even if PBE cannot stand on its own."[12] If that is the case, then virtue ethics would seem to occupy a centrally important place in moral philosophy in general and in organizational and business ethics in particular. But to see further why this might be the case, we need to understand more fully what exactly virtue ethics involves.

1. ELEMENTS OF VIRTUE ETHICS

Perhaps the most usual way of drawing the distinction between virtue ethics and PBE is to observe that virtue ethics is centered on the actor while PBE is centered on the action itself or its consequences. Certainly, it is true that in virtue ethics, the actor, and in particular the character of the actor, takes a central place. But that is not to say that actions are unimportant, and this for at least two reasons. First, the action has consequences that will usually affect others as well as the actor, and these consequences will assist or otherwise in enabling those involved toward their true *telos*, or purpose, in life. Koehn observes that Aristotle's system of thought "places tremendous weight upon the act because life itself is an *energeia* or activity of performing various acts."[13] Second, the action will have further consequences for the actor, since it will play a part in reinforcing or undermining the actor's character. "Aristotle . . . views every act as inevitably developing a character who performs an act well or poorly [and] will not treat an outcome in isolation from past and future outcomes. An outcome is not just a consequence of an act but a consequence for one or more agents engaged in a series of actions."[14] Thus while act utilitarianism will often concentrate on the outcomes of one act in isolation, virtue ethics will seek to understand both the precursors and outcomes of the act for the agent in question: "Past actions, by moulding character, become the cause of future actions."[15]

A second element of virtue ethics, evident from the above discussion, is that it is teleological in nature. The ultimate purpose for each individual is, in Aristotle's terms, *eudaimonia*—defined by MacIntyre as something like "blessedness, happiness, prosperity. It is the state of being well and doing well, of a man's being well-favoured himself and in relation to the divine." This definition leads MacIntyre to define the virtues as "precisely those qualities the possession of which will enable an individual to achieve *eudaimonia* and the lack of which will frustrate his movement toward that *telos*."[16] Associated with this teleological approach is the concept of a narrative quest—that as storytelling animals we make sense of our lives through our individual and communal journeys, through which we try to realize our own *telos*.[17]

A third element of virtue ethics follows from these first two. Koehn describes it as a focus "on the conformity between right thinking and desire. . . . [T]he virtuous agent simply is the person habituated to desire to do what is good and noble."[18] MacIntyre similarly offers an extension of his definition of virtue given above. He writes that "virtues are dispositions not only to act in particular ways but also to feel in particular ways. To act virtuously . . . is to act from inclination formed by the cultivation of the virtues."[19] And Porter, following Aquinas, describes the person of true virtue as being "characterised by harmonious unanimity among her feelings, judgments and will" such that there is no conflict between the passions and the will.[20] Thus virtues are enduring character traits (as, of course, are vices) and this focus on character and its development, and the associated possession and exercise of the virtues (or vices), also characterizes an ethic of virtue. We should also note that the requirements of virtue are such that, in the ideal, the truly virtuous individual must possess all of the virtues; there must be a harmony or unity about the individual in which the whole of his or her life is directed toward his or her *telos*, and this can arise only if all the virtues are possessed and exercised in concert.[21]

It might be inferred from the discussion so far that virtues have everything to do with the person *qua* individual and nothing to do with life in the community. A fourth element of virtue ethics, however, is that the community occupies a central part. It is, for example, axiomatic in Aristotle's frame of reference (with the city-state as the basis of society) that "the virtues find their place not just in the life of the individual, but in the life of the city and that the individual is indeed intelligible only as a *politikon zoon* [a political animal]."[22] Solomon likewise emphasizes this point: "The concept of the virtues provides the conceptual linkage between the individual and his or her society. A virtue is a pervasive trait of character that allows one to 'fit into' a particular society and to excel in it. . . . The virtues [are], on the one hand, essential aspects of the individual. On the other hand they [are] precisely the 'excellences' that a certain society require[s]."[23] As Morse puts it, extending the argument to the political sphere, "[v]irtue is cultivated in the proper political and social environment, such that excellence in a person comes from a state with well-ordered laws, and other individuals concerned with the development of virtue."[24]

Horvath makes the same point: "This traditional ethical paradigm begins with the community as the ethical base rather than individuals existing in isolation. Within a community, people occupy recognised roles, and these roles in turn include ethical obligations. To fulfil such roles well, people need to develop virtues within themselves."[25] This, then, affirms the essential intertwining of the individual, and his or her own narrative quest, with the community and its shared sense of *telos*. It is in community that the virtues are developed and (partially) for whose good they are exercised.

The fifth and final element of virtue ethics is that it focuses on excellence. The Greek word *arête* can be translated either as virtue or as excellence, and the latter points to the essentially positive nature of virtue ethics. Solomon contends that "virtue is doing one's best, excelling, and not merely 'toeing the line' and 'keeping one's nose clean.'"[26] Koehn similarly argues that virtue ethics' stress on excellence "helps counter the levelling tendency of deontological ethics."[27] We will return to this particular aspect of virtue ethics when we consider MacIntyre's concept of a practice. For now, however, we can note that the possession and exercise of virtues such as temperance, fortitude, justice, and practical wisdom—the four cardinal virtues—are not ends in themselves but are means to the end of excellence in all the practices in which an agent engages. It is through the pursuit of excellence in these practices that the agent's character is developed, and the agent is enabled on his or her journey toward his or her own *telos* within a community that provides the social context of the agent's life.

2. A CRITICISM

Having outlined the key elements of virtue ethics, we need immediately to consider a potentially fatal criticism that derives, not from other approaches to moral philosophy as might be expected, but from work in empirical social psychology. We have noted how "[t]he development of good character is of central importance, because the virtue ethicist thinks actions follow from one's character; thus, the person with a virtuous character will subsequently perform virtuous acts in a given moral situation."[28] But what if the notion of character is flawed and actions are determined more by response to *situation* than by *character*?

This is the argument propounded by Doris and debated subsequently between Solomon and Harman.[29] The debate is between "situationism,"[30] or alternatively the "fragmentation theory of character,"[31] and its opposite— "globalism"[32] or the "regulatory theory."[33] Harman, in summarizing the situationism side of the debate, argues that the evidence from social psychology suggests that "people . . . do not have broad and stable dispositions corresponding to the sorts of character and personality traits we normally suppose that people have."[34]

Solomon's robust defence of character is in three parts. First, much of the evidence cited in support of situationism is drawn from rather extraordinary and experimental contexts that, while informative, do not necessarily undermine the conventional understanding of character.[35] Second, the experiments providing the social psychological evidence were, by their nature, one-off short-term events, whereas character is necessarily a phenomenon to be practiced and observed over the long term.[36] Third, what is revealed in the empirical evidence is not so much lack of character as *conflict* between different character traits.[37] Hence, he argues for not throwing out the baby with the bath water.[38]

In his more detailed analysis of the empirical work cited in support of situationism, Webber also finds problems with the evidence; indeed he argues that some should be set aside as specious and that the remaining evidence does not necessarily support the arguments propounded.[39] The key part of Webber's argument, in line with Solomon's third point, is that the empirical evidence is indicative of *competing* character traits where those involved in the experiments have to choose between, for example, "the well-being of the learner and obedience or deference to authority of the experimenter, and so may have inclinations against administering the [electric] shocks, but also stronger inclinations towards obedience or deference"—referring to the Milgram obedience experiments.[40] He argues further, in reviewing data from an American study that was originally designed to explain the difference in homicide rates between northern and southern regions of the United States, that "the traditional notion of traits [globalism] therefore genuinely does have an explanatory and predictive power that the behaviourist notion [situationism] lacks."[41]

Weaver argues similarly. He draws on the concept of moral identity (a self-conception organized around a set of moral traits) "in which these moral traits are a deep and relatively stable part of one's self-concept or self-schema . . . and in which these traits are manifested in action."[42] He cites empirical research supporting a link between moral identity and morally significant behavior.

This is not to argue, however, that situations are unimportant or that context and environment have no part to play in character development or in actual behavior. They clearly do. Indeed, Solomon acknowledges that, while "[n]one of this implies that we should give up or give in on character," it does tell us "that circumstances and character cannot be pried apart and should not be used competitively as alternative explanations of virtuous or vicious behaviour."[43] And he further argues that while "character is vulnerable to environment . . . it is also a bulwark *against* environment."[44] Weaver similarly acknowledges that theories of moral identity "do not make unsustainable assumptions of stable, constantly effective behavioural personality types or traits"[45]; these theories accept that contextual factors can influence behavior. The mechanism by which this operates is that "these factors make persons relatively more aware of, and thus responsive to, less central elements of their moral identity."[46] Again, the potential for conflict between different character traits, here as a result of contextual factors, emerges. Weaver also links this to the responsibility of the moral agent, arguing that "[v]irtue theories hold people responsible for how their virtue is affected by the situations that they enter into"[47] and suggesting that proactive management of one's own environment to protect virtue is appropriate where this is possible. We will return to this whole issue below in the discussion of organizational ethics. For now, however, we can conclude that the concept of character survives its critique—albeit as a more nuanced concept in which situationism is acknowledged but not privileged over a globalist understanding.

3. THE APPLICATION OF VIRTUE ETHICS TO BUSINESS

I indicate above that there have been two somewhat different ways of approaching virtue ethics and business, and that I would put forward one of these two approaches based on the work of the moral philosopher Alasdair MacIntyre. It is worth, however, and by way of contrast, explaining briefly the alternative approach and identifying its central weakness. We can term this alternative an Aristotelian approach and, indeed, I have already cited from some of the work of its two main proponents, Daryl Koehn and Robert Solomon.

While this body of work might seem to be true to its Aristotelian origins, there is one particular part of it that we should note. Solomon in one of his early papers notes Aristotle's distinction between two types of economic activity. First, there is *oecinomicus*, or household trading, "which he approved of and thought essential to the working of any even moderately complex society." Second, there is "'*chrematisike*' which is trade for profit. Aristotle declared the latter activity wholly devoid of virtue and called those engaged in such purely selfish practices 'parasites.' All trade, he believed, was a kind of exploitation. Such was his view of what I call 'business.' [48] Solomon goes on, in effect, to dismiss Aristotle's "prejudices," which "underlie much of business criticism and the contempt for finance that preoccupies so much of Christian ethics even to this day. . . ."[49]

This dismissal, however, leads Solomon to produce an apparently seamless link between the individual, the business organization, and society, in which the aims of each are conveniently aligned. This is perhaps best illustrated by the title of one of his books: *A Better Way to Think about Business: How Personal Integrity Leads to Corporate Success*.[50] The danger in this approach, however, is that it suggests that success is the aim of integrity—the motivation is economic, not moral. This is, in other words, ethics for profit's sake rather than ethics for ethics' sake or, alternatively, what we might term a strategic approach to ethics.[51]

This is not to say that Solomon is entirely uncritical of modern corporations. While writing that his aim "is not to attack business or corporate life or to promote radical reforms that would undermine rather than improve the free enterprise system," he also argues that "[i]n place of the brutally competitive and disruptive imagery and narrowly 'bottom-line'-oriented thinking that is so pervasive these days, I want to underline the supreme importance of stability in the organization, to encourage a sense of community, which the best corporations already recognize (at least in their public relations), and to reinforce the importance of integrity in the individual,"[52] and he speaks against contemporary business culture as being about "making money . . . devoid of any larger sense of obligation or ethics," or "that a business must pursue its profits *no matter what*," or of the "infamous 'obligations to the stockholders.'"[53]

Morse, however, provides a telling critique.

> While Solomon correctly argues that virtues only flourish within a community, we must understand that there will be a congruence between civic and business virtue only if the business' ends are subordinate to society's ultimate end of producing good human beings. . . . Simply stated, a business encourages vicious persons when it both promotes desires for material goods above and beyond what is necessary for the good life, and when it requires that its members pursue excessive profit regardless of the normal confines of justice. In the scenario in which it creates vicious persons, it no longer performs its proper function in society, namely, to promote the good life by providing for the material necessities of its citizens.[54]

Koehn's work is both extensive in its evaluation of an Aristotelian approach and critical of it, noting, for example, "problems with the moral psychology implicit in Aristotelian virtue ethics" when applied in a corporate setting. I have offered a critique of this, and attempted to show how an ethics of virtue based on MacIntyre's work provides the revision to virtue ethics that Koehn calls for.[55] The basis of the weakness in taking a straightforward Aristotelian approach (a weakness Koehn acknowledges but does not resolve) lies in an insufficiently critical understanding of the nature of the modern corporation and of its essential part in influencing the ethics of modernity—something for which we can hardly blame Aristotle although, as in so many other things, we might well have heeded his warnings in relation to *chrematisike* as a particular form of economic activity. To better understand the nature of the modern corporation, we require a level of sophistication in our understanding of business organizations and of virtue ethics that Solomon's and Koehn's work does not offer and MacIntyre's neo-Aristotelian work does. It is to this that we now turn.

4. MACINTYRE'S VIRTUES-GOODS-PRACTICE-INSTITUTION SCHEMA[56]

The significance of MacIntyre's work in general and its application to contemporary organizations has been addressed elsewhere. From this it is clear that MacIntyre's arguments for and development of virtue ethics, and its application specifically to the area of business, are already well documented and have received critical review.[57] In order to explore this here we need to build up MacIntyre's schema stage by stage.

Goods, Practices, and Institutions

We begin to do so by turning to MacIntyre's oft-quoted definition of a practice, noting, as mentioned above, its emphasis on excellence. A practice is

> [a]ny coherent and complex form of socially established cooperative human activity through which goods internal to that form of activity are realized in the course of trying to achieve those standards of excellence which are appropriate to, and partially definitive of, that form of activity, with the result that human powers to achieve excellence, and human conceptions of the ends and goods involved, are systematically extended.[58]

Internal goods derived from practices, both the excellence of products that result and the perfection of the individual in the process, can be contrasted with external goods such as survival, fame, power, profit or, more generally, success. When achieved, MacIntyre argues, these external goods are "always some individual's property and possession. [They are] characteristically objects of competition in which there must be losers as well as winners." With internal goods, however, although there is competition in one sense; this is competition to excel, and so benefits all members of the community engaged in the practice.[59]

The internal goods of practices, then, stand in distinction to the external goods, and these external goods are particularly associated with the institutions that "house" the practice:

> Institutions are characteristically and necessarily concerned with . . . external goods. They are involved in acquiring money and other material goods; they are structured in terms of power and status, and they distribute money, power and status as rewards. Nor could they do otherwise if they are to sustain not only themselves, but also the practices of which they are the bearers. For no practices can survive for any length of time unsustained by institutions. Indeed so intimate is the relationship of practices to institutions—and consequently of the goods external to the goods internal to the practices in question—that institutions and practices characteristically form a single causal order in which the ideals and the creativity of the practice are always vulnerable to the acquisitiveness of the institution, in which the cooperative care for common goods of the practice is always vulnerable to the competitiveness of the institution. In this context the essential feature of the virtues is clear. Without them, without justice, courage and truthfulness, practices could not resist the corrupting power of institutions.[60]

MacIntyre's description of institutions and their relationship with practices can be applied in almost any context. MacIntyre himself indicates that "the range of practices is wide: arts, sciences, games, politics in the Aristotelian sense, the making and sustaining of family life, all fall under the concept."[61] The argument here is that this can be extended to include organizational life in general, and business organizations in particular, by redescribing organizations as practice-institution combinations. In other words, an organization consists of *both* a practice at its core *and* an institution that houses the practice. It should also be clear from this that the essential association and tension between practices and institutions, and between internal and external goods, gives the texture of organizational life a central dilemma. We can depict this as shown in figure 2.1 and will explore this dilemma further below.

First, however, let us clarify how this applies to business organizations. MacIntyre acknowledged that in *After Virtue* he did not pay particular attention to what he termed "productive practices." He later made good that lack of attention by referring specifically to productive crafts such as "farming and fishing, architecture and construction":

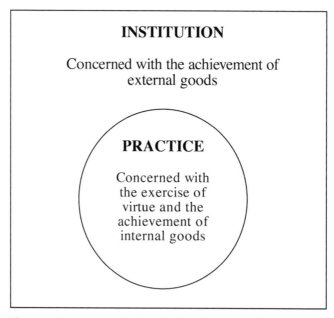

Figure 2.1. An organization depicted as a practice-institution combination.

The aim internal to such productive crafts, when they are in good order, is never only to catch fish, or to produce beef or milk, or to build houses. It is to do so in a manner consonant with the excellences of the craft, so that there is not only a good product, but the craftsperson is perfected through and in her or his activity.[62]

We can legitimately extend MacIntyre's notion of "productive crafts" to business organizations in general by noting that at the core of any such organization (and organizations in general) there is a practice. The particular practice may be fishing, or producing beef or milk, or building houses, or it may be providing financial services or mining or retailing. The entirely common feature, however, is that all such activities fall within MacIntyre's definition of a practice as "any coherent and complex form of socially established cooperative human activity."

Furthermore, it follows that individuals who work in such organizations would do well to view themselves as craftspeople and their work as set in the context of a practice. This would be only one of a number of practices in which they engage, but is no less important than any other practice—indeed, quite possibly more important given the amount of time and energy, physical and emotional, expended there. If they endeavor to maintain an integrity of character by exercising the virtues here as elsewhere, gaining such internal goods as are available, thereby helping them in their narrative quest toward their own *telos*, then not only would the individuals benefit (be "perfected through and in her or his activity") but they would, in the very act of doing all of this, also play a necessary part in the humanizing of business from within.[63]

But what is it that enables the individual in a business organization, the craftsperson, to seek and realize such perfection, or indeed to have that aim frustrated? To answer this question requires further commentary on MacIntyre's notion of virtue and its relationship to goods, practices, and institutions.

Virtues and Institutional Governance

We have noted above MacIntyre's initial definitions of the virtues (as enabling an individual to achieve *eudaimonia* and as dispositions not only to act in particular ways but also to feel in particular ways), but he later links virtues, goods, and practices more specifically:

> A virtue is an acquired human quality the possession and exercise of which tends to enable us to achieve those goods which are internal to practices and the lack of which effectively prevents us from achieving any such goods.[64]

Virtues, therefore, as enduring character traits are not practice-specific, but span and are necessary to the flourishing of any practice. The virtues enable the individual to achieve the goods internal to practices, and the achievement of those goods *across a variety of practices and over time* is instrumental in the individual's search for and movement (the individual's narrative quest) toward his or her own *telos*.

However, this leads to another important point in MacIntyre's schema, which it is as well to cover here:

> [T]he making and sustaining of forms of human community—*and therefore of institutions*—itself has all the characteristics of a practice, and moreover of a practice which stands in a peculiarly close relationship to the exercise of the virtues. . . . For the ability of a practice to retain its integrity will depend on the way in which the virtues can be and are exercised in sustaining the institutional forms which are the social bearers of the practice.[65]

In other words, senior managers—those who have, in one sense, outgrown the practice at the core of the institution and now represent the institution that houses it—also have the same opportunity to exercise the virtues in the practice of the making and sustaining of that institution, enabling them on their narrative quest toward their own *telos*. This more complex schema is represented in figure 2.2, where the smaller circle with the "P" inside represents the practice of making and sustaining the institution.[66]

However, MacIntyre, in drawing attention to the central dilemma of his schema—the tension between the practice and the institution, despite their forming "a single causal order," and the associated tension between internal and external goods—notes that "practices are often distorted by their modes of institutionalisation, when irrelevant considerations relating to money, power and status are allowed to invade the practice."[67] The point in relation to individuals being craftspeople—whether in the core practice at the heart of the institution, or in the making and sustaining of the institution itself—is that aside from their own virtuous character, the mode of institutionalization and the extent to which it mistakenly prioritizes external goods is fundamental to enabling craftspeople to seek and realize perfection in their practice, or indeed to have that aim frustrated. This is, as we noted earlier, the importance of context or environment to the exercise of virtue. An important part of the whole virtues-goods-practice-institution schema is to focus on the institution in order to assess what features of the institution will better enable it not to distort the practice that it houses. There is, as well, a need to focus on the virtues necessary to sustain what we might call such virtuous institutional forms. We can therefore ask what would characterize an institution in good order, one that protects and perhaps extends the excellences of the practice it houses.

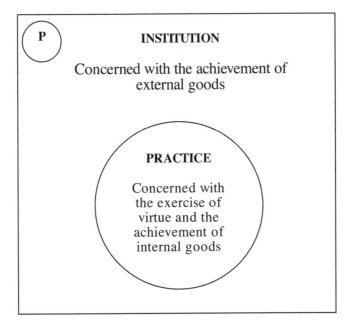

Figure 2.2. An organization depicted as a practice-institution combination together with the second practice of making and sustaining the institution.

5. THE CHARACTER OF THE VIRTUOUS INSTITUTION

Evidence from a variety of studies[68] highlights the importance of peer and superior influence on the ethical behavior of managers. It has been argued[69] that an appropriate way of conceptualizing this is to think not just in terms of particular individuals and their exercise (or not) of the virtues at the institutional level, as MacIntyre does, but also in terms of *institutional* level virtues (and vices), and hence of institutional *character*. Just as MacIntyre talks of the concern for external goods and the acquisitiveness and competitiveness *of the institution*, it seems perfectly possible, by way of analogy or projection, or by way of metaphor,[70] to speak of the institution as having a virtuous or vicious character, or a character that is somewhere between these two extremes. Klein comments that "formal organizations can function like a moral person. . . . [T]hey potentially have something analogous to character, which can be evaluated as virtuous or vicious."[71]

A virtuous institutional character, then, might be defined as the seat of the virtues necessary for an institution to engage in practices with excellence, focusing on those internal goods thereby obtainable, while warding off threats from its own inordinate pursuit of external goods and from the corrupting power of other institutions in its environment with which it engages.[72]

Taking business organizations as a particular form of practice-institution combination (one housing what MacIntyre, as we have seen, calls "productive crafts") and drawing from the definition of virtuous institutional character given above, the concept of the virtuous business organization can be explored further. The first requirement of a business organization with a virtuous character would be that there is a good purpose for the particular practice-institution combination that it comprises. Given the teleological nature of virtue ethics, it will come as no surprise that this consideration poses a challenge to certain businesses—those engaged in tobacco or arms manufacture, for example, might find this requirement particularly challenging. Second, the institution would be aware that it is founded on and has as its most important function the sustenance of the particular business practice that it houses. Third, and following from this, the institution would encourage the pursuit of excellence in that practice, whatever that may mean for the particular practice in question. Fourth, the institution would focus on external goods (such as profit and reputation) as both a necessary and worthwhile function of the organization (they are *goods*, not *bads*), but only to the extent necessary to the sustenance and development of the practice. Finally, the institution would be such as to be able to resist the corrupting power of institutions in its environment with which it in turn relates, such as competitors, suppliers, or those which represent the financial market, where these encourage a single-minded concentration on external goods.

Which particular virtues would characterize virtuous business organizations? Although we might consider a list such as the four cardinal virtues, it is clear that justice, courage, and truthfulness are the *sine qua non* of MacIntyre's schema,[73] together with the virtues of integrity and constancy,[74] which refer to their consistent application of these other virtues across practices and over time. The virtuous business organization would require courage in order to resist the corrupting power of institutions with which it relates and to minimize the effects of the environment on its character where these might be damaging. It would require justice in order to distribute external goods appropriately, to weigh its own advantage with that of the wider community, to foster its own excellence through (for example) an allocation of roles that ensures that those who are truly best at particular tasks are appointed to do them, and to generate internal harmony through ensuring that subordinates accept the justice of their place.[75] Solomon's[76] emphasis on trust (by which we should infer the virtue of both offering trust to others and being trustworthy oneself) points to the necessity of truthfulness for the conduct of business.

Such virtues would find their institutional embodiment in a number of features.[77] These are the development of a *power-balanced structure* that will ensure that the views and desires of particular constituencies are not privileged over those of others, and decision-making *systems and processes* that enable rational critical dialogue having the effect of countering biases and enabling the questioning of the hitherto unquestioned. In particular, these will allow the organization not to see itself as compartmentalized[78] from other institutions in society but as one part of a larger whole. While to some extent outside of its control, the encouragement of a supportive *culture* will also be a feature of the character of a virtuous business organization.[79]

6. PRECONDITIONS FOR
VIRTUOUS BUSINESS ORGANIZATIONS

According to MacIntyre, as we have already seen, "the ability of a practice to retain its integrity will depend on the way in which the virtues can be and are exercised in sustaining the institutional forms which are the social bearers of the practice." He then continues, "The integrity of a practice causally requires the exercise of the virtues by at least some of the individuals who embody it in their activities; and conversely the corruption of institutions is always in part at least an effect of the vices."[80] Hence, there is the need to focus on individual agents, to which we will return.

At another level, MacIntyre illustrates the contrast between virtuous and vicious business organizations, by describing two fishing crews. One is motivated only or overridingly by the pursuit of external goods and hence aims at wages for the crew and profit for the owners. The second pursues internal goods and is devoted to the particular excellences required by the practice of fishing.[81] In the first case, both owners and workers would abandon the activity should they find other means of enhancing their income. The second crew, however, would subordinate economic goods to an allegiance to the continuation of the practice of fishing and the way of life it entails. It is, in other words, the *prioritization* of external goods that corrupts the institution and threatens the practice. If this is so, the question then becomes what can be done institutionally to maintain an appropriate *balance* between the pursuit of internal and external goods in such a way that the institution is able to preserve its practices by ensuring that they are not eroded by the inordinate pursuit of external goods.

This, however, raises a further issue. To return to MacIntyre's fishing crews, because both crews fish it is clear that in the very short term the conduct of the practice *requires* neither the virtues of the practitioners and owners, nor the flourishing of the institutions that house the practice—technical expertise and equipment is all that is required. However, in the medium to long term at least one commentator[82] suggests that without an appropriate regulatory environment the virtuous fishing crew instanced here would not long survive the effects of the other sort—crews that would overfish and then leave in grim parody of the tragedy of the commons.

This, then, raises an important question: Why do some businesses actively protect the virtues even when this is to the detriment of the pursuit of external goods such as profit? It turns out that the description of MacIntyre's work given above attests to a familiar triad—that of the agent, the institution, and the environment. Any adequate characterization of either virtuous or vicious business organizations will require us to comment on all three of these.

Virtuous Agents

The first precondition for a virtuous business organization, then, is the presence of virtuous agents at the level of both the practice and the institution, for without agents who possess and exercise the virtues the practice itself would no longer be fostered internally through the pursuit of excellence, and at the institutional level the corruption of the institution and the consequent distortion of the practice would seem to be inevitable. This is particularly the case for those agents who hold decision-making authority in the institution. But the presence of such agents at both practice and institutional (managerial) levels is clearly insufficient to guarantee the presence of organizational virtue.[83]

A Conducive Mode of Institutionalization

The second precondition for a virtuous business organization is the mode of institutionalization, which distributes both decision-making authority and decision criteria within institutions. In other words, we would expect that different institutional forms will support to different extents the practices that they house, and thereby enable the exercise of the virtues and the attainment of internal goods to a greater or lesser degree. Weaver makes this point well and links it back to the moral agency of individuals: "[O]rganizations themselves—and the way they normalise and reproduce virtue or vice—become the primary influence on the moral identity of their employees, and thus on the degree of virtue characterizing those employees."[84]

This precondition in particular has led to much discussion about the possibility or otherwise of applying MacIntyre's virtues-goods-practice-institution schema to *capitalist* business organizations, and this warrants further discussion at this point. MacIntyre's contention is that capitalist forms of business organization have, in effect, institutionally "won" over the practice—its justification is the pursuit of external goods—such that "much modern industrial productive and service work is organized so as to exclude the features distinctive of a practice," and in such a way that this type of activity is "at once alien and antagonistic to practices."[85]

Three related points contribute to this view. First, Public Limited Companies (PLCs) operate under a variety of legal obligations, but their purpose has (at least within Anglo-American capitalism) been clear since the judgment in the 1919 *Dodge v. Ford Motor Co.* case compelled Henry Ford to issue a dividend rather than cut product prices on the basis that "a business corporation is organized and carried on primarily for the profit of stockholders."[86] Borrowing MacIntyre's terms again, where the capitalist system operates effectively, it represents the victory of external goods over internal goods, of effectiveness over excellence.

Second is the range of intellectual and moral errors in the process of decision-making through which such a victory is institutionalized. Utilitarianism, which as was argued above acts as the primary decision-making method in business organizations, disguises value choices in presenting both the ranking of harms and benefits and the impacts of decisions over time as simple facts, subordinates means to ends, and routinely excludes externalities from the list of consequences to be weighed. In the ordinary conduct of relations in such contexts, the distinction between manipulative and non-manipulative behavior is thus dissolved.[87]

Third is the impact of this on the prospects for moral agency that we have already noted. Here the exclusion of both questions and persons from participation in decision making[88] becomes a feature, perhaps *the* feature, of the moral life of persons whose character is compartmentalized[89] and whose moral agency, the conditions for which require a narrative unity, are critically undermined.[90] As a result, "capitalism . . . provides systematic incentives to develop a type of character that has a propensity to injustice."[91]

These three points provide a very serious critique of capitalist business organizations in the form with which MacIntyre is familiar. Despite this, however, the counterargument has been made[92] that *all* business activities, irrespective of their form of institutionalization, must contain the vestiges of a practice and the virtues to some degree, for if they did not—that is, if the institution had "won" so completely that the virtues had suffered "something near total effacement"[93]—then the institution would have, in effect, killed itself from the inside by failing to sustain the practice on which it itself is founded. In other words, while in capitalist forms of business organization the practice may be potentially and continually under threat from the acquisitiveness and competitiveness of the corporation, it still exists. This counterargument, of course, suggests that MacIntyre is overly pessimistic in his assessment. That particular forms of institutionalization may be more or less conducive to the sustenance and development of the practices they house, however, would seem to be self-evident.

A Conducive Environment

The third precondition for a virtuous business organization is a conducive environment. It is clear that MacIntyre regards institutions as open systems that are both affected by other institutions in society and are capable (in both positive and negative ways) of compartmentalizing themselves from them. It is apparent therefore that a particularly significant factor in any organization's ability to maintain and exercise the virtues and support the practice it houses is the extent to which the environment is more or less conducive to such activity. As we have noted, character at the individual level, and by extension at the institutional level, is "vulnerable to environment" as well as being "a bulwark *against* environment."[94] Hence, we would expect that an unconducive environment would be problematic for organizational virtue.

An ethically responsive environment will encourage institutions to act virtuously. An ethically neutral environment will provide no utilitarian reasons for institutions to act virtuously, and a vicious environment will encourage the institution to function viciously.

The mechanism by which this operates is through the variation in the distribution of external goods in the market. Thus, an institution that is subject to poor economic performance, for example, is likely to be under increased pressure to act viciously—the economic vulnerability of the institution is likely to affect the exercise of the virtues by those with decision-making authority. Hence, Dobson's forlorn comment that the virtuous firm, if placed in a competitive market environment, "would rapidly perish"[95] is predicated on an ethically neutral or vicious environment. MacIntyre himself warns: "We should therefore expect that, if in a particular society the pursuit of external goods were to become dominant, the concept of the virtues might suffer first attrition and then perhaps something near total effacement, although simulacra might abound."[96]

In other words, a society in which a vice such as avarice has been, in effect, legitimized in capitalist business organizations would provide such an unhealthy environment that even the presence of virtuous agents together with a supportive mode of institutionalization might not be sufficient to ensure the existence of organizational virtue. It is MacIntyre's contention that such legitimizing of avarice has become ubiquitous in modern capitalist society.[97] And while, again, MacIntyre's assessment may be viewed as overly pessimistic, it points to the importance of a conducive environment within which organizational virtue may flourish.

One further point that merits consideration here relates to the work of institutional theorists. DiMaggio and Powell's seminal article questioned the "startling homogeneity of organizational forms and practices"[98] and defined institutional isomorphism as "a constraining process that forces one unit in a population to resemble other units that face the same set of environmental conditions."[99] However, as Nelson and Gopalan have observed, while organizations are subject to isomorphic pressures, "they also maintain boundaries, which distinguish them from their environment and provide a separate identity"; indeed, "[w]ithout such boundary maintenance, the organization will dissolve."[100] They also note the existence (in the sociology of religion and social movements rather than in organization studies) of "reciprocal opposition," in which organizational values and institutional forms are developed "whose features form an inverse image of each other. . . . The oppositional group adopts symbols and social structures that are the reciprocal opposite of those used by the dominant group."[101] This suggests that, while a conducive environment is clearly beneficial to organizational virtue, it may be possible for organizations to resist a neutral or vicious environment and potentially to create around themselves a more conducive environment than most other organizations experience.

7. CONCLUSION

In this chapter I have outlined a particular approach to the application of virtue ethics to business organizations. My intention has been to show how MacIntyre's virtues-goods-practice-institution schema provides a robust conceptual framework and a set of terminology with which to explore these issues. Within MacIntyre's schema the focal point for the exercise of virtue is the practice, but all practices require institutions to house them, giving rise to business organizations as practice-institution combinations. Within any such practice-institution combination, however, there are, in fact, two practices. The first is the practice at the core of the activity—be it farming or fishing, architecture or construction, the provision of financial services, mining, retailing, or whatever. The second is the practice of making and sustaining the institution itself. Within both practices craftspeople, whether engaged principally in the practice at the core or principally with the institution, can endeavor to maintain an integrity of character by exercising the virtues and producing excellent goods or services or institutions, while also themselves gaining such internal goods as are available, thereby helping them in their narrative quest toward their own *telos*.

I then explored the characteristics of the virtuous business organization—its good purpose, its focus on the excellence of the practice at its core, its ability to strike an appropriate balance between internal and external goods, and its ability to resist the corrupting power of other institutions in its environment. I also explored the corporate virtues necessary to sustain such virtuous organizations and identified three preconditions necessary for virtuous business organizations: the presence of virtuous agents at both the practice and institutional levels, a conducive mode of institutionalization, and a conducive environment within which organizational virtue might flourish.

This conceptual framework and set of preconditions provides, I would argue, the necessary level of sophistication in our understanding of business organizations and of virtue ethics in this context that Koehn's and Solomon's works do not provide, as well as offering a sufficiently critical understanding of the nature of the modern corporation and of its significant part in influencing the ethics of modernity. In contrast to PBE, it provides the necessary particularity of application to the specific context of organizational and business ethics, while providing a conceptual framework within which to situate any analysis of particular business ethics issues. In addition, and importantly, it provides a terminology with which to discuss these issues, a terminology that is derived from Aristotle but is at the same time readily applicable to modernity.

Drawing on this terminology and the conceptual framework it supports, the task, for those who are convinced that virtue ethics offers the best way forward in the urgent task of reforming our business organizations, is to provide examples of its current application and to encourage its wider adoption.[102] In such a task, I would argue, we are engaged in a genuine search for excellence.

NOTES

1. See, for example, Philippa Foot, *Virtues and Vices and Other Essays in Moral Philosophy* (Oxford, UK: Blackwell, 1978); Alasdair MacIntyre, *After Virtue*, 2nd ed. (London: Duckworth, 1985); C. Swanton, *Virtue Ethics: A Pluralistic View* (New York: Oxford University Press, 2003).

2. Early examples are Joseph DesJardins, "Virtues and Business Ethics," in *An Introduction to Business Ethics*, ed. G. Chryssides and J. Kaler (London: Chapman and Hall, 1993), 136–42, and first published in *Corporate Governance and Institutional-*

ising Ethics, ed. M. Hoffman (Lanham, Md.: Lexington Books, 1984); Robert Solomon, *Ethics and Excellence: Cooperation and Integrity in Business* (New York: Oxford University Press, 1992); and Robert Solomon, "Corporate Roles, Personal Virtues: An Aristotelean Approach to Business Ethics," *Business Ethics Quarterly* 2, no. 3 (1992): 317–39.

3. DesJardins, "Virtues"; C. Horvath, "Excellence v. Effectiveness: MacIntyre's Critique of Business," *Business Ethics Quarterly* 5, no. 3 (1995): 499–532.

4. DesJardins, "Virtues," 137.

5. Horvath, "Excellence v. Effectiveness," 500–501.

6. Horvath, "Excellence v. Effectiveness," 511.

7. MacIntyre, *After Virtue*, 7, 11–12, 24, respectively.

8. During the writing of this chapter the untimely death of Robert Solomon was announced. His contribution to business ethics, particularly through a virtue ethics lens, was considerable. One particular regret is that, since I later in this chapter criticize his particular approach, he will not now have an opportunity to respond. He would doubtless have done so in the robust fashion that so characterized his work.

9. Solomon, "Corporate Roles," 323.

10. Solomon, "Corporate Roles," 324.

11. Daryl Koehn, "The Role of Virtue Ethics in the Analysis of Business Practice," paper presented at the annual conference of the Society for Business Ethics, Atlanta, Georgia, 1993.

12. Horvath, "Excellence v. Effectiveness," 524.

13. Daryl Koehn, "A Role for Virtue Ethics in the Analysis of Business Practice," *Business Ethics Quarterly* 5, no. 3 (1995): 534.

14. Koehn, "A Role for Virtue Ethics," 534.

15. Koehn, "A Role for Virtue Ethics," 536.

16. MacIntyre, *After Virtue*, 148.

17. MacIntyre, *After Virtue*, 216–20.

18. Koehn, "A Role for Virtue Ethics," 536.

19. MacIntyre, *After Virtue*, 149.

20. J. Porter, *The Recovery of Virtue* (London: SPCK, 1994), 114.

21. J. Porter, *Recovery of Virtue*, 121–23.

22. MacIntyre, *After Virtue*, 150.

23. Solomon, *Ethics and Excellence*, 107; see also R. Solomon, "Aristotle, Ethics and Business Organizations," *Organization Studies* 25, no. 6 (2004): 1021–43.

24. J. Morse, "The Missing Link between Virtue Theory and Business Ethics," *Journal of Applied Philosophy* 16, no. 1 (1999): 52.

25. Horvath, "Excellence v. Effectiveness," 505.

26. Solomon, "Corporate Roles," 327.

27. Koehn, "Role for Virtue Ethics," 537. Koehn cites the Kantian O'Nora O'Neill's argument that competitions in which the winner intends to win are immoral because winner and loser are not treated with equal respect. She argues that virtue ethics, by contrast, celebrates the human capacity to develop a noble soul in and through friendly competition and so does not contain the same equalizing tendency.

28. Morse, "Missing Link," 50.

29. J. Doris, *Lack of Character: Personality and Moral Behaviour* (New York: Cambridge University Press, 2002); R. Solomon, "Victims of Circumstances? A Defense of Virtue Ethics in Business," *Business Ethics Quarterly* 13, no. 1 (2003): 43–62; Gilbert Harman, "No Character or Personality," *Business Ethics Quarterly* 13, no. 1 (2003): 87–94.

30. Doris, *Lack of Character*, 23–26.

31. J. Webber, "Virtue, Character and Situation," *Journal of Moral Philosophy* 3, no. 2 (2006): 194.

32. Doris, *Lack of Character*, 22–23.

33. Webber, "Virtue, Character and Situation," 205.

34. Harman, "No Character or Personality," 92.

35. Solomon, "Victims of Circumstances?" 49.

36. Solomon, "Victims of Circumstances?" 51.

37. Solomon, "Victims of Circumstances?" 56.

38. Solomon, "Victims of Circumstances?" 45.

39. The Dime-in-the-Slot Experiment and the Zimbardo Stanford Prison Experiment are specious according to Webber. The Milgram Obedience Experiment, the Bystander Experiment, and the Samaritan Experiment do not necessarily support the arguments propounded. See Webber, "Virtue, Character and Situation," 195–98 and 198–201, respectively.

40. Webber, "Virtue, Character and Situation," 204.

41. Webber, "Virtue, Character and Situation," 211.

42. G. Weaver, "Virtue in Organizations: Moral Agencies as a Foundation for Moral Agency," *Organization Studies* 27, no. 3 (2006): 345.

43. Solomon, "Victims of Circumstances?" 56.

44. Solomon, "Victims of Circumstances?" 46.

45. Weaver, "Virtue in Organizations," 346.

46. Weaver, "Virtue in Organizations," 347.

47. Weaver, "Virtue in Organizations," 353.

48. Solomon, "Corporate Roles," 321.

49. Solomon, "Corporate Roles," 322.

50. R. Solomon, *A Better Way to Think about Business: How Personal Integrity Leads to Corporate Success* (New York: Oxford University Press, 1999).

51. I am indebted to John Dobson for these insights in an undated working paper from California Polytechnic State University titled "Virtue Ethics as a Foundation for Business Ethics: A 'MacIntyre-Based' Critique."

52. Solomon, *Ethics and Excellence*, 20.

53. R. Solomon, "Business with Virtue: Maybe Next Year?" *Business Ethics Quarterly* 10, no. 1 (2000): 340–41.

54. Morse, "Missing Link," 54–55.

55. See Daryl Koehn, "Virtue Ethics, the Firm and Moral Psychology," *Business Ethics Quarterly* 8, no. 3 (1998): 501; and G. Moore, "Corporate Character: Modern Virtue Ethics and the Virtuous Corporation," *Business Ethics Quarterly* 15, no. 4 (2005): 659–85.

56. The following sections draw largely on a previous paper, G. Moore and R. Beadle, "In Search of Organizational Virtue in Business: Agents, Goods, Practices, Institutions and Environments," *Organization Studies* 27, no. 3 (2006): 369–89, which is used with the kind permission of Sage Publications Ltd. Copyright © Sage Publications Ltd., 2006. My debt to and the permission of Ron Beadle are also duly acknowledged.

57. See R. Beadle and G. Moore, "MacIntyre on Virtue and Organization," *Organization Studies* 27, no. 3 (2006): 323–40; R. Beadle, "The Misappropriation of MacIntyre," *Reason in Practice* 2, no. 2 (2002): 45–54; Geoff Moore, "On the Implications of the Practice-Institution Distinction: MacIntyre and the Application of Modern Virtue Ethics to Business," *Business Ethics Quarterly* 12, no. 1 (2002): 19–32; Moore, "Corporate Character"; Geoff Moore, "Humanizing Business: A Modern Virtue Ethics Approach," *Business Ethics Quarterly* 15, no. 2 (2005): 237–55.

58. MacIntyre, *After Virtue*, 187.

59. See MacIntyre, *After Virtue*, 189–91, and also A. MacIntyre, "A Partial Response to My Critics," in *After MacIntyre*, ed. J. Horton and S. Mendus (Cambridge, UK: Polity Press, 1994), 284.

60. MacIntyre, *After Virtue*, 194.

61. MacIntyre, *After Virtue*, 188.

62. MacIntyre, "Partial Response," 284.

63. For further exploration of what it means to be a craftsperson operating in a practice, see Moore, "Humanizing Business."

64. MacIntyre, *After Virtue*, 191.

65. MacIntyre, *After Virtue*, 194–95 (my italics).

66. It is quite likely that many institutions will house more than one practice. For simplicity, however, I assume a single practice within any particular institution. It should also be noted that this second practice of making and sustaining institutions will also require its own institutionalization. There is not space here to consider the legal, governance, social custom, and other elements of this informal institutionalization.

67. MacIntyre, "Partial Response," 289.

68. See, for example, I. Akaah and E. Riordan, "Judgments of Professionals about Ethical Issues in Marketing Research: A Replication and Extension," *Journal of Marketing Research* 26, no. 1 (1989): 112–20; R. Baumhart, "Problems in Review: How Ethical Are Businessmen?" *Harvard Business Review* 39, no. 4 (1961): 6–9; and S. Brenner and E. Molander, "Is the Ethics of Business Changing?" *Harvard Business Review* 55, no. 1 (1977): 57–71.

69. See S. Klein, "Is a Moral Organization Possible?" *Business and Professional Ethics Journal* 7, no. 1 (1988): 51–73, and Moore, "Corporate Character."

70. See Kenneth Goodpaster and J. Matthews, "Can a Corporation Have a Conscience?" *Harvard Business Review* 60, no. 1 (1982): 135, and G. Morgan, *Images of Organization* (Thousand Oaks, Calif.: Sage, 1997), 4-8 and *passim*, respectively.

71. Klein, "Is a Moral Organization Possible?" 56.

72. See Moore, "Corporate Character."

73. MacIntyre, *After Virtue*, 194.

74. A. MacIntyre, "Social Structures and Their Threats to Moral Agency," *Philosophy* 7, no. 4 (1999): 317–18.

75. Klein, "Is a Moral Organization Possible?" 60.

76. See Solomon, *Ethics and Excellence*.

77. See Moore, "Corporate Character."

78. MacIntyre, "Social Structures," 322.

79. See Moore, "Corporate Character," for more on the distinction and relationship between culture and character.

80. MacIntyre, *After Virtue*, 194–95.

81. MacIntyre, "Partial Response," 285–86.

82. J. Dobson, "MacIntyre's Position on Business: A Response to Wicks," *Business Ethics Quarterly* 7, no. 4 (1997): 125–32.

83. I do not have sufficient space here to deal specifically with the role of management within MacIntyre's schema. See Geoff Moore, "Re-imagining the Morality of Management: A Modern Virtue Ethics Approach," paper presented at "Alasdair MacIntyre's Revolutionary Aristotelianism: Ethics, Resistance and Utopia," London Metropolitan University, 2007, where I deal more fully with this aspect of the conceptual framework developed here.

84. Weaver, "Virtue in Organizations," 356.

85. MacIntyre, "Partial Response," 286.

86. Cited in E. Dodd, "For Whom are Corporate Managers Trustees?" *Harvard Law Review* 45, no. 7 (1932): 1145–63.

87. This is a consistent feature of MacIntyre's work. See A. MacIntyre, "Against Utilitarianism," in *Aims in Education*, ed. S. Wiseman (Manchester, UK: University of Manchester Press, 1964), 1–23; A. MacIntyre, "Utilitarianism and Cost Benefit Analysis," in *Values in the Electric Power Industry*, ed. K. Sayre (Notre Dame, Ind.: University of Notre Dame Press, 1977), 217–37; A. MacIntyre, "Corporate Modernity and Moral Judgment: Are They Mutually Exclusive?" in *Ethics and Problems of the Twenty-First Century*, ed. Kenneth Goodpaster and K. Sayre (Notre Dame, Ind.: University of Notre Dame Press, 1979), 122–33; MacIntyre, *After Virtue*; MacIntyre, "Social Structures."

88. See Robert Jackall, *Moral Mazes* (New York: Oxford University Press, 1988), 6.

89. MacIntyre, "Utilitarianism and Cost Benefit Analysis"; MacIntyre, "Corporate Modernity"; MacIntyre, "Social Structures."

90. MacIntyre, "Social Structures," *passim*.

91. A. MacIntyre, *Marxism and Christianity* (London: Duckworth, 1995), xiv.

92. Moore, "Corporate Character."

93. MacIntyre, *After Virtue*, 196.

94. Solomon, "Victims of Circumstances?" 46.

95. John Dobson, "The Feminist Firm: A Comment," *Business Ethics Quarterly* 6, no. 2 (1996): 227.

96. MacIntyre, *After Virtue*, 196.

97. MacIntyre, *Marxism and Christianity*, xiii.

98. P. DiMaggio and W. Powell, "The Iron Cage Revisited: Institutional Isomorphism and Collective Rationality in Organizational Fields," *American Sociological Review* 48, no. 2 (1983): 148.

99. DiMaggio and Powell, "Iron Cage," 149.

100. Reed Nelson and S. Gopalan, "Do Organizational Cultures Replicate National Cultures? Isomorphism, Rejection and Reciprocal Opposition in the Corporate Values of Three Countries," *Organization Studies* 24, no. 7 (2003): 1119.

101. Nelson and Gopalan, "Organizational Cultures," 1120.

102. For particular examples see Moore, "Corporate Character," and Moore and Beadle, "In Search of Organizational Virtue."

Chapter Three

The Human Rights Obligations of Multinational Corporations

Denis G. Arnold, University of
North Carolina–Charlotte

We live in an era of increasing economic globalization. While trade among nations has been an important feature of the global economy for centuries, recent years have seen a rapid increase in international trade. Multinational corporations (MNCs) operate in a multitude of political jurisdictions and so are subject to a multitude of legal frameworks. Frequently, the laws regarding such matters as the treatment of customers, the treatment of employees, and protection for the environment are significantly different in different host nations. In the case of developing economies, consumer protection, worker safety, and environmental safeguards are often poorly developed or nonexistent. Even when such laws exist in developing nations, the law enforcement and judicial apparatus necessary to ensure compliance often does not exist. MNCs operating in such nations are often free to determine for themselves whether or not they will adhere to host nation laws. As a result, MNCs must determine for themselves what minimum moral standards ought to be adhered to in their global operations. One standard that is increasingly being used to determine the minimum ethical obligations to which MNCs should adhere in their global operations is that of human rights.

1. HUMAN RIGHTS VS. LEGAL RIGHTS

Human rights differ from legal rights in that, unlike legal rights, the existence of human rights is not contingent upon any institution. Many nations grant their citizens certain constitutional or legal rights via foundational documents or legal precedent. However, the rights that are protected vary among nations. Some nations ensure that the rights of citizens are protected via effective policing and an independent judiciary. Frequently, however, poor citizens and disfavored groups are not provided with the same level of protection for their legal rights as the economic and political elite. Persons who are deprived of their rights do not thereby cease to have those rights. As A. I. Melden has argued:

> [T]he complaint that persons are deprived of their human rights when, for example, they are subjected to forced indenture by their employers, is a complaint that their rights have been violated and implies, clearly, that they have rights they are unjustly prevented from exercising. If one were deprived of one's rights in the sense in which one would be deprived of things in one's physical possession by having them taken away, one would no longer have the rights, and there would be no grounds for the complaint. So it is with the denial of a person's right—this does not consist in denying that he has the right but, rather, in denying him, by withholding from him, that to which he has the right or the means or opportunity for its exercise.[1]

Employers may deny employees or other stakeholders their rights whether or not local governments are complicit, but in doing so they in no way diminish the legitimacy of the claims of their employees to those rights. However, by virtue of their failure to properly respect these stakeholders, such employers succeed in diminishing their own standing in the community of rights holders.

In the weak and failed states where many multinational corporations operate, they are often the most powerful institutions in existence. In such cases, corporate managers are uniquely situated to help ensure that the basic rights of individuals within their spheres of influence are protected. Many corporations have embraced this obligation. For example, Mattel ensures that all of the factories in its global supply chains meet basic human rights standards. Nike provides microloans to community members in the areas where it has large contract factories, thus providing additional help to improve the economic well-being of these communities. And Adidas ensures that the basic rights of workers in its contract factories are respected, while using its occupational safety expertise to help noncontract factories in those same communities improve working conditions.

2. THE UNITED NATIONS "DRAFT NORMS"

The promulgation of the United Nations Universal Declaration of Human Rights, together with the advocacy of organizations such as Amnesty International and Human Rights Watch, has led to the widespread acceptance of human rights as a basic tool of moral evaluation by individuals of widely divergent political and religious beliefs. However, the UN Universal Declaration has well-known conceptual limitations and is of limited use in assessing the ethical obligations of multinational corporations. First, it presents a list of rights that would ideally be granted to individuals (e.g., the right to paid vacation time) rather than a rigorously grounded set of core ethical obligations. In a world of scarce resources and competitive markets, such an ideal list fails to provide clear ethical standards for the conduct of business. Second, the UN Universal Declaration does not distinguish between the ethical obligations of different global actors, and instead implicitly concerns itself with the obligations of nation-states to their citizens. In particular, it does not distinguish between individuals, corporations, nongovernmental organizations, and states.

Recently, the UN Working Group on the Methods and Activities of Transnational Corporations has produced Draft Norms on the Responsibilities of Corporations and Other Business Enterprises with Respect to Human Rights. These draft norms articulate a robust list of ethical obligations and specifically identify MNCs as responsible for their fulfilment. Furthermore, once adopted, adherence to these norms on the part of corporations is to be monitored and verified by the UN. The list of basic rights identified by the working group includes rights that enjoy relatively universal acknowledgment in a wide range of regional and international codes and agreements such as equal opportunity, nondiscrimination, collective bargaining, and safe and healthy working environments. However, the Draft Norms go well beyond this, stipulating for example that corporations must:

- Seek to ensure that "the goods and services they provide will not be used to abuse human rights."
- Contribute to "the highest attainable standard of physical and mental health; adequate housing; privacy; education; freedom of thought, conscience and religion" for all people.
- Ensure that "human rights, public health and safety, bioethics, and the precautionary principle" are respected in all of their environmental practices.

Unsurprisingly, the Draft Norms have met with strenuous resistance from business interests. Part of this resistance is due to the fact that the Draft Norms attribute such a wide and imprecise range of obligations to MNCs, and do so without the benefit of a conceptual scheme for distinguishing between the basic ethical obligations of MNCs on the one hand and states on the other. The Draft Norms seem to be aspirational in the same manner as the Universal Declaration. However, it is important that a clear distinction be drawn between the minimum duties of MNCs and their managers, and those actions that it would be good to perform but which are not morally required. The latter sort of activities, if performed consistently over time, might serve as a basis for describing an MNC as a good global citizen—or a good citizen of those nations in which it operates—but the failure to perform such actions does not mean that an MNC fails to meet its minimum moral duties. What is needed, then, is an account of the basic human rights obligations of MNCs.

3. BASIC RIGHTS

Human rights are moral rights that apply to all persons in all nations, regardless of whether the nation in which a person resides acknowledges and protects those rights. It is in this sense that human rights are said to be *inalienable*. In order to gain clarity about basic human rights, it is necessary to answer certain philosophical questions about their nature. Two of the most basic questions are the following: How can basic human rights be justified? What basic human rights exist? Let us consider each question in turn.

Human rights are rights enjoyed by humans not because we are members of the species *Homo sapiens sapiens*, but because fully functional members of our species are persons. Personhood is a metaphysical category that may or may not be unique to *Homo sapiens sapiens*. To be a person one must be capable of reflecting on one's desires at a second-order level, and one must be capable of acting in a manner consistent with one's considered preferences.[2] The capacity to reflect on one's competing preferences and to act in a manner consistent with one's second-order preferences is a key feature of personhood and one that distinguishes persons from mere animals. It is in this sense that the idea of personhood is properly understood as metaphysical rather than biological.[3]

Theorists with a wide range of commitments readily agree that persons enjoy a basic right to individual freedom, and that other persons have a duty not to restrict or constrain the freedom of others without strong justification.[4] This right is grounded in Kant's second formulation of the categorical imperative: "Act so that you treat humanity, whether in your own person or in that of another, always as an end and never as a means only."[5] The popular expression of this principle is that morality requires that we respect people. Kant provides a sustained defense of the doctrine of respect for persons, and he and his interpreters specify in detail its practical implications. Respecting other persons requires that one refrain from interfering with their decisions and actions. Typically one person is justified in limiting the freedom of another only when his or her own freedom is unjustly restricted by that person. One traditional way of capturing this sense of a liberty right is that individuals should be free to as much liberty or freedom as is compatible with like liberty or freedom for all.

There is little controversy regarding the negative right to liberty or freedom. However, there is significant controversy over whether or not there are positive rights to certain economic and social goods. Positive rights entail not merely negative obligations on the part of others to refrain from certain actions, but a positive obligation to fulfill the right of the rights holder. For example, if individuals have a right to employment or health care in order to ensure their subsistence and well-being, then others have an obligation to provide them with health care or employment. The state may be called upon to fulfill these duties, but in weak or corrupt states such duties may be neglected. And in states where market values trump consideration for basic human rights, such rights may also be neglected. Under such conditions the burden of fulfilling such obligations seems to fall on individuals, but most individuals are not well positioned to meet such obligations. Furthermore, even in cases where the state does meet such alleged obligations, traditional libertarians would argue that it is illegitimate to tax some citizens in order to ensure the subsistence and well-being of others.[6] Have we then reached an impasse?

Arguably there are at least two philosophically sound reasons for thinking that we can move beyond this apparent impasse. First, there is an influential and persuasive argument against the idea that the distinction between negative and positive rights is unsustainable. Second, there is a widely influential set of positive arguments that can be used to support both a right to freedom and minimal welfare rights such as the right to subsistence. Let us consider each argument in turn.

Henry Shue has famously argued that the very distinction between negative and positive rights which the preceding analysis presumes is artificial and inconsistent with social reality.[7] For example, consider the right to physical security (i.e., the right not to be harmed). It is possible to avoid violating a person's right not to be harmed by refraining from certain actions. However, it is not possible to protect a person from harm without taking proactive steps. At a minimum, law enforcement agencies and a criminal justice system are required so that individuals are not left to defend themselves against forces that they are unable to defeat on their own. The existence of these social institutions is predicated on positive actions in the forms of design, implementation, administration, and taxation. In this way it can be seen that the protection of a prototypical negative right requires positive actions, and not merely the avoidance of particular actions. Since negative rights entail both negative and positive duties, the notion of negative vs. positive rights loses its meaning. There are only rights and corresponding obligations, but the obligations that correspond to these rights are both negative and positive. There is then a strong argument against a theory of rights that includes negative but not positive rights.

Now let us turn to the positive arguments. Much of the most important and influential work on human rights has been produced by Kantians. Rather than beginning with rights claims, Kantians begin with obligations or duties to respect other persons. These duties constrain the pursuit of ends, whether they are self-interested goals or projects pursued on behalf of other parties such as shareholders. Respecting persons involves both negative obligations, such as refraining from using others as mere tools via physical force, coercion, or manipulation, and positive obligations, such as supporting physical well-being and the development of basic human capacities. When they stand in the appropriate relationship to an obligation-bearer, persons have rationally justified rights-claims against them. Rights take the form of side-constraints that bound the moral space in which agents may pursue ends without unjustified interference by other agents or institutions. For example, a minor child has legitimate rights-claims against his or her parents regarding his or her physical well-being and the development of his or her human capacities, by virtue of the child's relation to them. The morally legitimate ends of parents do not include actions that substantially undermine the physical well-being or normal development of their child. Similarly, a convenience store owner has a rights-claim against those in his community to be free from assault and robbery. The morally legitimate ends of other community members do not include actions that would undermine the freedom of the store owner.

Wherever corporations do business, they are already in special relationships with a variety of stakeholders, such as workers, customers, and local communities. In their global operations and in their global supply chains, corporations have a duty to respect those with whom they have relationships. Corporate managers, then, have obligations to both ensure that they do not illegitimately undermine the liberty of any persons, and the additional obligation to help ensure that minimal welfare rights to physical well-being and the development of basic human capacities are met within their spheres of influence. For example, corporations have sufficient power and coercive influence to ignore the labor and environmental laws in many developing nations. These host nations typically lack the police and judicial infrastructure necessary to enforce such laws. Host nation governments may also be fearful that if they enforce their own laws, then the corporations may move their operations to nations that are willing to ignore local laws. However, such laws are essential for the protection of the basic rights of the citizens of developing nations. For this reason, corporate managers have an obligation to ensure that local host nations laws are respected.

4. THE MINIMUM MORAL DUTIES OF MNCS

For pragmatic purposes it will be helpful to specify the minimal moral duties of MNCs. Let us begin with those duties regarding liberty or freedom rights. Previously we characterized freedom as controlling one's behavior via one's unforced choice while having knowledge of relevant circumstances. Freedom may be characterized in the following terms:

> This consists in a person's controlling his actions and his participation in trans-actions by his own unforced choice or consent and with knowledge of relevant circumstances, so that his behavior is neither compelled nor prevented by the actions of other persons. Hence, a person's right to freedom is violated if he is subjected to violence, coercion, deception, or any other procedures that attack or remove his informed control of his behavior by his own unforced choice. This right includes having a sphere of personal autonomy and privacy whereby one is let alone by others unless and until he unforcedly consents to undergo their action.[8]

Possessing freedom entails having the general abilities and conditions required for a person to be able to act in a manner consistent with his or her second-order preferences. A right to freedom, then, involves the right to pursue one's own goals and preferences without interference from others. Specifically, it includes control over one's own physical integrity, freedom of belief and expression, and freedom of association. Traditionally, the right to freedom is thought to be as extensive as is compatible with a like right to freedom for all. Such freedom may be rightfully curtailed if a person's actions illegitimately infringe upon the rights of others.

The rights one enjoys as a person are not unlimited in the sense that one is free to exercise all of them under any circumstances. Legitimate restrictions may be placed on the exercise of one's rights by both the state and private enterprise. It is, for example, not an illegitimate infringement of one's right to freedom of expression if an employer prohibits proselytizing on behalf of one's religious convictions while at work. Such activity is typically disruptive and as such incompatible with the purposes for which employees are hired. Furthermore, employees are typically free to engage in such activity when they are not working. Restricting employee activity in this manner does not infringe on an employee's dignity as a person. There are, however, certain restrictions on employee freedom that always violate human dignity because they treat the employee as a tool rather than as a person. Control over one's physical integrity is one such example. This freedom could, for example, be violated by a rule that permitted only one bathroom break each day.

As we have seen, physical and psychological well-being are required for a person to be able to act autonomously. The most important human needs in this regard concern basic goods. Basic goods are the general physical and psychological capabilities necessary for human functioning. In recent years, the relationship between well-being and human functioning has received a great deal of attention from economists and philosophers. Some of the most important work on this topic has been produced by Amartya Sen and Martha Nussbaum.[9] Their distinctive variety of quality-of-life assessment, known as the capabilities approach, has become increasingly influential.

Nussbaum identifies the capabilities necessary for humans to enjoy well-being. Drawing from Nussbaum's work we may identify the most important of these as life, physical health and integrity, freedom of thought and expression, freedom of affiliation, and the ability to exercise practical reason and pursue one's conception of the good. The argument defended here is not that MNCs have an obligation to ensure that stakeholders function well. Instead, the argument is that MNC managers have an obligation to ensure that they do not inhibit employees, customers, community members, and other stakeholders from the opportunity to pursue their basic capabilities.

Given the duty to respect persons with whom they interact, we may conclude that MNCs have minimal duties to ensure that the following rights are respected in their global operations:

- The right to physical security and freedom of movement.
- The right to non-discrimination on the basis of arbitrary characteristics such as race, sex, religion, ethnicity, and sexual orientation.
- The right to freedom of association and collective bargaining.
- The right to fair treatment.
- The right to subsistence.
- The right to develop basic human capabilities.

The first four rights that must be respected are comparatively straightforward. There is little disagreement over whether employees can legitimately be forced to work or locked into factories, or whether customers may legitimately be discriminated against because of their race or sex. And despite the strenuous efforts of companies such as Wal-Mart to resist a union presence in their stores, there is little disagreement that it is morally illegitimate to prohibit employees from collective organizing. With respect to fair treatment, few would disagree that employee evaluations ought to be based on performance and not on personal relationships, and that executive compensation ought to be based on merit and fair market comparisons rather than on membership in "good old boy" networks. The right to subsistence is somewhat more controversial. If it is taken to mean—as it must be—that employees are sometimes entitled to wages above both the legally mandated minimum wage and the prevailing market wage, then there is substantial disagreement about whether or not this is a duty.

Finally, some might object that a duty not to interfere with the development of basic human capacities is far too broad to be regarded as a duty of MNCs. For example, it might be objected that if poor people cannot afford an MNC's products (e.g., a portable water filter), then the MNC undermines access to potable water, and clearly water is a necessary good for the development of human capacities. This is not the case. To see this we need to notice the distinction between refraining from providing someone with the partial means for functioning and interfering with their ability to function. The arguments provided thus far do not support the conclusion that MNCs have obligations to provide citizens in the communities in which they operate with goods or services they need to function. This is an example of an action that might be morally praiseworthy but is not morally required. It is to be differentiated from, for example, the case of selling a portable water filter to people in the rural sectors of developing nations, people who if they could afford the filters at all could do so only after months and perhaps years of savings, only to have the filters fail to perform as advertised because of errors in the manufacturing processes or design flaws. In such cases the MNC would have a duty to compensate customers for the harm it caused and retrieve and either repair or destroy all faulty filters.

5. ARE HUMAN RIGHTS A WESTERN CONCEPT?

At this point in our discussion, it is worthwhile to consider an objection to the foregoing argument concerning human rights. This criticism stems from the observation that the idea of human rights emerged from the Western philosophical tradition but is taken to be universal in its applicability. The claim is then made that human rights are of less importance in the value systems of other cultures. For example, it is argued that "Asian values" emphasize order, discipline, and social harmony, as opposed to individual rights. In this view, the freedom and well-being of individuals should not be allowed to interfere with the harmony of the community—as might be the case, for example, when workers engage in disruptive collective action in an effort to secure their rights. This view might also be used to defend the claim that the moral norms that govern Asian factory operations should emphasize order and discipline, not freedom and well-being.

Several points may be made in reply to this objection. First, Asia is a large region with a vast and heterogeneous population. As Amartya Sen and others have argued, to claim that all, or even most, Asians share a uniform set of values is to impose a level of uniformity that does not exist at present and has not existed in the past.[10] Second, in secular, democratic Asian societies such as India, respect for individual rights has a long tradition. Indeed, there are significant antecedents in the history of the civilizations of the Indian subcontinent that emphasize individual freedom and well-being. For example, in the third century BC, the emperor Ashoka granted his citizens the freedom to embrace whatever religious or philosophical system they might choose, while at the same time he emphasized the importance of tolerance and respect for philosophical and religious beliefs different from one's own.[11] Third, even if it was the case that Asian cultures shared a uniform set of values that deemphasized human rights, this would not by itself provide good reasons for denying or disrespecting the rights to freedom and well-being. This is because the justification of human rights provided above is grounded in rational arguments that are valid across cultures. The critic is likely to retort that such a view reflects Western prejudices grounded in Enlightenment ideals. This response is unpersuasive. Diverse intellectual traditions have emphasized the importance of values derived from reason, rather than from mythology, traditionalism, mere sentiment, or some other source.

6. CONCLUSION

Some MNCs, such as Alcoa, Royal Dutch Shell, and Adidas, have developed their own human rights standards and implemented them in their global operations. Other MNCs, such as Dole Foods, Cutter & Buck, and Toys R Us, have worked with nonprofit organizations such as Social Accountability International to institutionalize human rights standards in their global operations and to certify the continued implementation of such standards. Companies in different sectors of the global economy face distinctive challenges when they seek to ensure that human rights are respected in their operations. However, it is implausible for any company to claim that the protection of basic human rights is exclusively the province of governments. MNCs are capable of protecting human rights and thereby contributing to the promotion of global justice. Those that do so are rightly praised and rewarded; those that fail to do so are rightly condemned and targeted for boycotts and other punitive measures.

NOTES

© Denis G. Arnold. Elements of this essay are excerpted from Denis G. Arnold, "Moral Reasoning, Human Rights, and Global Labor Practices," in *Rising above*

Sweatshops: Innovative Management Approaches to Global Labor Practices, ed. Laura P. Hartman, Denis G. Arnold, and Richard Wolkutch (Westport, Conn.: Praeger, 2003), and Denis G. Arnold, *The Ethics of Global Business* (Malden, Mass.: Blackwell, forthcoming).

1. A. I. Melden, *Rights and Persons* (Berkeley: University of California Press, 1977), 167–68.

2. Harry Frankfurt, *The Importance of What We Care About* (New York: Cambridge University Press, 1988); Gerald Dworkin, *The Theory and Practice of Autonomy* (New York: Cambridge University Press, 1988).

3. Melden, *Rights and Persons*.

4. Robert Nozick, *Anarchy, State, and Utopia* (New York: Basic, 1974); Loren Lomasky, *Persons, Rights, and the Moral Community* (New York: Oxford University Press, 1987); Onora O'Neill, *Bounds of Justice* (New York: Cambridge University Press, 2000).

5. Immanuel Kant, *Groundwork for the Metaphysics of Morals*, ed. Mary McGregor (New York: Cambridge University Press, 1998), section II.

6. Nozick, *Anarchy, State, and Utopia*.

7. Henry Shue, *Basic Rights: Subsistence, Affluence, and U.S. Foreign Policy*, 2nd ed. (Princeton, N.J.: Princeton University Press, 1996).

8. Alan Gewirth, *Human Rights: Essays on Justification and Applications* (Chicago: University of Chicago Press, 1982), 56–57.

9. Amartya Sen, "Well-Being, Agency and Freedom: The Dewey Lectures 1984," *Journal of Philosophy* 82, no. 4 (April 1985): 169–221; Martha Nussbaum, *Women and Human Development* (New York: Cambridge University Press, 2001).

10. Amartya Sen, "Human Rights and Asian Values," in *Business Ethics in the Global Marketplace*, ed. Tibor Machan (Stanford, Calif.: Hoover, 1999), 37–62; Amartya Sen, "East and West: The Reach of Reason," *New York Review of Books* (July 20, 2000): 33–38; Jack Donnely, "Human Rights and Asian Values: A Defense of 'Western' Universalism," in *The East Asian Challenge for Human Rights*, ed. Joanne R. Bauer and Daniel A. Bell (New York: Cambridge University Press, 1999), 60–87; Tatsuo Inoue, "Liberal Democracy and Asian Orientalism," in *The East Asian Challenge for Human Rights*, ed. Joanne R. Bauer and Daniel A. Bell (New York: Cambridge University Press, 1999), 27–59.

11. Sen, "Human Rights and Asian Values."

Chapter Four

Contractarian Business Ethics Today

Ben Wempe, Erasmus University

In the course of Western moral and political philosophy, the social contract model has been invoked in support of a wide variety of theoretical and practical aims. Consider the following instances of social contract argumentation from the history of political theory. In a preliminary dialogue of *Politeia*, Plato uses the social contract argument to challenge Socrates' first attempts at a definition of justice.[1] At the time of the Investiture Controversy, Manegold of Lautenbach, an Alsatian monk living in the eleventh century, evoked the social contract argument to contest bishop appointments by the emperor Henri IV and to support the papal prerogative in this regard.[2] But it was on the occasion of the great political revolutions of the seventeenth and eighteenth century that the social contract tradition grew to full stature, when classical contractarians, such as Hobbes, Locke, and Rousseau, used the contract model to specify conditions under which the national state can legitimately exercise its power. An important new impulse to the social contract tradition came in the course of the twentieth century, when modern contractarians evoked the model as a basis for theories of a just basic structure of society.[3] Most famously, John Rawls breathed new life into the social contract model in order to specify two principles of social justice with which any rational contractor would have to agree. Working contemporaneously to Rawls, Thomas Scanlon developed a methodology of reasonable rejection to delineate the domain of morality itself.

Continuing this multifarious tradition, the most recent application of the social contract argument was its use as a foundation for a theory of business ethics.[4] Analogous to classical and modern contract theories, contractarian business ethics (CBE) seeks to specify principles of organizational ethics on the basis of a social contract model especially adapted for this purpose.

CBE is in vogue among those who study organizational ethics. But one may well wonder how convincing this particular application of the contract model remains. Taking stock of this newest offshoot, we see a diverse and relatively loose usage of the social contract model in the various current CBE proposals. In this chapter I will assess the credentials of CBE as a social contract argument by drawing upon primary sources of the social contract tradition in the history of moral and political theory as well as the secondary literature on contractarianism.[5] I will elaborate on an earlier comparative analysis of the manner in which the contract model has been used in political theory and social justice to suggest four application conditions for any future CBE. Three of these conditions would seem to follow from the inherent logic of the contract model and can be substantiated from the manner in which it was employed by some of the well-established earlier contractarians; a fourth condition stems from the defining characteristics of the business ethics domain. To apply the contract model properly to the domain of business ethics, it should be (1) self-disciplined, i.e., it should not aspire to results beyond what the contract model can realistically establish; (2) argumentative, i.e., it should primarily be used as a "moral proof procedure"[6] and should seek to provide publicly justified reasons[7] that are demonstrative results of the contractarian method; (3) task-directed, i.e., it should be clear what the social contract thought-experiment is intended to model; and (4) domain-specific, i.e., the contractarian choice situation should be tailored to the defining problems of business ethics. These four conditions turn out to be at once points of criticism of current CBE, as well as design criteria for all future work on CBE.

To defend these four application conditions, I will first survey some key contributions to the emerging tradition of CBE and undertake a somewhat more in-depth analysis of Thomas Donaldson and Thomas Dunfee's so-called integrative social contracts theory (ISCT) as an exemplar of the use of social contract thinking in business ethics. I will then review the results of a comparative analysis of the use of the contract model in theories of political authority and of social justice. On the basis of this comparative analysis I will develop and discuss the four design criteria that need to be taken into account when transposing the contract model to the domain of business ethics. I will conclude with a brief review of some of the research topics flowing from this analysis to suggest foci for future discussions.

1. CONTEMPORARY CONTRIBUTIONS TO CBE

The idea of a social contract has often been invoked in connection with questions concerning the legitimacy of business firms, either with or without the explicit use of that label. For example, elements of a social contract argument readily emerge in one of the two contending theories that are traditionally used to argue for corporate legitimacy, commonly known as the "inherence" theory and the "concession" theory.[8] According to the former theory, corporations are entitled to operate on the basis of transfer of rights possessed by individual members of the corporation. According to the latter, corporations completely owe their existence to governmental permission. "[T]hrough its charter a corporation obtains certain special privileges, such as limited liability, which only government can confer."[9] Ideas about what exactly a corporation can exchange for this "license to operate" vary considerably, but it is clear that the relationship of government and corporation is conceived here as a contractual one.

A relatively early elaboration of the social contract idea can be found in the work of Drucker, one of the first authors to suggest that managerial authority is obtained by a process identical with that depicted by the great contract theorists in the tradition of political theory:

> The modern corporation is thus a political institution; its purpose is the creation of legitimate power in the industrial sphere. . . . The political purpose of the corporation is the creation of a legitimate social government on the basis of the original power of the individual property rights of its shareholders. The corporation is the *contrat social* in its purest form.[10]

Another author who explicitly referred to the idea of a social contract as an agreement between business institutions and the enveloping society was Anshen, who argued that

> The system confers legitimacy on business institutions, defines the bounds and rules of their performance, and in a variety of ways evaluates the aggregate cost-benefit trade-off that is the result of business activity. The conclusion is inescapable that the corporation receives its permission to operate from the society and ultimately is accountable to the society for what it does and how it does it.[11]

This author moreover points out a significant shift in the terms of the contract in recent years. Under the terms of the old contract business could freely seek to maximize its profits. "Economic growth . . . was widely accepted as the source of all progress—social as well as economic. The only significant restriction laid upon business was that it must be competitive."[12] But under the new contract

> we are becoming sensitive as a society to the unpleasant and sometimes wounding by-products of unrestricted economic growth. We are beginning to be

concerned about economic and social burdens not recorded in the accounting records of business organizations and not reflected in their costs and prices. Increasingly, this concern is feeding a popular demand that corporations internalize their social costs, that they make positive contributions to minimizing or removing environmental contamination and dangerous and unhealthy working conditions, that they assure to their customers the quality and safety of their products, and that they act affirmatively to provide equal access to jobs and careers to members of all groups in our society.[13]

Anshen's rendition of the social contract argument illustrates the type of substantive obligations that may be imposed upon corporations under the social contract for business. These passages also underscore that the contract between business and society can apparently be renegotiated over the years. What Anshen did not propose was *justification* tied to *reasoned agreement* between interested parties, as in the method of classical and modern contractarians. This idea was first introduced to CBE by Donaldson.[14] His version of the contract between business and society was construed as a relatively direct analogue to classical social contract theories, aiming again to establish the conditions under which corporations could operate legitimately. Donaldson argued that, in exchange for a license to operate, corporations are obliged to "maximize prima facie benefits" for consumers and employees such as efficiency and income, while "minimizing drawbacks" such as depletion and alienation.[15]

Werhane does not explicitly use the term social contract, but she discusses the idea of moral rights[16] and implied contracts[17] in connection with labor relations. This approach allows us to place her in the moral rights and the natural law traditions, which were standard ingredients of classical social contract theories; however, whereas Donaldson's contract extends to the relationship with interest constituencies outside the corporation, such as customers and environmentalists concerned with the prevention of depletion of natural resources, Werhane's focuses on the relationship between the corporation and its internal stakeholders, in particular employees. Her position requires a detailed bill of rights for both employees and employers, such as procedural and substantial due process.[18]

While Keeley explicitly mentions the term "social contract" in the very title of his book and draws upon some central elements from the contract tradition, such as the idea of voluntary consent to social rules binding participants in cooperative social arrangements, it is helpful to situate his work within the interactionist tradition of American sociology or to relate it to the idea that organizations involve multiple actors with conflicting interests that are not entirely resolved by the employment contract.[19]

Keeley invokes the social contract essentially as a metaphor to support a plea for a rights-based approach to the study of organizations, so as to replace the presently dominant goal-based view. Organizations have no goals, Keeley argues, even though their participants may have goals *for* the organization. This is best summed up by his analogy of an organization as an ongoing game, like football or chess. The game has no purpose and its participants may change, but it does have rules that give participants certain rights. Similarly, the organization is an arena in which participants, endowed with certain rights, pursue their individual goals. According to Keeley, this perspective is superior to the goal-based view in descriptive, normative, as well as heuristic terms. Organizations do not need a comprehensive purpose shared by all participants but operate by virtue of agreement on the going activities, which must be seen as "joint means to separate purpose."[20]

Keeley explicitly mentions Hessen and Anshen as two bad examples of the social contract for business; however, his own rendering of the contract argument is open to criticism, too. In his battle against the goal-based paradigm in organization studies he portrays the corporation as an institution that eventually is only of value to the extent it safeguards individual capacities and freedoms. In this fashion he especially emphasizes classical individual rights and "negative" freedoms so that his rendition of the social contract for business quickly assumes the form of classical contractarian theories. Keeley's interpretation might suffice were organizations simply a form of civil polity of citizens pursuing their interests in a loosely defined association. But organizations are focused instruments, constituted by the tightly coordinated actions of their participants. The moral imperative appropriate to this form of association is not merely to eschew coercion, but to foster constructive participation in shared endeavors. The reverse of organizational compulsion is not unimpeded exit but willing cooperation. Keeley's social contract model fails to cater for this most basic function of organizations.

Dunfee draws on the social contract idea by coining the concept of "extant social contracts," by which he means the bottom-up process of convergence of ethical norms among members of the same communities or groups of individuals with common goals. These shared norms give rise to a prima facie duty of compliance on the part of members. If individuals simultaneously participate in multiple communities, then this may give rise to conflicting community-specific norms. In Dunfee's proposal such conflicts can be resolved through the application of priority rules.[21]

Freeman, writing alone and with his coauthor Evan,[22] used the Rawlsian device of a "veil of ignorance" to elaborate a doctrine of "fair contracts," consisting of the six ground rules for corporate conduct. These are labeled as (1) the principle of entry and exit, stipulating that corporations must have clearly defined entry, exit, and renegotiation conditions; (2) the principle of governance, which requires that the procedure for changing the rules of the game must be agreed upon by unanimous consent; (3) the principle of externalities, which asserts that if a contract imposes a cost on external parties, these have the option to become a party to the contract, and the terms are renegotiated; (4) the principle of contracting costs, i.e., all parties to the contract must share in the cost of contracting; (5) the agency principle, i.e., any agent must serve the interests of all stakeholders and adjudicate conflicts within the bounds of the other principals; and finally, (6) the principle of limited immortality, which prescribes managers to act as fiduciaries to the interests of all separate stakeholders and the collective. In the coauthored version,[23] the idea of "fair contracts" is directly used to refute Williamson's classical transaction cost analysis of corporate governance.[24] Pace Williamson, Freeman and Evan argue that shareholders do not have a unique position in the corporate governance equation, so that there is no reason to privilege them at the cost of securities for other key actors in the corporation, as can be gathered from the aforementioned principles.

We may conclude that there is no lack of reference to the contractarian method in the present literature on corporate legitimacy and business ethics. There is no doubt, however, that the most widely cited version of CBE grew out of the eventual cooperation of two of the authors just listed, Donaldson and Dunfee, resulting in their proposal for an integrative social contracts theory (ISCT).[25] Since ISCT is in many ways the best-known and most acclaimed instance of CBE, I will use it as an exemplar from which its credentials and design criteria can be illustrated.

The leading idea of the ISCT project was to reconcile conflicts between norms that may come about in the context of international business, activities involving different occupational groups or across economic communities. In any practice of international business there may well arise conflicts between (usually stricter) moral norms in the home country of the corporation and the (generally more lenient) standards practiced in the host country. A concrete example is the UK-based tobacco giant British American Tobacco. It has a very restrictive policy on underage smoking in its European markets in line with the relevant tobacco control legislation, but in developing markets without such restrictions, British American Tobacco does not adhere to strict policies that limit underage access to cigarettes.[26]

The important point to which ISCT draws our attention is that the more multinational corporations work across national borders, the more likely these conflicts between community-specific moral norms will surface. In the vocabulary of ISCT, such local norms are referred to as microsocial contracts, a notion which largely coincides with Dunfee's idea of extant social contracts. Microsocial contracts, which are characteristically discussed in the plural, refer to the set of "extant, actual agreements existing within and among industries, national economic systems, corporations, trade associations, and so on."[27] The contractual element in this name underscores that the moral force of such a norm within an economic community rests on the consent and support of individual members of that community for that norm. The principal ambition of ISCT, then, is to seek to adjudicate possible conflicts between microsocial contracts originating from different economic communities by means of identifying universal, more fundamental principles, called hypernorms.

In view of this general description of the project an average business practitioner will naturally wonder what prompts the need for these hypernorms. And why would we obey them? In what follows I will examine how ISCT develops an answer to these two questions and the precise role the social contract plays in ISCT. These efforts will ultimately assist in the development of criteria for any future work on CBE.

2. FURTHER ANALYSIS OF THE ICST ARGUMENT

ISCT proceeds from an inventory of the current state of normative business ethics by arguing that it is insufficiently equipped to deal with typical problems of the present-day business world. In this respect, ISCT seeks to improve upon currently available "pivotal" ethical theories, such as utilitarianism, Kantianism, virtue ethics, or the stakeholder model. By their very nature, these general ethical theories are incapable of ever rising above a "view from nowhere." Donaldson and Dunfee point out:

> No single theory has emerged that is fully capable of providing guidance about the gamut of challenging business ethics matters. . . . For want of a usable theory, many academics . . . have turned to the pivotal traditions of ethical theory — in other words, to the broad normative theories of consequentialism, virtue ethics, Kantian deontology, and pragmatism. . . . Yet, none of these philosophically inspired attempts has been fully satisfactory. What has gone wrong? Why has no one been able to use these singly or in combination, to establish a single, generally accepted paradigm in business ethics?[28]

Their diagnosis runs as follows:

> We believe the difficulty of such approaches lies largely in their imprecision. As sometimes happens when grand, broadly drawn theories are applied to specific

issues, the results are blurry. . . . [T]he pivotal traditions of ethical theory, when applied in undiluted form to real-world problems, have offered a "view from nowhere." They have been incapable of locating the complex, particular problems of corporations, industries, economic systems, marketing strategies, etc., in a way that would provide an institutional "somewhere."[29]

Donaldson and Dunfee present ISCT as a remedy that aspires to bridge the gap between the sterile universalism of "the view from nowhere" and the danger of relativism that always accompanies an emphasis on context in the development of ethical norms. ISCT's remedy is based on the identification of a series of hypernorms. But how are these to be established?

Hypernorms and the Social Contract

The social contract model generally functions as a framework for justification in ethics. This framework is based on the liberal idea that the legitimacy of social rules and institutions depends on their being freely and publicly acceptable to all individuals bound by them. If rational individuals in appropriately defined circumstances (the contractors) could or would agree to certain rules or institutions, then insofar as we identify with these individuals and their interests, what they accept should also be acceptable to us now as a basis for our cooperation.

In the ISCT project this general idea of a social contract is elaborated in two entirely different senses. Alongside microsocial contracts, which we already came across in the work of Dunfee, ISCT introduces a macrosocial contract. Within the boundaries of the community, microsocial contracts have normative force because a sufficient number of individual members subscribe to them. In contrast, the macrosocial contract, which is typically discussed in the singular, stands for the hypothetical style of contracting in the manner of some well-established social contract theories. The latter device serves as an adjudicatory mechanism to reconcile actual conflicts between conflicting microsocial contracts.

By analogy to classical and modern social contract theories, one would expect the authors to use the macrosocial contract thought-experiment to derive relevant hypernorms. ISCT, however, introduces a further layer of complexity. Donaldson and Dunfee distinguish three types of hypernorms: procedural, structural, and substantive.[30] Procedural hypernorms refer to the preconditions of exit and voice that are required to establish authentic local norms; structural hypernorms deal with organizing all matters necessary for the organization of the economic community, irrespective of any specific preferences of individual members; only substantive hypernorms serve directly to accommodate conflicting community-specific norms.

The point to observe here is that only the first two categories of hyper-norms result from the thought-experiment and the ensuing agreement of the contractors to the macrosocial contract. The substantive hypernorms, how-ever—the type of principles that do the real work in the ISCT framework—can be discovered by anyone who goes to the trouble of surveying the rele-vant evidence. Substantive hypernorms do not so much result from the contract, but they are to be *recognized*—not only by the contractors, but also by you and me. If we may take recognition to be a weaker form of agreement than rational consent, this distinction tends to loosen the connection between the substantive hypernorms and the macrosocial contract. It renders the func-tion of the macrosocial contract less prominent within the conceptual ma-chinery of ISCT. As far as the identification of substantive hypernorms is con-cerned, we can do without the macrosocial contract altogether.[31]

ISCT's Practical Guidance

We may now return to the question of whether ISCT actually succeeds in de-livering on its promise to provide more concrete practical guidance. Donald-son and Dunfee draw conclusions on four concrete examples, but in these cases the actual content of the covering hypernorms are not specified. These examples of substantive hypernorms concern bribery, gender discrimination, workplace safety, and ethics in marketing research.[32] They also indicate that the relevant hypernorms that are found in this manner have a *presumptive* sta-tus, i.e., they can always be refuted again if the balance of the evidence for and against changes. While this may look like and is in fact praised as, an at-tractive and flexible procedure,[33] it is unlikely to make substantive hyper-norms any more practical.

It is no surprise, therefore, that several commentators have criticized ISCT for the lack of more concrete substantive hypernorms.[34] In spite of these ex-hortations, Donaldson and Dunfee have so far declined to provide a list of substantive hypernorms, pointing out that

> more precise definition of the issue, stemming from the process in which one first identifies the ethical decision and then seeks to identify relevant hyper-norms, is more likely to produce results than a top-down analysis in which a simple, preexisting "definitive list" list of hypernorms is used with deductive reasoning.[35]

This presumably also means that Donaldson and Dunfee consider the compi-lation of a list of hypernorms to be a task for the community of business ethics scholars, and not merely a task resting on their shoulders. This may turn out to be a sensible proposal. This complicates, however, ISCT's initial claim to be able to provide better practical guidance than the "pivotal" general theories.

It is the combination of this claim and its omission not yet to have come up with more concrete substantive hypernorms, which leads us to the conclusion that, as it presently stands, ISCT fails in its own terms. The question, hence, immediately arises: How can CBE do a better job at providing practical guidance? One suggestion would be to simply carry on with the work of identifying more substantive hypernorms following the four examples set out in the book so as to come to some system or perhaps a provisional list of substantive hypernorms. In light of the above line in inquiry it is also important to consider a revised CBE that makes a more complete application of the social contract argument. In order to prepare the way for a more robust CBE, I will end this chapter with a sketch of four design criteria that should be taken into account in developing CBE to its full potential.

3. DESIGN CRITERIA FOR CBE

The suggestion developed in the preceding section of this chapter was that most problems of ISCT can be traced to a misunderstanding of the *nature* of the contract device as a method of justification. In a previous paper I have suggested a neutral and robust method for this purpose on the basis of an inventory of some of the existing contract theories.[36] This was based on a comparative analysis of the method of argument employed in two established groups of social contract theories. Classical theories dating from the seventeenth and eighteenth centuries used the contract device to establish the conditions for a legitimate exercise of political authority. Modern theories from the twentieth century evoked the contract device to formulate principles of social justice. This comparative analysis of the two families of established social contract theories suggests a number of main criticisms of current CBE, which can in turn be stated in the form of design criteria for any future CBE, as the elements of an architect's program of demands. These criteria may be seen as boundary conditions for a well-formed CBE and will be discussed as the criteria of self-discipline, argumentative method, task-directedness, and domain-specificity, respectively.

Self-Disciplinedness

The idea of self-discipline serves to remind us that, when applied to the domains of political authority or just institutional arrangement, the contract model was characteristically used to establish some regulatory ideals or formal results. In the case of classical social contract theories, the contract was characteristically used to specify the conditions of legitimate political authority, but not any concrete legislation.[37] Similarly, modern contract theories of social justice used the contract to work out a set of formal principles in terms of which existing basic institutions could be evaluated. Rawls, for example, specifies two general principles for the basic structure but he leaves the contents of the laws to be established in the legislative stage, where the contract model no longer has a part to play.[38] The social contract for business should similarly be restricted to establishing formal rather than substantive results.

Various CBE proposals seem to fall short of the self-discipline standard. Werhane, for example, comes up with a useful but quite minute bill of rights, which she argues are all implied in the relationship between employers and employees.[39] And in the ISCT project, the contract also seems to be invoked to establish some fairly substantive results. This can be seen from the four examples of presumptive hypernorms.[40] Apparently, in the authors' view, the ISCT methodology can be used to make out that there is a presumptive hypernorm against corrupt practices such as the airplane manufacturer paying money to the minister of defense of a developing country, to facilitate winning a contract for jet fighters. Another hypernorm forbids discrimination, as in the case of the female drivers of a global express delivery firm in Saudi Arabia.

Many of the commentaries on ISCT are critical of Donaldson and Dunfee's reluctance to provide more examples of substantive hypernorms. For instance, Mayer and Cava have sought to employ the ISCT framework to the problem of international gender discrimination to point out that it fails to resolves this issue satisfactorily.[41] Husted has also signaled problems in the application of the empirical methods used by the ISCT project, which he illustrates on the basis of discriminatory practices in Mexico.[42] Rowan has concluded that failure to specify more concrete hypernorms is at odds with the promise to attend issues of business ethics more adequately than the extant general ethical theories. At the very least ISCT would need to put together a "formalized partial list" of hypernorms that apply to functional areas of business operation.[43] Soule compared ISCT with the project of Rawls, pointing out that this influential political philosopher would have done only half of his job had he not specified his two principles of justice. Like Rawls, Donaldson and Dunfee ought to make their project complete by providing "a few good managerial principles."[44] Hartman has sought to apply the ISCT framework to the issue of global labor standards and concluded that it is capable of supporting universal labor rights, such as the rights to life and freedom from slavery, but it does not provide sufficient guidance for the more context-embedded "relative" rights, such as the minimal level of safety consistent with a particular culture or specific conditions.[45]

All these commentators therefore seem keen on making *more concrete* the practical significance of the ISCT framework. If the idea of a self-disciplined CBE is sound, then this would suggest that a more realistic way in which the contract model for business can provide practical guidance is along the lines of establishing "mid-level bridging principles"[46] or the model of specification elaborated by Richardson.[47] This way more substantive content may be added to the hypernorms, providing us with a better sense of the general norms of the macrosocial contract without spelling out *concrete policy issues*, such as are at stake in the examples discussed by the authors of ISCT and their critics.

Argumentative Method

Whereas the idea of self-discipline suggests that the social contract model should be used restrictively as a formal argument, the criterion of argumentative method reminds us that, in the hands of political theorists, the contract model was typically used in an argumentative fashion. Classical social contracts make a hypothetical case. And it is precisely this hypothetical character of the contract argument that makes it imperative for these theorists to argue why, given the conditions of the state of nature, *certain obligations* ought to be enforced, *rather than others*. Failing any such specific reasons, the contract model would actually be reduced to a device for stipulating norms or guidelines the theorist thinks to be appropriate. Now, everyone is of course free to employ the contract argument in such a fashion. My argument here is that only in its argumentative form can the contract model generate genuine added value. In its stipulative form, exemplified by ISCT, the contract model does not contribute anything essential beyond a loose contractual metaphor.

To make optimal use of the social contract model, it must be used as a "moral proof procedure."[48] That is to say, the contract must somehow render intelligible *why* the terms of the contract deserve to be subscribed to by the contractors, and hence why they deserve to be adopted by the audience that the contract theorist addresses. Moreover, these contractual terms must be based on reasons to which all interested parties are (or should be) susceptible, a condition which is discussed in the literature on the contractarian method as public justification or free public reason.[49]

The idea of a distinctively contractarian argumentative method can clearly be seen from established classical and modern contract theories. Hobbes's version of the social contract, for example, proceeds from a demonstration to all rational individuals (as characterized in part I of *Leviathan*) that it is for everyone's benefit to transfer his rights under the law of nature to a sovereign. Similarly, the basic method of Rawls's version of the social contract consists in deriving the famous principles of social justice from an ideal initial situation where individuals are free and equal. Given our conception of ourselves as free and equal, he asks how principles specifying the basic organization of society can be premised on public reasons that each contracting individual can, in principle, recognize. Proceeding from these widely accepted but weak premises about the initial situation, the thought-experiment renders intelligible why his famous principles of equal political liberty, equal opportunity, and the difference principle will be chosen.

Unfortunately, current versions of CBE fail to employ this basic argumentative method. Freeman simply takes the idea of a Rawlsian veil of ignorance and then starts imagining what contractors would agree to, without any of the sophisticated and very detailed conceptual machinery that Rawls puts into place in order to get to his intended results. The method employed by the ISCT project also appears less than logically compelling. Although the setup of the ISCT thought-experiment[50] is more elaborate than Freeman's version of CBE, it simply does not warrant the resulting terms of the contract.[51] Given the parameters as set, it is not at all clear why the contractors would opt for the procedural and structural hypernorms as specified; more importantly, the social contract model turned out to be redundant for the identification of the vitally important category of substantive hypernorms. There is no use of the social contract's hypothethical argumentative method in Donaldson and Dunfee's so-called macrosocial contract.

Task-Directedness

The third point to consider involves the degree to which CBE exhibits what I will call task-directedness. In the more successful examples of the use of the social contract model, theorists appear to work on the basis of a fairly precise task that the contract is supposed to fulfill. All classical social contract theories of lasting value were intending to drive home a certain counterintuitive conclusion that rational individuals would be better off establishing the proposed form of social authority. The contract served to resolve the problem of collective action inherent in the organization of a political community, thereby bridging the opposition between individual and collective rationality.[52] Viewed from a purely individual perspective, it is not attractive to give up the natural rights one enjoys under the state of nature. It is only through the contract perspective that the specific solutions defended by Hobbes or Locke can be justified to individual agents.

With modern social contract theories, the contract model served to provide a more solid foundation to certain intuitive judgments about social justice. This may again be illustrated from Rawls's theory. Most people will intuitively subscribe to the view that effort should be rewarded in the distribution of the cooperative surplus. We can justify that people who work hard will be rewarded better than people who are born tired. Most people will also subscribe to the view that advantages which are purely based on one's social background, gender, or race ought not to be rewarded. But not everyone will be convinced directly that the same also applies to talents. Yet, according to Rawls, advantages that are purely based on talents ought not to be taken into account when dividing the cooperative surplus. The compelling reason he provides for this point of view is that, like race, class, and gender, talent is not something the individual agent can influence. In this example, the thought-experiment of the social contract thus helps to bring out more clearly some implications concerning our intuitive ideas about social justice that by themselves may be less self-evident. The idea of an original position helps, as he says, to "extract the consequences" of our notion of fairness.[53] It seems evident that if we want to find proper employment for the contract argument in the context of organizational ethics we should be clear about what we want to establish before we can start modeling. So what could be possible tasks that the social contract model could perform for us within the domain of organizational ethics?

One obvious application may be illustrated from the present study of corporate governance. Roe focuses our attention on the different ways in which various national economies accommodate conflicts of interests between various constituencies in a corporation.[54] Aguilera and Jackson sought to enlarge the simplistic outlook of economic theory by drawing on the institutional theory perspective.[55] The challenge for them is to find a golden mean between the "undersocialized" view of *Homo economicus* and the "oversocialized" view that institutional theory casts on the question of corporate governance. On that basis these authors give a more detailed analysis of the interaction between three key actors in the corporation: capital, management, and labor. In this manner, the suggested improvement of the corporate governance debate is cast in descriptive/explanatory terms. The social contract perspective, on the other hand, is preeminently suited to give a more normative content to the "corporate governance equation," which plays a role in adjudication of conflicting interests of key actors within and outside the corporation. This is precisely the sort of function performed by the social contract model in classical and modern projects such as in the work of Hobbes, Kant, and Rawls.

Domain-Specificity

The fourth and final insight that can be derived from the comparative analysis concerns the fact that the contract model needs to be properly adapted to the domain to which it is applied. This insight goes under the label of domain-specificity. In each of the classical and social justice domains, the contract model was accurately focused on the appropriate domain characteristics. Classical social contract theories were able to allow relatively many degrees of freedom. The only hard criterion for a well-formed political contract was how life under the authority of the state can be made more attractive than life without such authority. It follows from this relatively open structure that more than one solution fulfills this condition. Or, to put the same point in different words, as long as life in the state of nature is thought to be grim, the theorist could easily imagine an agreement that justifies political authority. By itself, Hobbes's *Leviathan* does not at all look appealing, but it still is attractive as compared to the horrors of the state of nature.

As compared to the relatively coarse-grained argumentation of the various classical theories, modern social contract theories are much more precise. These theories are more refined in the kind of social arrangements that they seek to justify. For classical social contract theories it was sufficient to argue that the establishment of political authority was advantageous to everyone when compared to the state of nature. Modern social contract theories have to evoke a far more fine-grained argument to establish the conditions for a fair distribution of the fruits of social cooperation. Hence Rawls's conceptual apparatus had to be far more elaborate than that of Hobbes or Locke.

In the case of CBE, the contract model also needs to be fine-tuned to the domain to which it is applied. Defining issues of business ethics are set against the backdrop of collective production aimed at the creation of added value. These activities presuppose an effective political authority to see to it that contractual obligations are honored and to sanction promises made. Typical issues for business ethics arise out of the attempt to weigh interests reaching beyond purely legal matters and hence not covered by political authority. Typical issues for business ethics moreover involve considerations beyond economic calculus. The options of access and exit to the community that CBE addresses are entirely different from the access and exit conditions of the other domains. Characteristic issues of business ethics cannot rely on a clear-cut set of stakeholders that will be affected by a specific company activity, as was the case with classical and modern social contract endeavors. For example, the question of supply chain responsibility and to what extent a company in a rich industrial economy should take into account the issue of exploitation of workers in a cheap labor country is distinctively less straightforward than Locke's argument on property rights or Rawls's deduction of principles of justice within a domestic society. Hence a refined CBE should first and foremost address the problem of stakeholder identification.

The argument from domain-specificity should also serve as a warning for aspirant CBE theories not to rely on too direct copies of the contract model imported from other domains. This may be seen, for example, from the doctrine of "fair contracts," the attempt at a CBE presented in Freeman[56] and again in Freeman and Evan[57] that essentially involves a misguided attempt to isolate the Rawlsian device of a "veil of ignorance" and to apply it directly to the problems of organizational ethics.

4. CONCLUSION

The aim of this chapter is to assess the social contract credentials of some current members of the family of contractarian theories of business ethics (CBE). In the process of establishing these credentials, it draws attention to four crucial shortcomings that can be discerned in the application of the contract model to the domain of organizational ethics, as was done in the various current instances of CBE.

A comparative analysis of the manner in which the social contract model was applied by classical and modern contractarians serves to make clear that this model always works within certain application conditions. Three of these follow from the logic of the contract model; the fourth has to do with the domain to which the contract argument is applied. The first three ideas, of self-discipline, argumentative method, and task-directedness, serve to remind us that there is something like an optimal use that can be made of the social contract argument. The criterion of self-discipline suggests that if the model tries to reach beyond its purpose and is employed to defend too specific results, the contract model will be unable to get to a sufficient level of generality. In the same way as Rawls intended his project specifically to support his particular conception of justice for the basic structure of society, organizational ethicists interested in the use of the contract model should not seek to derive concrete substantive principles of organizational ethics from the contract, but rather a particular conception of justice for the practice of cooperative production.

The criterion of argumentative method specifies that a contract model properly so-called seeks to persuade its audience by providing reasons to which the audience is (or should be) susceptible. In this manner, it can also be used to exclude extraneous factors from the reasoning process; for example, it would seem just reasonable that any trade or production, however profitable to the parties cooperating in that enterprise, may not harm other parties without adequate and sufficient compensation or voice. For the corporate governance debate this means a shift of emphasis from institutional analysis to more deliberative forms of accommodation between the claims of conflicting stakeholder groups.

The criterion of task-directedness refers to the intended task to which CBE is directed, and what would be appropriate candidates for the extraneous factors in the context of typical organizational ethics problems for which we should be controlling. Again, I point to the subject of corporate governance as an area in which the contract model could provide normative principles to accommodate conflicts over the distribution of the cooperative surplus. Typical corporate governance issues, such as just distribution of the advantages and (internal and external) costs of production, and the avoidance of collective action problems, were traditional tasks to which the social contract model was set.

The fourth and final condition to be taken into account is that the model must be adapted to suit the defining problems in business ethics. Many characteristics of the domain of organizational ethics differ from the setting in which classical and modern social contract theories operated. Defining problems of business ethics reach beyond national borders and beyond the enforceable legal regulations. Therefore an organizational ethics equivalent of the Rawlsian idea of circumstances of justice must be worked out by way of a sketch of the relevant factors that give rise to the characteristic questions of business ethics. The corporate governance assumes certain conditions such as social peace and productive cooperation, which will crucially determine the nature of the interactions between these key actors. Only if the contract argument is set up in accordance with these conditions, can it do what it is supposed to do, i.e., help us to shape and reflectively equilibrate our intuitions about organizational ethics.

NOTES

1. Plato, *The Republic* (Harmondsworth: Penguin, 1982), 104.

2. Michael Lessnoff, *Social Contract* (London: Macmillan, 1986), 5.

3. Bruce Ackerman, *Social Justice in the Liberal State* (New Haven, Conn.: Yale University Press, 1980); David Gauthier, *Morals by Agreement* (Oxford, UK: Clarendon Press, 1986); Jürgen Habermas, *The Theory of Communicative Action*, 2 vols. (Boston: Beacon Press, 1987); Habermas, *Moral Consciousness and Communicative Action*, trans. Christian Lenhardt and Shierry Weber Nicholsen (Cambridge, Mass.: MIT Press, 1990); John Rawls, *A Theory of Justice* (Oxford, UK: Oxford University Press, 1971); Rawls, *Political Liberalism* (New York: Columbia University Press, 1993); Rawls, *Justice as Fairness: A Restatement*, ed. Erin Kelly (Cambridge, Mass.: Harvard University Press, 2001); Thomas Scanlon, *What We Owe to Each Other* (Cambridge, Mass.: Harvard University Press, 1998).

4. Melvin Anshen, *Corporate Strategies for Social Performance* (London: MacMillan, 1980); Thomas Donaldson, *Corporations and Morality* (Englewood Cliffs, N.J.: Prentice-Hall, 1982); Donaldson, *The Ethics of International Business* (New York: Oxford University Press, 1989); Thomas Donaldson and Thomas W. Dunfee, *Ties That Bind: A Social Contracts Approach to Business Ethics* (Cambridge, Mass.: Harvard Business School Press, 1999); Michael Keeley, *A Social-Contract Theory of Organizations* (Notre Dame, Ind.: University of Notre Dame Press, 1988).

5. See, e.g., Brian Barry, *Theories of Justice* (London: Harvester-Wheatsheaf, 1989); Barry, *Justice as Impartiality* (Oxford, UK: Clarendon, 1995); David Boucher and Paul Kelly, eds., *The Social Contract from Hobbes to Rawls* (London: Routledge, 1994); Norman Daniels, ed., *Reading Rawls: Critical Studies on Rawls's* A Theory of Justice (Stanford, Calif.: Stanford University Press, 1989); J. W. Gough, *The Social Contract* (Oxford, UK: Clarendon Press, 1957); Jean Hampton, *Political Philosophy* (Boulder, Colo.: Westview Press, 1997); Hampton, "Contract and Consent," in *A Companion to Contemporary Political Philosophy*, ed. Robert E. Goodin and Philip Pettit (Oxford, UK: Blackwell, 1993), 379–93; Will Kymlicka, "The Social Contract Tradition," in *A Companion to Ethics*, ed. Peter Singer (Oxford, UK: Basil Blackwell, 1991), 186–204; Patrick Riley, *Will and Political Legitimacy: A Critical Exposition of Social Contract Theory in Hobbes, Locke, Rousseau, Kant, and Hegel* (Cambridge, Mass.: Harvard University Press, 1982).

6. Scanlon, *What We Owe to Each Other*.

7. Fred D'Agostino, *Free Public Reason: Making It Up As We Go* (New York: Oxford University Press, 1996); Gerald F. Gaus, *Value and Justification: The Foundations of Liberal Theory* (New York: Cambridge University Press, 1990); Gaus, *Justificatory Liberalism: An Essay on Epistemology and Political Theory* (New York: Oxford University Press, 1996); David Gauthier, "Public Reason," *Social Philosophy and Policy* 12 (1995): 19–42; John Rawls, *Political Liberalism*.

8. See, e.g., Robert Hessen, *In Defense of the Corporation* (Stanford, Calif.: Hoover, 1979); Margaret M. Blair, *Ownership and Control: Rethinking Corporate Governance for the Twenty-First Century* (Washington, D.C.: Brookings, 1995).

9. Hessen, *In Defense of the Corporation*, xiii.

10. Peter Drucker, *The Practice of Management* (London: Heinemann, 1956).

11. Anshen, *Corporate Strategies*, 6.

12. Anshen, *Corporate Strategies*, 7.

13. Anshen, *Corporate Strategies*, 8–9.

14. Donaldson, *Corporations and Morality*; Donaldson, *Ethics of International Business*.

15. Donaldson, *Corporations and Morality*, 45–52.

16. Patricia Werhane, *Persons, Rights, and Corporations* (Englewood Cliffs, N.J.: Prentice Hall, 1985), 60–76.

17. Werhane, *Persons, Rights, and Corporations*, 143–52.

18. Werhane, *Persons, Rights, and Corporations*, 168–70.

19. Richard M. Cyert and James March, *A Behavioral Theory of the Firm*, 2nd ed. (1963; Oxford, UK: Blackwell, 1992).

20. Keeley, *Social Contract Theory of Organizations*, 12.

21. Keeley, *Social Contract Theory of Organizations*, 12.

22. R. Edward Freeman, "The Politics of Stakeholder Theory: Some Future Directions," *Business Ethics Quarterly* 4 (1994): 409–21; Freeman, "A Stakeholder Theory of the Modern Corporation," in *Perspectives in Business Ethics*, ed. L. P. Hartman (New York: McGraw-Hill, 2002), 171–81.

23. R. Edward Freeman and William M. Evan, "Corporate Governance: A Stakeholder Interpretation," *Journal of Behavioral Economics*, 19, no. 4 (1990): 337–59.

24. Oliver E. Williamson, *The Economic Institutions of Capitalism* (New York: Free Press, 1985).

25. Donaldson and Dunfee, *Ties That Bind*.

26. Action on Smoking and Health (ASH), "British American Tobacco: Exporting Misery to the Poor." http://www.ash.org.uk/html/press/060427.html (accessed April 27, 2006).

27. Donaldson and Dunfee, *Ties That Bind*, 19.

28. Donaldson and Dunfee, *Ties That Bind*, 12–13.

29. Donaldson and Dunfee, *Ties That Bind*, 13.

30. Donaldson and Dunfee, *Ties That Bind*, 53.

31. Ed Soule, "Managerial Moral Strategies: In Search of a Few Good Principles," *Academy of Management Review* 27 (2002), 117.

32. Donaldson and Dunfee, *Ties That Bind*, 61–62.

33. Donaldson and Dunfee, *Ties That Bind*, 74.

34. John R. Rowan, "How Binding the Ties? Business Ethics as Integrative Social Contracts," *Business Ethics Quarterly* 11 (2001): 379–90; Soule, "Managerial Moral Strategies"; Laura P. Hartman, William Shaw, and Rodney Stevenson, "Exploring the Ethics and Economics of Global Labor Standards: A Challenge to Integrated Social Contract Theory," *Business Ethics Quarterly* 13 (2003): 193–220.

35. Donaldson and Dunfee, *Ties That Bind*, 75.

36. Ben Wempe, "In Defense of a Self-Disciplined, Domain-Specific Social Contract Theory of Business Ethics," *Business Ethics Quarterly* 15 (2005): 113–35.

37. J. S. McClelland, *A History of Western Political Thought* (London: Routledge, 1996), 176.

38. Rawls, *Theory of Justice*, 195–201; Rawls, *Political Liberalism*, 338.

39. Werhane, *Persons, Rights, and Corporations*, 168–70.

40. Donaldson and Dunfee, *Ties That Bind*, 61–62.

41. Don Mayer and Anita Cava, "Social Contract Theory and Gender Discrimination," *Business Ethics Quarterly* 5 (1995): 258.

42. Brian Husted, "A Critique of the Empirical Methods of Integrative Social Contracts Theory," *Journal of Business Ethics* 20 (1999): 227–35.

43. Rowan, "How Binding the Ties?" 386.

44. Soule, "Managerial Moral Strategies," 118–19.

45. Hartman, Shaw, and Stevenson, "Exploring the Ethics and Economics of Global Labor Standards," 208–10.

46. Michael D. Bayles, "Moral Theory and Application," *Social Theory and Practice* 10 (1984): 97–120.

47. Henry S. Richardson, "Specifying Norms as a Way to Resolve Concrete Ethical Problems," *Philosophy and Public Affairs* 19 (1990): 279–310.

48. Thomas Scanlon, quoted in Hampton, *Political Philosophy*, 135.

49. Ackerman, *Social Justice in the Liberal State*; D'Agostino, *Free Public Reason*; Gaus, *Value and Justification*; David Gauthier, *Morals by Agreement* (Oxford, UK: Clarendon Press, 1986); Habermas, *Theory of Communicative Action*; Rawls, *Political Liberalism*.

50. Donaldson and Dunfee, *Ties That Bind*, 28–36.

51. Donaldson and Dunfee, *Ties That Bind*, 37–46.

52. Mancur Olson, *The Logic of Collective Action* (Cambridge, Mass.: Harvard University Press, 1965).

53. Rawls, *Theory of Justice*, 21.

54. Mark J. Roe, *Political Determinants of Corporate Governance: Political Context, Corporate Impact* (New York: Oxford University Press, 2003).

55. Ruth Aguilera and Gregory Jackson, "The Cross-National Diversity of Corporate Governance: Dimensions and Determinants," *Academy of Management Review* 28 (June 2003): 447–65.

56. Freeman, "Politics of Stakeholder Theory."

57. Freeman and Evan, "Corporate Governance."

Chapter Five

The Normative Study of Business Organizations: A Rawlsian Approach

Nien-hê Hsieh, The Wharton School,
University of Pennsylvania

The appeal of grounding our normative understanding of business in the work of John Rawls should come as no surprise. Given the status of Rawls's thought in contemporary moral and political philosophy, such an approach promises to be influential and to command broad support.[1] The nature of Rawls's theory, however, presents an important challenge: Rawls takes social institutions to be the subject of his analysis whereas much of the normative study of business organizations focuses at the level of the individual or the organization.

This chapter examines what this challenge suggests for attempts to develop a Rawlsian approach to the normative study of business organizations. The chapter argues that despite this challenge, there is much to be gained for the normative study of business organizations from developing such an approach. At the same time, adopting a Rawlsian approach may require us to revise the scope of contemporary study of business organizations and revisit commonly held assumptions. Specifically, a thorough-going Rawlsian approach to the normative study of business organizations raises questions about the contemporary ownership structure of publicly traded corporations and, more generally, the economic institutions associated with capitalism.

There are limits to how much any one chapter can convey about a scholar's work. In the case of Rawls, these limits are all the more apparent. This chapter aims to convey the breadth of issues to which Rawls's work applies without losing sight of the depth and sophistication of his work. Section one highlights some key themes and concepts in Rawls's work and discusses the appeal in applying his thought to the normative study of business organizations. Section two discusses an important challenge to the development of a

Rawlsian approach to the normative study of business organizations. Sections three through six illustrate ways to develop a Rawlsian approach with respect to key questions in the normative study of business organizations. These questions concern the responsibilities of multinational enterprises, Rawls's account of natural duties as they apply to individual business actors, employee compensation, and the internal organization of business enterprises. Sections six and seven turn to the more general question of whether a thorough-going Rawlsian approach to the normative study of business organizations requires us to rethink the contemporary ownership structure of publicly traded corporations and the economic institutions associated with capitalism.

1. THE WORK OF RAWLS

In *A Theory of Justice*, Rawls aims to articulate an account of justice that "best approximates our considered judgments of justice and constitutes the most appropriate moral basis for a democratic society." Specifically, he aims "to generalize and to carry to a higher order of abstraction the traditional theory of the social contract as represented by Locke, Rousseau, and Kant."[2] "The guiding idea," writes Rawls, "is that the principles of justice for the basic structure of society are the object of the original agreement. They are the principles that free and rational persons concerned to further their own interests would accept in an initial position of equality as defining the fundamental terms of their association."[3]

Rawls refers to his conception of justice as "justice as fairness." The subject of justice, as noted above, is the "basic structure," by which Rawls means, roughly, the social and political institutions that structure the terms on which members of society interact and cooperate.[4] In the initial position of equality he describes—otherwise known as the "original position"—the parties lack knowledge about (1) their place in society, class position, or social status; (2) their natural assets and abilities; (3) their conception of the good and their own life plans; (4) the particular circumstances of their society, including the political and economic situation and the level of civilization and culture; (5) the generation to which they belong.[5] In other words, the parties to the agreement lack knowledge about "the specific contingencies" that put them at odds with one another and "tempt them to exploit social and natural circumstances to their own advantage."[6] In lacking such knowledge, the parties are characterized as situated behind a "veil of ignorance."[7]

Rawls puts forward two principles of justice that characterize justice as fairness. The first principle states, "each person has the same indefeasible claim to a fully adequate scheme of equal basic liberties, which scheme is compatible with the same scheme of liberties for all."[8] The basic liberties and rights are subject to constitutional protection; they include liberties such as political liberty, freedom of speech, and freedom of the person.[9] The second principle requires social and economic inequalities to be arranged such that they satisfy two conditions: "first, they are to be attached to offices and positions open to all under conditions of fair equality of opportunity; and second, they are to be to the greatest benefit of the least-advantaged members of society."[10] This second principle is often referred to as "the difference principle." Central to Rawls's account is that the first principle takes priority over the second principle. Infringements of the basic liberties can be justified only on grounds of liberty; they cannot be justified on grounds of greater social or economic advantage. With its commitment to equal liberty for citizens and a degree of social and economic equality, Rawls's theory of justice is illustrative of the class of theories of justice often referred to as "liberal egalitarian."[11]

In *A Theory of Justice*, Rawls is concerned to articulate an account that stands as an alternative to utilitarianism and to perfectionism as moral theories. Justice as fairness, in other words, is presented as part of a moral doctrine. Modern societies, however, are characterized by a plurality of comprehensive philosophical, moral, and religious doctrines. Furthermore, many of the doctrines may be incompatible and yet equally reasonable, a situation Rawls describes as "reasonable pluralism."[12] In the face of reasonable pluralism, in order to be justified, a conception of justice cannot be presented simply as a moral doctrine. The task is one of how to articulate a conception of justice that is feasible in the light of reasonable pluralism.

In *Political Liberalism*, Rawls takes up this task by defending justice as fairness as a political conception of justice. Although a political conception of justice is moral in the sense that it depends upon ideals and principles for its content, three features serve to distinguish it from a comprehensive moral, religious, or philosophical doctrine. First, unlike a comprehensive doctrine — which aims to guide much, if not all, of our behavior — a political conception of justice aims to regulate only the basic structure. It takes no position on questions that are likely to distinguish comprehensive doctrines, such as questions about what is of value in life or ideals of associational relationships. Second, a political conception of justice is presented without reference to any specific comprehensive moral, religious, or philosophical doctrine. The idea is that it can be supported by a variety of reasonable comprehensive doctrines, but can be presented without specifying what doctrines may support it. It is presented as a "freestanding view."[13] Third, the content of a political conception of justice is expressed in terms of ideas that are implicit in the public political culture of a democratic society. Rawls begins with a specific political culture that takes as fundamental the idea of society as "a fair system of cooperation over time" along with the idea of treating persons as free and equal.[14] He argues that in such a culture, justice as fairness, when understood as a political conception of justice, can gain the support of an "overlapping consensus," which consists of all the reasonable moral, religious, or philosophical doctrines that are likely to continue over time under a constitutional regime that takes the account of justice in question as its political conception of justice.[15]

In *The Law of Peoples*, Rawls extends the scope of a liberal political conception of justice, such as justice as fairness, from a purely domestic context to an international one.[16] Just as Rawls takes reasonable pluralism to characterize modern democratic states, so does he take the international context to be characterized by a plurality of reasonable, yet incompatible, moral, philosophical, and religious doctrines. In such a context, Rawls asks what principles and norms ought to guide liberal societies in their interaction with other liberal societies. He also asks what principles and norms ought to guide liberal societies in their interaction with nonliberal societies that are not just according to a liberal political conception of justice. Taken together, these principles and norms of international law and practice comprise what he calls the "Law of Peoples."

As Samuel Freeman points out in *The Cambridge Companion to Rawls*, "to appreciate the development of Rawls's views it is essential to understand that all along he has sought to work out a realistic ideal of justice (a 'realistic utopia')."[17] Rawls's account of justice is ideal in being designed for a "well-ordered society," namely one in which "everyone accepts and knows that the others accept the same principles of justice, and the basic social institutions satisfy and are known to satisfy these principles."[18] At the same time, his account is realistic in that "it is designed to apply neither to moral saints or perfect altruists on the one hand, nor to natural sinners or rational egoists on the other, but to what humans at their best are capable of, given their nature, under normal conditions of social life."[19]

The aim of articulating a realistic ideal of justice is in part what makes Rawls's theory so attractive as a basis for evaluating social institutions and practices. Indeed, Rawls's work has inspired a vast inquiry into not only what justice as fairness, but also what justice more generally, requires for various social institutions and practices.[20] It is not difficult to understand the appeal of extending Rawls's theory to the normative study of business organizations.

2. THE CHALLENGE FOR A RAWLSIAN APPROACH TO THE STUDY OF BUSINESS ORGANIZATIONS

The most prominent application of Rawls's thought to the normative study of business organizations is found in the defense of stakeholder theory advanced by R. Edward Freeman and William Evan.[21] Recall that in *A Theory of Justice*, Rawls relies upon the concept of the "original position" in his defense of the principles of justice. Adapting the concept of the original position to the level of business organizations, Freeman and Evan ask us to imagine the groups affected by managerial decisions as parties to a hypothetical contract that specifies the principles to govern managerial decision-making.[22] Arguing that the parties would reject a contract that required managers to act exclusively in the interests of shareholders, Freeman and Evan conclude that justice requires business organizations to be managed in the interests of all key stakeholders.[23]

Critics have raised a variety of objections against Freeman and Evan's defense of stakeholder theory. For example, James Child and Alexei Marcoux argue that the kind of knowledge that parties would need to determine their rational interests as stakeholders far exceeds that which parties know in the original position, thereby making the application of Rawls inappropriate.[24] Another criticism, highlighted by Robert Phillips and Joshua Margolis, is that Rawls's account rules out arrangements that depend upon the possibility of exit for their acceptance, but business organizations allow for exit. Phillips and Margolis also note that business organizations are purposive organizations, whereas society is open-ended with regard to its aims.[25] The authors conclude that "organizations require an ethics of their own, an ethics which reflects the significant differences that distinguish organizations from nation-states and individuals."[26]

These criticisms each highlight what they take to be differences between business organizations and states that make it inappropriate to apply Rawls's theory to business organizations. Justice as fairness, according to Rawls, takes as its subject the basic structure, which functions at the level of the state. Because the social contract differs from other types of agreements, the principles developed to govern the basic structure are distinct from those that apply to agreements in general.[27] Given that Rawls takes social institutions to be the subject of his analysis, there arises a challenge in applying Rawls's theory of justice to the normative study of business organizations, given its focus at the level of the individual or the organization.

Three lines of response can be found in the literature. One response is that the distinction between states and business organizations is drawn too sharply. Edwin Hartman, for example, argues that voluntary associations share enough similarities with states to make it appropriate to apply a conception of justice such as Rawls's to business organizations.[28] Jeffery Moriarty advances a similar claim.[29] As a point of clarification, this line of response should be distinguished from an objection discussed in section five of this chapter. This objection is not that an analogy should be drawn between states and other associations, such as business organizations, which is in effect what authors such as Hartman propose. The objection is not, for example, that a version of the difference principle ought to be applied within a business organization such that inequalities in pay work to the advantage of the lowest paid worker in that organization. Rather, the objection is that private associations and individual-level choices ought to be considered part of the basic structure so that decisions made within associations and by individuals also are governed by the principles of justice. One objection along these lines, in response to which Rawls amended his account, was that the basic structure ought to include the family, given its importance in determining the life prospects of individuals.[30]

A second line of response is represented by Robert Phillips's defense of stakeholder theory.[31] In contrast with Freeman and Evan, Phillips does not transpose Rawls's account of justice from the level of society directly to the level of organizations. Rather, he brings to bear at the level of organizations one of the motivating ideas in Rawls's account. This is the idea of reciprocity. Phillips adopts a conception of reciprocity articulated in Rawls's early work as "the principle of fair play." The principle states, roughly, that a person who has accepted the benefits of a scheme of cooperation has a duty of fair play to do her part in supporting the scheme and not taking advantage of the benefits without cooperation.[32] According to Phillips, organizations benefit in their relations with stakeholders in such a way that they have obligations to their stakeholders on grounds of fair play. Although the content of these obligations is specified by further considerations, the principle of fair play provides the normative foundation for the sorts of obligations attributed to organizations by stakeholder theory. Phillips's account represents a broadly Rawlsian approach to the normative study of business organizations that seems to avoid the challenge described above.

A third line of response is to adopt a contractarian approach to the normative study of business organizations that is not specifically Rawlsian in its incarnation. This approach locates the appeal of Rawls's theory in the use of the social contract. Accounts in this vein aim to adapt social contract theory to take into consideration the differences between states and business organizations. Thomas Donaldson and Thomas Dunfee's Integrative Social Contracts Theory (ISCT) is one such account.[33] For example, Donaldson and Dunfee propose norms to govern business activity based on what would be acceptable to economic actors who are ignorant of their role in economic life. In contrast to Rawls's account, the parties in their account are knowledgeable of their non-economic interests, values, and commitments. Furthermore, contracts in general play a much greater role in Donaldson and Dunfee's account. As part of their account, Donaldson and Dunfee specify conditions under which the norms determined by contracts at the individual and organizational levels ought to be respected. Developing a Rawlsian approach to the normative study of business organizations along these lines raises two questions. The first concerns the role of the social contract in Rawls's account and the extent to which accounts that adapt social contract theory to the normative study of business remain distinctively Rawlsian in their approach.[34] The second concerns the appropriateness of applying social contract theory to the normative study of business.[35]

These lines of response involve important questions: Is it appropriate to draw an analogy between states and business organizations, and how plausible are hypothetical contract approaches to the normative study of business organizations? These and related questions are the subject of much debate and merit attention. However, there is reason to hold that we can develop a Rawlsian approach to the normative study of business organizations without having to settle them and that we can do so in a manner in keeping with Rawls's focus on the basic structure of society. The remainder of this chapter outlines the development of such an approach with reference to key questions in the normative study of business organizations.

3. NON-IDEAL THEORY AND GLOBAL JUSTICE

One reason that Phillips and Margolis cite for developing an ethics specific to organizations is that Rawls's account focuses on "ideal theory." Ideal theory assumes "that (nearly) everyone strictly complies with, and so abides by, the principles of justice."[36] "Organizations," according to Phillips and Margolis, however, "are products of a non-ideal world." According to Phillips and Margolis, "they arise, operate, and serve the purposes they do in the way that they do in large part because the basic structure of society is not just and because individual agents are imperfect."[37]

Phillips and Margolis are right to emphasize that Rawls focuses on ideal theory. There is reason to doubt, however, that the focus on ideal theory rules out consideration of business organizations from within Rawls's account of justice. To begin, in defining the subject of justice, Rawls makes clear that institutions and associations such as "firms and labor unions, churches, universities, and the family" are not part of the basic structure.[38] That Rawls should define the basic structure in this manner suggests that institutions and associations, which include business organizations, are part of a just society. That seems correct. Even under conditions of full compliance with the principles of justice, it is difficult to imagine no need for business organizations. For example, economic theorists argue that business organizations are needed because certain kinds of economic activity are better achieved through organizations rather than through arm's-length market transactions.[39] This need may be interpreted as arising from a kind of imperfection, but this is not the kind of imperfection that Rawls has in mind when discussing non-ideal theory, which concerns the compliance of individuals with the principles of justice. To be certain, it remains a question as to what extent the principles of justice apply to the internal operation of business enterprises, but this is not a question about the distinction between ideal and non-ideal theory.

There is one area in which Rawls discusses non-ideal theory in a way that holds promise for informing the normative study of business organizations. This is found in his account of global justice as discussed in *The Law of Peoples*.[40] In this work, Rawls distinguishes between societies in the realm of ideal theory and societies in the realm of non-ideal theory. Societies in the realm of ideal theory obey the Law of Peoples, by which Rawls means a "particular political conception of right and justice that applies to the principles and norms of international law and practice."[41] These societies are also "well-ordered," meaning that, at a minimum, they secure human rights for all of their citizens and have an effective legal system that is guided by a common good idea of justice.[42] In the realm of non-ideal theory Rawls discusses two kinds of societies: "outlaw states" and "burdened societies." Outlaw states do not comply with the Law of Peoples and regard the advancement of their own interests to be a sufficient reason to engage in war with other states. Burdened societies are such that "historical, social, and economic circumstances make their achieving a well-ordered regime, whether liberal or decent, difficult if not impossible." According to Rawls, well-ordered societies owe a "duty of assistance" to help burdened societies establish reasonably just or decent institutions.[43]

One debate in the normative study of business organizations that Rawls's account has the potential to inform is the debate concerning the responsibilities of multinational corporations (MNCs). For example, one question is whether MNCs have a responsibility to provide aid to persons in developing economies—that is, to provide them with resources beyond what they receive in market transactions, for example, in the form of a living wage or schools for local children. Drawing on Rawls's account, it has been argued that there are conditions under which MNCs have a role in discharging the duty of assistance and thereby a responsibility to provide such aid.[44] This example illustrates one way in which Rawls's account of justice has the potential to inform a key debate in the normative study of business.

4. NATURAL DUTIES

The second line of inquiry along which to develop a Rawlsian account of the normative study of business organizations involves the principles for individuals specified by Rawls's account of justice. In his discussion of the principles that apply to individuals, Rawls distinguishes between "obligations" and "natural duties." Obligations are defined as arising from the result of our voluntary acts and "their content is always defined by an institution or practice the rules of which specify what it is that one is required to do."[45] Natural duties, in contrast, apply to persons regardless of their voluntary acts and their content is normally independent of the rules of institutions or social practices.[46] Examples include a duty to aid others when the cost is not excessive to us and a duty not to cause unnecessary suffering to others.[47] Of all the natural duties, the "most important," according to Rawls, is the natural duty "to support and to further just institutions."[48]

Three examples help to illustrate ways in which the account of natural duties contributes to developing a Rawlsian account of the normative study of business organizations. The first example continues the above discussion regarding the provision of aid by MNCs. It has been argued that the provision of aid on the part of MNCs can be grounded in a duty of rescue that applies to managers of MNCs.[49] Insofar as a duty to engage in rescue is the same as a natural duty to aid others, then Rawls's account of natural duties also grounds responsibilities on the part of MNCs according to this argument.

The second example involves the natural duty to support and to further just institutions. Rawls defines this duty as having two parts: "first, we are to comply with and to do our share in just institutions when they exist and apply to us; and second we are to assist in the establishment of just arrangements when they do not exist, at least where this can be done at little cost to ourselves."[50] Attributing to MNCs something like a natural duty to support and to further just institutions, Onora O'Neill argues that MNCs have a responsibility to help bring about conditions of justice in countries in which states lack the means to establish just domestic arrangements. "Justice," she writes, "has to be built by a diversity of agents and agencies," and MNCs, according to O'Neill, are among those agents.[51]

The third example concerns the appropriate relationship between business actors and legal and political institutions. The relationship between business actors and legal and political institutions extends beyond mere compliance with the law. Business actors face decisions about how to use the law to their advantage. They also face decisions about whether and how to influence the formulation and enforcement of regulations and policies. There is reason to believe that a natural duty to support and to further just institutions has implications for the decisions that business actors ought to take with respect to these and related areas. For example, it seems that a natural duty has implications for a variety of activities, including lobbying by business interests, corporate contributions to political campaigns, and the establishment of tax shelters. Drawing upon Rawls to investigate the appropriate relationship between business actors and legal and political institutions seems to be a promising and informative line of inquiry.

Whatever the specific outcome of that investigation, there is good reason to anticipate that such an investigation will attribute to managers a responsibility to respect important interests of various stakeholders in addition to shareholders. The reasoning is as follows. In Rawls's account, basic rights are those rights subject to constitutional protection. Although the right to personal property is among the basic rights, Rawls is clear that rights regarding the ownership and control of productive property are not. Rawls writes, "two wider conceptions of the right to property are not taken as basic: namely, (i) the right to private property in natural resources and means of production generally, including rights of acquisition and bequest; (ii) the right to property as including the equal right to participate in the control of the means of production and of natural resources, both of which are to be socially, not privately, owned."[52] Property rights and other institutional arrangements that regulate the functioning of the economy are to be determined in accordance with the principles of justice. The content of the natural duties in Rawls's account is independent of these institutional arrangements; the natural duties are, in a sense, prior to them. Hence, even if institutional arrangements require managers to act in the interests of shareholders, unless discharging natural duties always coincides with the interests of shareholders, there are likely to be instances in which discharging natural duties involves respecting important interests of parties other than shareholders.

This section and the previous one outlined ways in which elements of Rawls's theory of justice have been and could be extended to address key questions in the normative study of business organizations. In the following two sections, the chapter takes a slightly different approach. It turns to consider ongoing debates within the scholarship on Rawls that involve key questions in the normative study of business organizations. Section five concerns the principles that ought to guide how much to pay employees. Section six concerns the claim of workers to participate in the management of business organizations.

5. WAGES AND COMPENSATION

The question of what principles ought to guide how much to pay employees is a question for the normative study of business organizations. In the light of the above discussion about the challenge to developing a Rawlsian approach to the normative study of business organizations, it might seem that this question falls outside the scope of such an approach. As discussed, the principles of justice are held by Rawls to apply only to the basic structure. Accordingly, decisions about how much to pay employees are not subject to direct regulation by the principles of justice so long as they are in accordance with the laws set by the legislature operating within the context of the basic structure. Apart from setting this context, it would seem that justice as fairness allows for great discretion with regard to how much to pay employees.

G. A. Cohen argues that this is not the case.[53] Cohen challenges Rawls's stated view that the principles of justice apply only to the basic structure on grounds that this view is inconsistent with Rawls's account of justice as fairness. Cohen argues that the principles of justice apply not only to the basic structure, but also to the choices that individuals make within the basic structure. In Cohen's view, there is little discretion with regard to the principles that ought to guide how much to pay employees. The principles that ought to apply are precisely those principles of justice that regulate the basic structure.

Cohen advances his argument with reference to the difference principle and the way in which it is commonly thought to justify inequality. Recall that according to the difference principle inequalities are justified if, and only if, they are necessary to make the least advantaged better off than they would otherwise be.[54] According to Cohen, "it is commonly thought, for example by Rawls, that the difference principle licenses an argument for inequality which centers on the device of material incentives."[55] Inequality is justified because it occurs within a system that is structured to allow the least advantaged to be as well off as possible by providing the more advantaged members of society with incentives to utilize their greater advantages to the fullest. The idea is that unless the more advantaged members of society receive these incentives, their productive output will not be as great as it would otherwise be, thereby leaving the least advantaged even worse off. The difference principle selects the set of institutional and legal arrangements, that, given the choices made by individuals under them, result in the least advantaged being as well off as possible (relative to whoever are the least advantaged under any other arrangement).

Cohen raises the following question for the way in which the difference principle is thought to sanction inequality. "The talented can be asked," he writes, "whether the extra they get is *necessary* to enhance the position of the worst off. . . . Is it necessary *tout court*, that is independently of human will, . . Or is it necessary only insofar as the talented would *decide* to produce less than they now do, or not to take up posts where they are in special demand?"[56] Cohen argues that while there may be circumstances in which the more advantaged could not use their advantages to the fullest, in most circumstances it would appear that the more advantaged could do so without being paid extra. Inequality then is required to make the least advantaged better off only because the more advantaged "*make* those rewards necessary, through their own unwillingness to work for ordinary rewards as productively as they do for exceptionally high ones."[57] In a just society on Rawls's account, however, citizens affirm the principles of justice, so the more advantaged ought to be willing to work at the same level of productivity for ordinary rewards, because the least advantaged could be made even better off. In this manner, Cohen argues that "there is hardly any serious inequality that satisfies the requirement set by the difference principle."[58]

According to Cohen, if it is applied in a manner consistent with Rawls's theory of justice, the difference principle ought to apply not only to the basic structure, but also to the choices of individuals. This means that wages and compensation ought to be set not in terms of what employees are able to command in the market, but rather in terms of what is required to make the least advantaged members of society as well off as possible. To be certain, implementing this approach introduces a number of practical difficulties; the underlying concern is with the least advantaged members of society and equality as a whole, not the least advantaged or the distribution within any one organization. With that said, it is hard to imagine that the contemporary distribution of wages and contemporary levels of executive compensation in the United States, for example, could be justified under Cohen's argument. In fact, trying to equalize the pay structure within an organization may go quite some way to implementing the approach outlined in Cohen's argument. The more fundamental point for the normative study of business organizations, however, is quite clear. There is much less discretion than commonly thought in determining the principles that ought to inform decisions about wages and compensation. Instead, the difference principle is the relevant principle.

Cohen's argument is not without its critics. Andrew Williams, for example, argues that because the principles of justice are to apply to public rules, they do not apply to an individual's choice between bargaining for the highest wage possible and accepting lower pay as a committed egalitarian. That choice, according to Williams, fails to be "public" in the relevant sense. Not only do we lack a meaningful standard against which to measure the burden of work apart from the worker's willingness to engage in that work, we also lack a way to determine whether an individual is using her greater advantage to the fullest.[59] K. C. Tan offers a different objection. He argues that Cohen's approach fails to provide individuals with space in which to pursue personal projects within reasonable limits and that Cohen himself is committed to the view that individuals ought to have such space.[60] Joshua Cohen,[61] David Estlund,[62] and Thomas Pogge[63] are others who have raised objections to Cohen's account. It is beyond the scope of this chapter to rehearse these and other objections. Instead, in highlighting these objections, the aim of this discussion is to point to an ongoing and fundamental area of debate within the scholarship on Rawls that directly concerns a key question in the normative study of business organizations.

6. WORKERS AND MANAGEMENT

This section turns to another debate in the scholarship on Rawls that concerns a key question in the normative study of business organizations. A number of scholars have suggested that in focusing on the distribution of economic benefits, Rawls's theory overlooks important questions regarding the production of those benefits, including the question of whether justice as fairness requires that workers have a formal claim to participate in the management and governance of business organizations.[64] In fact, in *Justice as Fairness: A Restatement*, Rawls writes that it is "a major difficulty" that his account "has not considered the importance of democracy in the workplace and in shaping the general course of the economy." Although Rawls concludes that he "shall not pursue these questions," he writes that "certainly these questions call for careful examination. The long-run prospects of a just constitutional regime may depend on them."[65]

Recall that Rawls is clear that rights regarding the ownership and control of productive property are not considered among the basic rights.[66] In light of this point, there are two ways in which the case has been made that justice as fairness requires some form of worker participation in the management of business organizations. The first is to re-evaluate the extent to which such participation is required, as an empirical matter, to realize the principles of justice. The second is to examine the possibility that there are basic rights whose realization may require some form of worker participation in the management of business organizations. This section outlines arguments under each of these two approaches.

Under the first approach, there are three arguments that might be taken to show that a regime of worker participation is better suited, and perhaps required, to realize the requirements of justice under prevailing social and economic conditions. One such argument is what Joshua Cohen calls the "structural constraints argument."[67] Recall that the principles of justice require that basic liberties be realized in a fair, and not merely formal, sense. Realizing the fair value of political liberties means that "citizens similarly gifted and motivated have roughly an equal chance of influencing the government's policy and of attaining positions of authority irrespective of their economic and social class."[68] The structural constraints argument begins with the premise that in a capitalist economy, it is in society's collective interest to support policies that maintain a climate favorable to capitalist investment. Given this, worker control of business organizations is required to limit the undue influence of capitalists on the state and to realize the fair value of political liberties.

A second argument is based upon the idea that people's attitudes and capacities are influenced by their work environment.[69] Recall that in Rawls's account, treating persons as free and equal is inherent in what it means to be a citizen in a democracy. Such treatment is said to involve ensuring that citizens come to possess two moral powers. The first "is the capacity to understand, to apply, and to act from (and not merely in accordance with) the principles of political justice that specify the fair terms of social cooperation." The second is "the capacity to have, to revise, and rationally to pursue a conception of the good."[70] The argument here is that the lack of democratic participation in the workplace may adversely affect the development of these moral powers, which are in turn required for a well-functioning democracy.

A third argument is located in Rawls's rejection of perfectionism as the grounds for an account of justice. One way to interpret the rejection of perfection is to hold that the state ought to remain neutral with respect to conceptions of the good life. That is, the state should not promote one conception of the good life over another.[71] Suppose that capitalist firms place negative externalities on the operation of worker-managed firms. Then a state that does not subsidize worker-managed firms promotes a capitalist conception of the good with respect to work, which violates the principle that a liberal state ought to remain neutral with respect to conceptions of the good life.[72]

The second approach to grounding a formal claim on the part of workers to participate in the management of business organizations has been to examine the possibility that there are basic rights whose realization may ground that claim. One argument along these lines has been advanced by Iris Marion Young. Young argues that among the principles of justice is a "principle of self-determination" which requires that "individuals participate equally in the making of the decisions which will govern their actions within institutions of social cooperation."[73] The principle of self-determination is meant to apply to all institutions of social cooperation, including business organizations. Young advances four arguments for the principle of self-determination. First, Rawls argues that the principle for equal participation in politics transfers the conditions of equality and fair representation from the original position to a society's constitution. If so, argues Young, then equal participation should be extended as widely as possible.[74] Second, Young argues that it is in the interests of the least advantaged person to organize society such that one has a claim to participate equally in basic decisions within an organization.[75] Young's third argument is that only by allowing for self-determination at every level of social cooperation can society be, in Rawls's words, "a social union of social unions." Without self-determination, the goals of a given instance of social cooperation cannot be shared in common.[76] Fourth, Young argues that self-determination at every level of social cooperation best promotes self-respect.[77] In Rawls's account, self-respect plays a foundational role. Specifically, Rawls includes the "social bases of self-respect" among the list of goods whose distribution is a concern of justice. By the social bases of self-respect, Rawls means "those aspects of basic institutions normally essential if citizens are to have a lively sense of their worth as persons and to be able to advance their ends with self-confidence."[78]

A second argument along these lines focuses on the possibility that there is a basic right to protection against arbitrary interference at work.[79] In Rawls's account, for a claim to be accorded the status of a basic right, it must be counted among the social bases of self-respect.[80] An instance of interference is understood as arbitrary if little or no justification can be given for it in terms of the worker's interests upon whom the interference is visited. The severity of interference has two dimensions: in terms of the lack of justification that can be given for it and in terms of its impact on workers' interests. Examples of interests to be considered are physical safety; occupational stability to enable maintaining ties to family, friends, and community; and pride in one's work.[81]

A number of features associated with such interference give us reason to place protection against arbitrary interference at work among the social bases of self-respect. Of particular concern is that the arbitrary interference under consideration is interference that is visited by the decision of one individual on another individual within the context of an institutionally sanctioned decision-making procedure. To visit arbitrary interference on another individual is to treat her as though her interests and judgments do not matter.[82] As such, arbitrary interference is to treat an individual as lacking in standing or in worth. It is the absence of treating another individual with respect. To lack protection against such interference is to be placed in a position in which it is permissible, by virtue of the basic structure, to be treated by another individual as lacking in standing or in worth. It is difficult to imagine situations more damaging to developing a sense of self-worth and self-confidence than to be in such a position.[83] In turn, there is reason to hold that just as there is a basic right to personal property on Rawls's account, so too should there be a basic right to protection against arbitrary interference at work.

Given that basic rights are subject to constitutional protection and institutional recognition, realization of a basic right to protection against arbitrary interference places constraints on the legal rules that specify what is permitted and required with regard to the formation and operation of economic enterprises. At a minimum, these rules would include limits on managerial discretion and a right to exit on the part of workers.

At the same time, there is reason to think that such provisions may not be adequate to realize a basic right to protection against arbitrary interference at work. In the case of limiting managerial discretion, much of the literature on the theory of the firm emphasizes the need for decision-making in the context of economic activity; what distinguishes business organizations from markets is that they involve decisions that cannot be specified at the outset of a contractual relationship.[84] If we accept this, then there is a limit to the extent to which managerial discretion can be restricted without eliminating altogether what makes business organizations distinct and desirable. In the case of exit, there are a number of reasons to hold that the cost of exit is sufficiently high such that it is unreasonable to require providers of labor to protect their interests by exercising their right to exit.

First, because a worker's contribution to the firm depends upon her investment in developing firm-specific human capital, she will not be able to command as high a return outside of the specific firm in which she works. Given that greater investment in firm-specific human capital increases a worker's productivity, from the standpoint of both the worker and the firm it may not even be desirable to eliminate the cost to exit.[85] Second, because the ability to monitor workers is costly, employers will find it in their interest to pay workers more than the market-clearing wage so that there is a cost to exiting one's place of employment.[86] Third, there are costs associated with locating a new job and making the transition to it. Fourth, even if the cost to exiting a specific firm is low, the cost of protecting against arbitrary interference through exit may still be unreasonably high. The reasoning is as follows: If what distinguishes business organizations is the exercise of managerial discretion, on leaving one enterprise to enter another, the worker remains subject to the capacity for arbitrary interference. Insofar as most employment occurs in an organizational context, unless a worker accepts severe limitations to her options for work, it seems that she remains subject to the capacity for arbitrary interference. On Rawls's account, there is reason to hold that having work is an important source of self-respect. Hence, it seems unreasonable to require workers to rely on exit to protect against arbitrary interference.

Given the limits to exit and restrictions on managerial discretion as ways to protect against arbitrary interference, recognition of a basic right to protection against arbitrary interference is said to require some form of worker participation, either directly or indirectly, in the decision-making process internal to business organizations. By allowing workers to contest managerial decisions that result in severe forms of interference as part of the decision-making process internal to business organizations, workers are able to protect themselves against arbitrary interference. The protection accorded by participation is especially important when the cost to pursuing external remedies is prohibitively expensive or when the interference is difficult to rectify *ex post*.[87]

7. PUTTING RAWLS IN BUSINESS

The discussion in the previous section highlights a straightforward way in which to explore further the development of a Rawlsian approach to the normative study of business organizations. This is by examining what justice as fairness requires of the institutional arrangements that structure economic activity. As alluded to above, many of the responsibilities of managers and business organizations are specified by institutional-level requirements and permissions. As part of the broader set of social, economic, and political institutions, these requirements and permissions are amenable to analysis from the perspective of Rawls's theory of justice. To engage in that analysis is in keeping with what Rawls understands to be the subject of justice.

Inquiry along these lines would benefit from and contribute to the existing philosophical literature on questions about justice. In the philosophical literature, questions about justice have tended to be viewed almost exclusively as questions about the distribution of rights, goods, and opportunities among citizens. Recently, scholars such as Iris Marion Young have called for expanding the scope of inquiry beyond this "distributive paradigm."[88] An investigation into what justice requires for the institutional arrangements that structure economic activity would be an important contribution to this expanded scope of inquiry.

In pursuing this line of inquiry, two points should be kept in mind. The first is the importance of empirical analysis and assumptions. Rawls makes clear that principles of justice do not uniquely specify the precise institutional arrangements governing economic activity. With regard to the choice of an economic regime on grounds of justice, Rawls writes that "there is presumably no general answer to this question, since it depends in large part on the traditions, institutions, and social forces of each country, and its particular historical circumstances." The role of a theory of justice, according to Rawls, is to "set out in a schematic way the outlines of a just economic system that admits of several variations."[89] Hence, the inquiry into what justice requires of economic institutions will involve a substantial empirical component to specify the underlying conditions that help determine which set of institutional arrangements better realizes the principles of justice.

The second point to keep in mind is that a thorough application of Rawls's theory of justice has the potential to call for fairly substantial reform of the institutional arrangements normally thought to structure business activity and frequently taken for granted in the normative study of business organizations. This point echoes a point raised by Richard Marens. According to Marens, Rawls's theory has been applied somewhat selectively in contemporary business scholarship. Whereas Rawls's method of the social contract is widely referenced, there is much less discussion about the requirements of justice. A fully articulated Rawlsian approach to business ethics, according to Marens, may have serious implications for how we practice business.[90]

The discussion in the previous section on worker participation helps to underscore this point. Although some form of worker participation is often thought to be desirable in normative accounts of business organizations, not all accounts regard a claim to participate on the part of workers to be an important right. Recognition of such a right is more commonly associated with regimes of corporate governance that stand as an alternative to Anglo-American models of shareholder capitalism. Consider, for example, the case of European regimes of co-determination. If the arguments in the previous section are correct, then it is not only the case that Rawls's theory speaks to key questions in the normative study of business organizations, but also the case that a Rawlsian approach to the normative study of business organizations may require us to rethink fairly fundamental features of economic regimes often taken for granted.

In fact, a consistent Rawlsian approach to the normative study of business organizations may require us to go even further. To be clear, Rawls notes that there is no general answer to the question of what justice requires for the choice of an economic regime. At the same time, he is clear that some regimes do not meet the requirements of justice. In *Justice as Fairness*, for example, Rawls considers five types of regimes: laissez-faire capitalism, welfare-state capitalism, state socialism, property-owning democracy, and liberal (democratic) socialism.[91] Of these five regimes, only the latter two meet the requirements of justice. The latter two, however, represent fairly strong departures from the forms of capitalism normally taken as the background for contemporary normative studies of business. They depart much further from recognizing a right on the part of workers to participate in the management and governance of business organizations.

In the case of liberal (democratic) socialism, the means of production are owned collectively by members of society. In the case of property-owning democracy, although it does not involve common ownership of the means of production, a central feature is that "the background institutions work to disperse the ownership of wealth and capital, and thus to prevent a small part of society from controlling the economy, and indirectly, political life as well."[92] Both cases represent stark departures from the economic institutions taken for granted in the normative study of business organizations. In other words, a thorough-going Rawlsian approach to the normative study of business organizations may call for putting capitalism, at least as we know it, out of business altogether.

8. CONCLUSION

This chapter has argued that Rawls's theory has much to say about key questions in the normative study of business organizations. If correct, we do not need just yet to develop an ethics specific to organizations. Nor do we need to draw an analogy between states and business organizations in order to draw upon the insights of political philosophy in the normative study of business organizations. This is not to suggest that a Rawlsian approach can provide answers to all of the questions that arise in the field. No doubt there are normative questions about business organizations that are not amenable to a Rawlsian analysis, at least along the lines put forward in this chapter. Instead, the point of this chapter is to suggest that there is still much to explore in developing a Rawlsian approach to the normative study of business organizations. There is, so to speak, much work to be done before Rawls can be said to be fully in business.

NOTES

1. For example, in *The Cambridge Companion to Rawls*, Samuel Freeman writes that Rawls's works "have come to define a substantial portion of the agenda for Anglo-American political philosophy, and they increasingly influence political philosophy in the rest of the world." Samuel Freeman, ed., "Introduction," in *The Cambridge Companion to Rawls* (New York: Cambridge University Press, 2003), 1.

2. John Rawls, *A Theory of Justice*, rev. ed. (Cambridge, Mass.: Harvard University Press, 1999), xviii.

3. Rawls, *Theory of Justice*, 10.

4. Rawls takes the proper subject of justice to be the "basic structure," which he defines as "the way in which the main political and social institutions of a society fit together into one system of social cooperation, and the way they assign basic rights and duties and regulate the division of advantages that arise from social cooperation

over time. The political constitution within an independent judiciary, the legally recognized forms of property, and the structure of the economy (for example, as a system of competitive markets with private property in the means of production), as well as the family in some form, all belong to the basic structure." John Rawls, *Justice as Fairness: A Restatement*, ed. Erin Kelly (Cambridge, Mass.: Harvard University Press, 2001), 10.

5. Rawls, *Justice as Fairness*, 137.

6. Rawls, *Justice as Fairness*, 118.

7. Rawls, *Justice as Fairness*, 11.

8. Rawls, *Justice as Fairness*, 42.

9. They are required to provide the "political and social conditions essential for the adequate development and full exercise of the two moral powers of free and equal persons," which are the capacity for a sense of justice and the capacity for a conception of the good. Rawls, *Justice as Fairness*, 45.

10. Rawls, *Justice as Fairness*, 42–43.

11. For a helpful discussion of liberal egalitarianism, see Will Kymlicka, *Contemporary Political Philosophy*, 2nd ed. (New York: Oxford University Press, 2002)..For a recent discussion of Rawls's relation to liberalism, see Thomas Nagel, "Rawls and Liberalism," in Freeman, *The Cambridge Companion to Rawls* (New York: Cambridge University Press, 2003), 62–85.

12. John Rawls, *Political Liberalism* (New York: Columbia University Press, 1993), xvii.

13. Rawls, *Political Liberalism*, 12.

14. Rawls, *Political Liberalism*, 14.

15. Rawls, *Political Liberalism*, 15.

16. John Rawls, *The Law of Peoples* (Cambridge, Mass.: Harvard University Press, 2001), 3–4.

17. Samuel Freeman, *Cambridge Companion to Rawls*, 2.

18. Rawls, *Theory of Justice*, 397.

19. Samuel Freeman, *Cambridge Companion to Rawls*, 2.

20. For a discussion on how Rawls's account applies to the political constitution, see Frank Michaelman, "Rawls on Constitutionalism and Constitutional Law," in *The Cambridge Companion to Rawls*, ed. Samuel Freeman (New York: Cambridge University Press, 2003). For a discussion on how Rawls's account applies to the family, see Martha Nussbaum, "Rawls and Feminism," in Samuel Freeman, *Cambridge Companion to Rawls*.

21. R. Edward Freeman and William M. Evan, "Corporate Governance: A Stakeholder Interpretation," *Journal of Behavioral Economics* 19, no. 4 (1990): 337–59.

22. R. Edward Freeman, "The Politics of Stakeholder Theory: Some Future Directions," *Business Ethics Quarterly* 4, no. 4 (1994): 417.

23. Arguments based upon drawing an analogy between the state and business organizations are not unique to the normative study of business organizations. Among the most prominent examples in political theory is the account put forward by Robert Dahl. "To say that [democracy] is *not* justified in governing economic enterprises," writes Dahl, "is to imply that it is not justified in governing the state." Robert Dahl,

A Preface to Economic Democracy (Berkeley: University of California Press, 1985), 111. Michael Walzer advances a similar argument. "An economic enterprise," according to Walzer, "seems very much like a town." In economic enterprises, according to Walzer, managers "claim a kind of power to which they have no right." Michael Walzer, *Spheres of Justice* (New York: Basic Books, 1983) 300. Joshua Cohen uses the term "parallel case argument" to describe arguments along these lines that defend the claim of workers to participate in the management and governance of business enterprises. Joshua Cohen, "The Economic Basis for Deliberative Democracy," *Social Philosophy and Policy* 6, no. 2 (1989): 27. For further analysis of parallel case arguments, see Nien-hê Hsieh, "Justice in Production," *Journal of Political Philosophy* 16, no. 1 (2008): 72–100.

24. James Child and Alexei Marcoux, "Freeman and Evan: Stakeholder Theory in the Original Position," *Business Ethics Quarterly* 9, no. 2 (1999): 211. On the applicability of hypothetical contract arguments, see, for example, Gordon Sollars, "The Corporation as Actual Agreement," *Business Ethics Quarterly* 12, no. 3 (2002): 351–71. Sollars argues that the fact that corporations are the result of actual, rather than hypothetical, agreements rules out the application of a hypothetical contract approach.

25. Robert Phillips and Joshua Margolis, "Toward an Ethics of Organizations," *Business Ethics Quarterly* 9, no. 4 (1999): 623.

26. Phillips and Margolis, "Toward an Ethics of Organizations," 633.

27. Rawls, *Political Liberalism*, 276.

28. Edwin Hartman, "Moral Philosophy, Political Philosophy, and Organizational Ethics: A Response to Phillips and Margolis," *Business Ethics Quarterly* 11, no. 4 (2001): 643–87.

29. Jeffery Moriarty, "On the Relevance of Political Philosophy to Business Ethics," *Business Ethics Quarterly* 15, no. 3 (2005): 453–71.

30. For a discussion of this, see Nussbaum, "Rawls and Feminism."

31. Robert Phillips, *Stakeholder Theory and Organizational Ethics* (San Francisco: Berrett-Koehler, 2003).

32. John Rawls, "Legal Obligation and the Duty of Fair Play," in *Law and Philosophy*, ed. Sidney Hook (New York: New York University Press, 1964), 9–10.

33. Thomas Donaldson and Thomas Dunfee, *Ties that Bind: A Social Contracts Approach to Business Ethics* (Cambridge, Mass.: Harvard Business School Press, 1999).

34. Samuel Freeman, *Cambridge Companion to Rawls*, 140–98.

35. There is a rather extensive debate on the applicability of hypothetical contract arguments to the normative study of business organizations. See, for example, Ben Wempe, "On the Use of the Social Contract Model in Business Ethics," *Business Ethics: A European Review* 13, no. 4 (2004): 322–41; and Wempe, "In Defense of a Self-Disciplined, Domain-Specific Social Contract Theory of Business Ethics," *Business Ethics Quarterly* 15, no. 1 (2005): 113–35.

36. Rawls, *Justice as Fairness*, 13.

37. Phillips and Margolis, "Toward an Ethics of Organizations," 630.

38. Rawls, *Justice as Fairness*, 10.

39. There is a large body of literature in this area. The basis for this view is found in Ronald Coase, "The Nature of the Firm," *Economica*, 4, no. 16 (1937): 386–405. For some recent surveys, see Pierre Garrouste and Stéphane Saussier, "Looking for a Theory of the Firm: Future Challenges," *Journal of Economic Behavior and Organization* 58, no. 2 (2005): 178–99, and Oliver Williamson, "The Theory of the Firm as Governance Structure: From Choice to Contract," *Journal of Economic Perspectives* 16, no. 3 (2002): 171–95.

40. Rawls, *Law of Peoples*.

41. Rawls, *Law of Peoples*, 1. The "Society of Peoples" refers to those peoples, or societies, that follow the ideals and principles of the Law of Peoples with regard to their mutual relations. Rawls, *Law of Peoples*, 3.

42. Rawls, *Law of Peoples*, 64–67. Rawls describes two kinds of well-ordered societies: *liberal peoples* and *decent hierarchical peoples*. *Liberal peoples* share "a reasonably just constitutional democratic government that serves their fundamental interests; citizens united by what Mill called 'common sympathies'; and finally, a moral nature." Rawls, *Law of Peoples*, 23. A *decent hierarchical people* are non-liberal. They are nonaggressive and meet three additional criteria: first, they secure human rights for all members of society; second, they have a system of law that is able to impose duties and obligations on all people within the territory of the society; and third, those who administer the legal system understand the law to be guided by a common good idea of justice. Rawls, *Law of Peoples*, 64–67.

43. Rawls, *Law of Peoples*, 90.

44. Nien-hê Hsieh, "The Obligations of Transnational Corporations: Rawlsian Justice and the Duty of Assistance," *Business Ethics Quarterly* 14, no. 4 (2004): 643–61.

45. Rawls, *Theory of Justice*, 97.

46. Rawls, *Theory of Justice*, 98.

47. Rawls, *Theory of Justice*.

48. Rawls, *Theory of Justice*, 293.

49. Thomas Dunfee, "Do Firms with Unique Compentencies for Rescuing Victims of Human Catastrophes Have Special Obligations?" *Business Ethics Quarterly* 16, no. 2 (2005): 185–210.

50. Rawls, *Theory of Justice*, 293–94.

51. Onora O'Neill, "Agents of Justice," in *Global Justice*, ed. Thomas Pogge (Oxford: Blackwell, 2001), 201. Onora O'Neill's account could also be grounded in the duty of assistance put forward in Rawls, *Law of Peoples*, 90.

52. Rawls, *Justice as Fairness*, 114.

53. G. A. Cohen, "Incentives, Inequality, and Community," in *The Tanner Lectures on Human Values*, vol. 13, ed. Grethe Peterson (Salt Lake City: University of Utah Press, 1992); "The Pareto Argument for Inequality," *Social Philosophy and Policy* 12, no. 1 (1995): 160–85; "Where the Action Is: On the Site of Distributive Justice," *Philosophy and Public Affairs* 26, no. 1 (1997): 3–30; and *If You're an Egalitarian, How Come You're So Rich?* (Cambridge, Mass.: Harvard University Press, 2000).

54. To be clear, Rawls provides a number of interpretations of the difference principle of which this is one. Cohen takes his argument to apply equally to all of these interpretations. Cohen, "Where the Action Is," 5.

55. Cohen, "Where the Action Is," 6.

56. Cohen, "Where the Action Is," 8–9 (Cohen's emphasis).

57. Cohen, "Where the Action Is," 9 (Cohen's emphasis).

58. Cohen, "Where the Action Is," 6.

59. Andrew Williams, "Incentives, Inequality, and Publicity," *Philosophy and Public Affairs* 27, no. 3 (1998): 238–41.

60. Kok-Chor Tan, "Justice and Personal Pursuits," *Journal of Philosophy* 101, no. 7 (2004): 335.

61. Joshua Cohen, "Taking People as They Are?" *Philosophy and Public Affairs* 30, no. 4 (2001): 361–86.

62. David Estlund, "Liberalism, Equality, and Fraternity in Cohen's Critique of Rawls," *Journal of Political Philosophy*, 6, no. 1 (1998): 99–112.

63. Thomas Pogge, "On the Site of Distributive Justice: Reflections on Cohen and Murphy," *Philosophy and Public Affairs*, 29, no. 2 (2000): 137–69.

64. Barry Clark and Herbert Gintis, "Rawlsian Justice and Economic Systems," *Philosophy and Public Affairs* 7, no. 4 (1978): 302–25; Rodney Peffer, "Towards a More Adequate Rawlsian Theory of Social Justice," *Pacific Philosophical Quarterly* 75, no. 3–4 (1994): 251–71; David Schweikart, "Should Rawls Be a Socialist? A Comparison of His Ideal Capitalism with Worker-Controlled Socialism," *Social Theory and Practice* 5, no. 1 (1978): 1–27; and Iris Young, "Self-determination as Principle of Justice," *Philosophical Forum* 11 (Fall 1979): 30–46.

65. Rawls, *Justice as Fairness*, 178. The discussion in this section draws on Nienhê Hsieh, "Rawlsian Justice and Workplace Republicanism," *Social Theory and Practice* 31, no. 1 (2005): 115–42, and Hsieh, "Justice in Production."

66. Rawls, *Justice as Fairness*, 114.

67. Cohen, "Economic Basis," 28.

68. Rawls, *Justice as Fairness*, 46.

69. Carole Pateman, *Participation and Democracy Theory* (New York: Cambridge University Press, 1970).

70. Rawls, *Justice as Fairness*, 18–19

71. For a discussion of neutrality, see Kymlicka, *Contemporary Political Philosophy*.

72. David Miller, *Market, State, and Community: Theoretical Foundations of Market Socialism* (Oxford, UK: Clarendon Press, 1989).

73. Young, "Self-determination," 30.

74. Young, "Self-determination," 39.

75. Young, "Self-determination," 39–40.

76. Young, "Self-determination," 40.

77. Young, "Self-determination," 40.

78. Rawls, *Justice as Fairness*, 59.

79. Hsieh, "Rawlsian Justice and Workplace Republicanism."

80. Rawls, *Justice as Fairness*, 59.

81. To be clear, an instance of interference can be arbitrary in this sense even if the interference follows from a decision that is justified in the context of the decision-making procedure internal to economic organizations. That is to say, I assume that it is possible to describe a decision-making procedure in a positive sense without reference to whether the economic regime that permits such a decision-making procedure is

consistent with the principles of justice. As a further point of clarification, it should be noted that the lack of justification in terms of the worker's interests upon which the interference is visited is understood only as a sufficient condition for the interference to be considered arbitrary.

82. Joseph Raz makes a similar point with respect to authority. He writes, "we have views of what interpersonal relations are morally acceptable. They involve mutual respect, reciprocity, etc. One-sided submission to the will of an authority seems to violate these precepts." Joseph Raz, "Introduction," *Authority*, ed. Joseph Raz (New York: New York University Press, 1990), 16.

83. Consider an example given by Stuart White in which a worker says to himself, "I had better not go to those gay clubs any more because if my boss finds out he might sack me, and I will then be destitute. Instead, I had better go to the Young Conservative's Association to impress him." Stuart White, *The Civic Minimum: On the Rights and Obligations of Economic Citizenship* (New York: Oxford University Press, 2003), 47.

84. For statements of what distinguishes economic enterprises from the market, see, for example, Coase, "The Nature of the Firm," and James March and Herbert Simon, *Organizations*, 2nd. ed. (Oxford: Blackwell, 1993).

85. On these and related points, see Raghuram Rajan and Luigi Zingales, "Power in a Theory of the Firm," *Quarterly Journal of Economics* 113, no. 2 (1998): 387–432; Margaret Blair and Lynn Stout, "A Team Production Theory of Corporate Law," *Virginia Law Review* 84 (March 1999): 247–328; and Margaret Blair and Thomas Kochan, ed., *The New Relationship: Human Capital in the American Corporation* (Washington, D.C.: Brookings Institution Press, 2000).

86. George Akerlof and Janet Yellen, ed., *Efficiency Wage Models of the Labor Market* (New York: Cambridge University Press, 1986).

87. Following Philip Pettit's interpretation of the essence of republicanism as the constraint of the state's exercise of discretionary power and the guarantee of a citizen's right to contest decisions made by the state, elsewhere I call such an economic regime a regime of *workplace republicanism*. Hsieh, "Rawlsian Justice." Pettit focuses on a specific aspect of the republican tradition, namely what he takes to be its conception of freedom. Philip Pettit, *Republicanism: A Theory of Freedom and Government* (New York: Oxford University Press, 1997). There are other elements of the republican tradition that scholars have come to see as integral. For an interpretation of the republican tradition that is along the lines that Pettit adopts, see Quentin Skinner, *Liberty before Liberalism* (New York: Cambridge University Press, 1998).

88. Iris Young, "Taking the Basic Structure Seriously," *Perspectives on Politics* 4, no. 1 (2006): 91.

89. Rawls, *Theory of Justice*, 242.

90. Richard Marens, "Burying the Past: The Neglected Legacy of Business Ethics from the Postwar Years," paper presented at the Society for Business Ethics Annual Meeting, August 2006, 22.

91. Rawls, *Justice as Fairness*, 36.

92. Rawls, *Justice as Fairness*, 139. For discussions of property-owning democracy and the differences between it and capitalism, see Richard Krouse and Michael

McPherson, "Capitalism, 'Property-Owning Democracy,' and the Welfare State," in *Democracy and the Welfare State*, ed. Amy Gutmann (Princeton, N.J.: Princeton University Press, 1988); Samuel Freeman, *Cambridge Companion to Rawls*, 219–35; and Samuel Freeman, *Justice and the Social Contract: Essays on Rawlsian Political Philosophy* (New York: Oxford University Press, 2007): 102–9.

Chapter Six

Deserving Jobs, Deserving Wages

Jeffrey Moriarty, Bowling Green State University

After a time on the philosophical scrap-heap,[1] the concept of desert—or deservingness—is the subject of renewed interest among moral and political philosophers. This chapter applies recent work on desert to two sets of issues in business ethics. The first set of issues concerns who ought to be hired, fired, promoted, and demoted. Call these issues of "job justice." The second set of issues concerns how much workers, including managers, ought to be paid. Call these issues of "wage justice."[2] I focus on job and wage justice because considerations of desert play an important, though sometimes tacit, role in discussions of these issues.[3]

Our analysis will yield insight into two broader themes. The first concerns the viability of appeals to desert in the context of business. Desert plays a minor role in most contemporary theories of distributive justice. I ask whether the objections that have led political philosophers to abandon desert should lead business ethicists to abandon it also. I argue that they should not. These objections are less potent in the context of business than in the context of the state. But appeals to desert in the context of business are not unproblematic. A second theme of my discussion is that desert is a more complicated concept than is generally recognized. A policy that appears to treat people as they deserve may, upon closer inspection, not do so. As a result, considerations of desert may support far different policies than might at first be thought.

This chapter proceeds as follows. I begin in section one by describing in more detail the concept of desert. In section two, I explain how common business practices regarding the distribution of jobs and wages can be seen as requiting people's deserts (i.e., giving people what they deserve). After briefly considering arguments in favor of requiting desert in section three, I consider in section four the two main reasons political philosophers, beginning with

John Rawls,[4] have abandoned desert as a distributive principle. In section five, I consider whether these arguments tell against appeals to desert in the context of business. In section six, I examine, in light of the nuanced conceptions of desert developed by philosophers, whether common business practices really do requite people's deserts. Section seven considers the relationship between desert and merit. Section eight concludes.

To forestall an objection, let me be clear about the scope of this chapter. I focus on what organizational theorists call "distributive justice," i.e., the justice of *outcomes*.[5] In particular, I consider whether, in these outcomes, people have the jobs and wages they deserve, and whether this matters. But, first, I do not suppose that desert is all that matters in distributive justice. Other values, such as equality and liberty, may also matter. Thus I do not claim that, all things considered, distributive justice *requires* that workers have the jobs and wages they deserve. Second, I do not suppose that distributive justice is all there is to justice. Questions of procedural justice—viz., the justice of the procedures firms use to decide whom to hire and how much to pay them—may also matter.[6] For the sake of brevity, I do not take up these issues.

Finally, let me clarify my argumentative strategy. My goal is to illuminate questions in business ethics using results from political philosophy. States and firms are similar in that both direct the activity of, and distribute resources to, their members and others. As a result, similar normative questions—for example, about legitimate authority and distributive justice—arise in both contexts.[7] It is only natural to suppose that the answers political philosophers have given to these questions will be useful in some way to business ethicists (and vice versa). I do not suppose, however, that states and firms are *parallel cases*, so that what is appropriate in one case is necessarily appropriate in the other.[8] Elsewhere I have suggested that states and firms are at least *similar* cases.[9] But this view is controversial,[10] so I do not assume here that it is sound. To the contrary, I recognize morally important differences between states and firms. I draw on the work of political philosophers simply because they have thought in detail about desert, and this concept is relevant to job and wage justice.

1. WHAT IS DESERT?

Desert is a three-place property uniting a subject, a thing or treatment, and a fact.[11] When certain facts are true of certain subjects, they have the property of being deserving of certain things or treatments. Thus claims that subjects deserve things (or, desert-claims) have the form "P has the property of being deserving of (or, deserves) T in virtue of F," where P is a subject, T is a thing or treatment, and F is a fact about P, also known as the "desert-base."

Desert's nature can be understood by contrasting it with the closely related concept of entitlement. First, desert is always, at least in part, a "pre-institutional" notion. Entitlement, by contrast, can be wholly "institutional." To say that desert is pre-institutional is to say that deservers are in a natural sense *worthy* of what they deserve.[12] Desert may incorporate institutional elements, but it is always in some sense independent of them. To say that entitlement can be wholly institutional is to say that what people are entitled to can be wholly a function of the rules and criteria of institutions. For example, if P wins a majority of the votes for a political office in a democracy, then he is entitled to it. But this does not entail that P deserves it. This depends on whether P is the best candidate, i.e., whether he is worthy of the office.

Not all cases of entitlement are institutional. If P has a natural right to T, then P is (naturally) entitled to T, whatever the relevant institutions say. This brings us to the second difference between desert and entitlement. Both are thought to have normative significance. That is, to say that P deserves or is entitled to T is to say that there is a reason—but not necessarily a conclusive reason—for P to have T. But the significance of entitlement is understood in terms of rights, while the significance of desert is understood in terms of the goodness of states of affairs. If P is entitled to T, then P has a right to T, and failing to give T to P would violate or override a right of P's. By contrast, if P deserves T, then the state of affairs in which P has it is better, other things equal, than the state of affairs in which P does not. But failing to give T to P would not violate or override a right of P's.

Having considered the nature of desert-claims, let us now consider the conditions under which it is appropriate to make them. We said that all desert-claims involve a subject, a thing or treatment, and a fact about the subject. But what subjects can be deserving, of what things, and in virtue of what facts?

Everyone agrees that persons can be deserving, as in "Jones deserves a pay raise," or "Smith deserves to be fired." There is disagreement, however, about whether nonpersons can be deserving. It is natural to ascribe desert to subjects other than persons, as in the claim "this drug deserves to be approved by the FDA."[13] But some writers consider this a misuse of "desert."[14] According to them, while a certain drug perhaps should be approved, it cannot strictly speaking deserve to be. Philosophers also agree that the things and treatments people are said to deserve are things and treatments of value. As Joel Feinberg says, "[I]f no event were ever more or less pleasing to us than any other, then there would be no use for the concept of desert."[15] The value of a deserved thing can be positive, as when we say that a worker deserves a promotion, or it can be negative, as when we say that a worker deserves to be fired. Of course, there is disagreement about what has value, but the concept of desert is neutral among the various theories of value.

The question of what types of facts can serve as desert-bases has received the most attention. There is widespread agreement that if P deserves T in virtue of F, then F is a fact *about* P. So P cannot deserve a pay raise in virtue of a fact about another person Q. In addition, there is considerable—but not uniform—agreement that desert-bases are subject to two further conditions.

The first is the value condition. David Schmidtz puts this simply: "[T]o judge a person deserving is to respond to features of the person that we judge to be of value."[16] Desert's connection with value is sometimes expressed as the idea that, for F to be a desert-base, F must be (appropriately) the subject of an appraising or evaluative attitude, such as admiration, disgust, gratitude, or resentment.[17] For a person to be deserving of a job in virtue of his personal qualities, for example, those qualities must be admirable, or more generally, good to have. For a person to be deserving of a demotion in virtue of his per-formance, that performance must be unworthy, or more generally, bad to have done. As these examples show, in desert-claims, the value of the desert-base is the same as the value of the deserved thing or treatment. In the claim "Jones deserves a job in virtue of his superior personal qualities," *superior qualities* are positively valued, as is *getting a job*. In the claim "Smith deserves to be fired in virtue of falling asleep on the job," *falling asleep on the job* is nega-tively valued, as is *being fired*.

Challenges to the value condition are rare. A few writers, however, have claimed that need is a desert-base, so that a person might deserve assistance simply in virtue of needing it.[18] This is incompatible with the value condition. To be sure, in certain circumstances, we do appraise needy people. For ex-ample, we think badly of those who are needy as a result of foolishly wasting all of their money. What we are appraising people for in this instance, how-ever, is their imprudence, not their need *per se*. We do not appraise people merely for having needs. Does this mean that a person who is needy through no fault of his or her own *doesn't* deserve assistance? This is, in fact, what most desert-theorists believe.[19] But there is nothing extraordinary about this. Desert-theorists need not deny that the person's need is a *reason* to assist her, only that it makes her *deserving* of assistance. There are all sorts of reasons to treat people in certain ways that have nothing to do with their deserts.

The second condition on the types of facts that can serve as desert-bases is the credit condition. According to it, P deserves T in virtue of F only if P can claim credit for F. Thus Robert Young suggests that "it is only where agents . . . can take credit for what they do, that any of the various desert bases can ground justifiable claims of desert."[20] Others express the credit condition in terms of responsibility. James Rachels says that "the concept of desert serves to signify ways of treating people that are appropriate responses to them, given that they are responsible for [certain] actions or states of affairs."[21] So, if a person deserves a job in virtue of his or her qualifications, then the person can claim credit, or is responsible, for his or her qualifications. Likewise, if a person deserves to be fired in virtue of his or her actions, then he or she is at fault, or responsible, for those actions.

Challenges to the credit condition are more common. For this condition appears to be incompatible with the familiar claim that people can be deserving in virtue of hardships they suffer. Fred Feldman argues that if a person contracts a serious illness, then he deserves sympathy from his neighbors.[22] And this is so precisely because he or she is *not* at fault for getting ill. The same goes for victims of accidents and crimes. In fact, some identify hardship as a basis for desert of income in particular,[23] so that how much pay a person deserves depends on how unpleasant or hazardous his or her work is, or how difficult it was to acquire the skills necessary to perform it.[24] In these cases, the credit condition seems to get things backward: not only is it is not required for the deserver to be responsible for that in virtue of which he or she is said to be deserving (viz., the hardship), it must be the case that the deserver is not responsible for it.[25]

Here appearances are misleading. Cases of so-called "compensatory desert" are compatible with the credit condition. A number of writers have argued for this conclusion,[26] but to my mind none has done so more successfully than Serena Olsaretti.[27] She notes that the judgment that people deserve compensation for suffering a hardship depends on the judgment that their suffering the hardship is bad or unjust. This badness or injustice can be understood in terms of the sort of desert described above, or in terms of other values such as equality or rights. Thus, if we think that it is good or just that a person suffer some misfortune—perhaps because, in virtue of doing many bad deeds, he or she deserves to suffer it—then we will not judge that he or she deserves compensation. This shows, according to Olsaretti, that judgments of compensatory desert are parasitic on judgments of what is independently good or just. Thus, talk of compensatory desert is shorthand for talk of the sort of desert we described above, according to which desert is subject to the credit condition, or for talk of goodness or justice defined independently of desert.[28]

At this point, I have clarified the conception of desert that will occupy us in this chapter, and I have addressed two challenges to it. I do not suppose I have said enough to silence debate on these issues (especially with respect to my claim that hardship is not a desert-base). However, the existence of this debate will not impede our inquiry. The kind of desert I have identified is the kind of desert that has played, sometimes tacitly, an important role in discussions of job and wage justice. If there are other kinds of desert, they are less important for these issues than the kind I have identified.

2. DESERT AND COMMON BUSINESS PRACTICES

Using our analysis of the concept of desert, I aim to show in this section how common business practices regarding the distribution of jobs and compensation can be seen as requiting people's deserts. What must be shown, more precisely, is that jobs and wages can be deserved, that persons can be deserving of them, and that persons get the jobs and wages they deserve. The first two claims are indisputable. It is clear that jobs and wages can be deserved (whether or not things other than jobs and wages can be), and that persons can be deserving of them (whether or not they can be deserving of other things). The third claim—that firms distribute jobs and compensation in such a way that people's deserts of them are requited—is controversial. There is reason, however, to believe that they do.

Consider first jobs. Businesses typically allocate jobs, and take them away, on the basis of people's qualifications. Promotions and jobs go to the most qualified. Those who are unqualified are not hired. If the unqualified are hired and their lack of qualification becomes apparent, they are demoted or fired. Assigning jobs on the basis of qualifications is, according to a popular view, a way of requiting desert. Writers have focused on the case of new hires to make this point. (For convenience, in the remainder of this chapter, I too focus on new hires. However, the results I reach can easily be extended to firings, promotions, and demotions.) Thus George Sher notes that "it is often said that persons deserve to be hired for jobs . . . because they are best qualified to do the work."[29] William Galston says that the idea that coveted positions should go to the most qualified applicants is "one of the historically and conceptually most important desert-claims."[30]

Consider next wages. Neoclassical economic theory tells us that how much compensation an employee receives will be in large part a function of the contribution he or she makes to the firm, i.e., what his or her marginal revenue product is.[31] Paying much more is irrational because it leads to a net loss for the firm: The employee gets paid more money than he or she generates for the firm. Paying much less is irrational because it will leave the firm open to the poaching of its employees by competitors, who see that it remains profitable to offer those employees higher wages.[32] Compensating employees according to their contributions can be seen as a way of requiting their deserts. For, according to several philosophers, the desert-base for wages is contribution. The most prominent of these is David Miller, who says that "[p]eople deserve the rewards of economic activity for their achievement, for the contribution they make to the welfare of others by providing goods and services that others want."[33]

I have now described how common business practices regarding the distribution of jobs and compensation can be seen as requiting desert. Note that I do not claim that this is the *only* way to conceive of these practices. Distributing jobs and compensation in accordance with qualifications and contributions, respectively, might be required by efficiency, whether or not it is required by desert. Nor do I claim that business managers *actually conceptualize* their hiring and compensation policies as ways of treating people as they deserve. My claim is just that they *can be*, and *have been*, conceived of this way. If in fact these practices do requite people's deserts, then they can be philosophically evaluated using the arguments about desert's importance that we will consider below. Later, I will subject this matter to closer scrutiny, and ask whether common business practices regarding the distribution of jobs and compensation *really do* requite desert. This will involve a consideration of alternative views about the desert-bases for jobs and wages. For now, let us assume that they do.

The question of whether firms do requite desert is, of course, different from the question of whether they should. As I noted, recent political philosophers have largely abandoned desert as a distributive ideal. Before considering their anti-desert arguments, I will briefly review three common arguments in favor of requiting desert.

3. ARGUMENTS FOR TREATING PEOPLE AS THEY DESERVE

Philosophers and laypersons once agreed on the importance of desert for questions of justice. J. S. Mill, for example, said that "it is universally considered just that each person should obtain that (whether good or evil) which he deserves."[34] Recent empirical research confirms the continuing popularity of this view among laypersons.[35] So, we might ask, what reason has there been to believe it? Three arguments for requiting desert have dominated the literature.

The first, found in J. R. Lucas and Sher, appeals to the Kantian idea of respect for persons.[36] According to this argument, treating people with respect requires treating them as autonomous beings, i.e., as beings who are responsible for their behavior. The argument's next premise is that treating people as autonomous beings requires treating them as they deserve. If, following Kant, we must treat people with respect, then we must treat them as they deserve.[37]

The second argument for requiting desert, found in Rachels and Schmidtz,[38] appeals to the good effects of doing so. Receiving a good treatment following certain behavior encourages that behavior. Since people are said to deserve good treatment for good behavior, treating people as they deserve, when what they deserve is good, encourages good behavior. Similarly, receiving a bad treatment following certain behavior discourages that behavior. Since people are said to deserve bad treatment for bad behavior, treating people as they deserve, when what they deserve is bad, discourages bad behavior. Requiting desert, then, has the good effects of increasing good behavior and decreasing bad behavior.

According to a third argument, endorsed by W. D. Ross and Miller,[39] people's having what they deserve is intrinsically good, i.e., it is good irrespective of the good effects of their having it. Ross gives a simple thought experiment to reinforce this intuition. He asks us to imagine "two imaginary states of the universe, alike in the total amounts of virtue and vice and of pleasure and pain present in the two, but in one of which the virtuous were all happy and the vicious miserable, while in the other the virtuous were miserable and the vicious happy."[40] He says "very few people would hesitate to say that the first was a much better state of the universe than the second."[41] Since all else is held constant, what explains our belief that the first world is better than the second is the intrinsic goodness of requiting desert.

Much more could be said about these arguments, but I will say no more here. I want to examine whether the arguments *against* desert—the ones that have led many contemporary political philosophers to reject it as a distributive principle—apply with equal force in the context of business.[42]

4. TWO OBJECTIONS TO DESERT

The most important contemporary political philosopher to deny desert's significance is Rawls. His liberal egalitarianism is criticized by Robert Nozick[43] and Michael Sandel,[44] but neither the former's libertarianism nor the latter's communitarianism assigns a role to desert at the level of fundamental principle. A more recent version of egalitarianism, the so-called "luck egalitarianism" of G. A. Cohen[45] and Larry Temkin,[46] is less hostile to desert. It is sensitive to considerations of choice and responsibility, which are important concerns of desert-theorists. But luck egalitarians still do not embrace desert as an ideal to distribute social goods. Below I present what I consider to be the two main objections that have led political philosophers to abandon desert. These correspond to the two major features of desert-bases: the value condition and the credit condition. In section five, I consider whether these arguments undermine the legitimacy of appeals to desert in the context of business.

The Value Objection

One objection to the use of desert as a distributive criterion focuses on the value condition. Desert-claims imply a variety of claims about value. But according to a prominent view in contemporary political philosophy—viz., neutralism—states should be neutral among competing conceptions of the good. (A conception of the good is a set of ideas about what a good life consists in, and can be informed by sometimes controversial moral, religious, or philosophical views.)

Neutralism is typically understood as a doctrine about the state's actions as opposed to its condition.[47] That is, neutralists do not claim that a just state is one in which all conceptions of the good can be pursued equally easily. Their claim is that the state should not aim to promote a particular conception of the good through its actions, or that it should not justify its actions by appealing to such a conception. Thus Rawls says his justice as fairness satisfies "neutrality of aim in the sense that basic institutions and public policy are not to be designed to favor any particular comprehensive doctrine."[48] And Charles Larmore says that a political decision counts "as neutral only if it can be justified without appealing to the presumed intrinsic superiority of any particular conception of the good life."[49] The neutralists' claim is not that states should aim to promote all conceptions of the good equally, or in an evenhanded manner. It is, rather, that the state should promote no conception of the good *at all*, at least when there is reasonable disagreement about what is good or valuable.[50]

In fact, few neutralists explicitly appeal to the nonneutrality of desert-claims as a reason to disregard them. Nevertheless, it seems to me that neutrality and desert are in tension, and that the relative importance of neutrality explains the relative unimportance of desert in recent political philosophy.

To see this, recall the ways in which desert-claims imply claims about value. First, the things or treatments people deserve must be valuable. They must be, as Feinberg says, "generally regarded with favor or disfavor."[51] Second, the facts about people in virtue of which they are deserving must be valuable. They must be appropriately the subject of an appraising or evaluative attitude. Third, to say that someone deserves something is to say that the state of affairs in which they have it is, other things equal, better than the state of affairs in which they do not. Since desert is connected in these ways to value, a state policy of requiting desert implies various claims about value. But, as Rawls—one of the few neutralists explicitly to reject a state policy of requiting desert on the basis of its nonneutrality—says, "having conflicting conceptions of the good, citizens cannot agree on a comprehensive doctrine to specify an idea of moral desert for political purposes."[52] Thus, on his view, a neutralist state cannot endorse a policy of requiting desert.[53]

This might be challenged. According to neutralists, the state should not aim to promote, or justify its policies by appealing to, a conception of the good only when what is good is subject to reasonable disagreement. It might be denied that there is reasonable disagreement about the values bound up with desert.

I grant that there is unlikely to be much disagreement about the value of the things people are said to deserve, especially jobs and wages. Rawls, in fact, includes choice of occupation and income among his "primary goods," i.e., "things that every rational man is presumed to want."[54] Moreover, empirical studies show that nearly everyone agrees that it is good that people get what they deserve (though there is disagreement about what makes people deserving and about how important desert is compared to other values, such as equality and liberty).[55] However, there is likely to be considerable disagreement about what facts about people can serve as desert-bases, and this disagreement will be in part the result of disagreement about what is valuable. Aristotle noted long ago that "all agree that the just in distributions must accord with some sort of worth, but what they call worth is not the same."[56] This is clearest in cases where the basis of desert is moral virtue.[57] Different moral theories specify different traits as moral virtues. But disagreement about value also occurs in cases involving nonmoral desert, including the cases we are concerned about. Julian Lamont diagnoses the debate about what the desert-base for wages is as a debate about what is valuable about work: effort or contribution.[58] And Iris Marion Young suggests that what counts as a job qualification will be "normative . . . rather than neutrally scientific."[59] Since a policy designed to distribute a thing according to desert must specify what the desert-base is, such a policy looks to be incompatible with neutralism.

The Credit Objection

The credit condition is the focus of the second main objection to using desert as a distributive criterion. According to this condition, for P to deserve T in virtue of F, P must be able to claim credit for F. The objection begins by questioning the extent to which people can claim credit for the facts in virtue of which they are said to be deserving. For example, we commonly say that a person deserves a job in virtue of his qualifications. But can people really claim credit for their qualifications? They are at least in part the result of natural and social factors, such as native intelligence and childhood upbringing, for which people cannot claim credit.

This line of argument has been developed in two ways. First, according to some writers, we cannot claim credit for *any* putative desert-base.[60] It is obvious that we cannot claim credit for our native intelligence and childhood upbringing. But even our choices, they say, are the result of natural and social factors outside of our control.[61] According to this argument, since no one can claim credit for anything, no one deserves anything, and desert cannot be used as a criterion for just distribution.[62] For a time, this was considered to be the main objection to using desert as a criterion in a theory of distributive justice.[63]

The second, more popular—and to my mind more plausible—way of developing the credit objection takes a less skeptical view of human agency. It grants that people have some control over the facts in virtue of which they are said to be deserving, but insists that these facts are also in part the result of natural and social factors beyond their control, such as genetic inheritance and social circumstances. But, it says, reconciling this fact with the credit condition leaves the desert-theorist with a dilemma: requiting desert is either impracticable or it is unfair.[64] Which criticism is made depends on how the credit condition is understood.

We might understand the credit condition in a weak way. On this understanding, for P to deserve T in virtue of F, it must be the case that P did or brought about F voluntarily. P need not be able to claim credit for F in a "metaphysically deep" sense. That is, it need not be the case that F is purely the product of P's free choices, as opposed to natural and social factors (if we can even make sense of this idea). Miller understands the credit condition this way. He says that while "voluntary control is a necessary condition for desert . . . the extent of desert may depend not merely on factors subject to voluntary control but also on other traits—native ability, say."[65] Call this, following Richard Arneson, the "coarse-grained" conception of desert.[66]

Understood this way, requiting desert may seem unfair. Suppose that P and Q both work equally hard to gain admission to college. Suppose, however, that because P is more naturally talented than Q, P's academic qualifications (e.g., grades and test scores) turn out to be better than Q's. Assuming that the desert-base for admission to college is academic qualifications, on the coarse-grained conception of desert, P is more deserving of admission than Q. But is it fair to admit P rather than Q on this basis? Arguably not. As Sidgwick says, "there seems to be no justice in making A happier than B, merely because circumstances beyond his own control have first made him better."[67] If the fact that P is more qualified than Q is fully explained by P's superior natural abilities, as opposed to a free choice P made (e.g., to work harder), then "there seems to be no justice" in admitting P rather than Q.

Second, we might understand the credit condition in a strong way. Arneson[68] and John Roemer[69] think that desert is "fine-grained" with respect to natural and social factors. On this view, people are deserving in virtue of *that part* of their putative desert-base (e.g., academic qualifications) that is the result of their own free choices, not *that part* that is the result of natural and social factors beyond their control. So, to use our previous example, P is more deserving than Q of college admission if his qualifications remain somehow "better" than Q's even after discounting for the effects of his superior natural abilities. For all we have said, of course, they may be. But they may not. The idea that justice requires giving people what they deserve, on this conception of desert, is more attractive. Here, to borrow Sidgwick's phrase, those whom we make happier are not those who have already been made better by circumstances beyond their control, but those who have made themselves better.

But while requiting fine-grained desert may seem fair, it may also seem impracticable. Several difficulties arise. First, how do we determine which factors to discount in the assessment of desert? We might agree that we should discount native intelligence and socioeconomic status, but what else? Second, how do we actually do the discounting? Finally, implementing a discounting procedure is likely to require an enormous amount of resources, and the collection of a great deal of sensitive information about people's lives. Are these financial and moral costs worth it? The difficulties of measuring a fine-grained desert have seemed to some insuperable. Thus Arneson, who thinks this is the right conception of desert, says that "deciding to what degree an individual is truly deserving can be hard, even intractable, even in a small-scale and local context that does not stretch out over time."[70] Rawls agrees. To determine what people deserve, he says, we have to "discount for [the] greater good fortune of the better endowed,"[71] (and of course the bad fortune of the worse endowed). As there "seems to be no way" to do this, "rewarding desert is impracticable."[72]

5. RELEVANCE TO BUSINESS

At this point, we have considered the two main objections that have led to desert's rejection by political philosophers. Let us now see whether they should lead to its rejection by business ethicists as well. Note that even if the value and credit objections undermine appeals to desert in the context of business, it does not follow that firms should stop distributing jobs on the basis of qualifications and compensation on the basis of contributions. We have not established that these practices actually do requite people's deserts. Moreover, there may be other good (not-desert-based) reasons for having them.

I begin with the value objection. To recall, it says that states should be neutral among competing conceptions of the good. Since a policy of requiting desert implies controversial claims about value, neutralist states should not endorse one. The first thing to note about this objection is that it is not an *ar-*

gument against desert. It is an articulation of a view that, I have suggested, is inconsistent with the use of desert as a distributive criterion. To show that desert should be rejected on the basis of the value objection, it would have to be shown that states should be neutral. This can be resisted.[73] For the sake of argument, however, let us grant that they should. Still, I suggest, nothing follows about the use of desert in the context of business.

What follows if neutralism is true is that the *state* should be neutral among competing conceptions of the good. Nothing follows about what associations within the state, such as businesses, should be like. In fact, most neutralists explicitly allow for associations *not* to be neutral among conceptions of the good. Larmore says that the neutralist "does not require that . . . institutions in society [other than the state] operate" in the spirit of neutralism. Instead, associations such as "[c]hurches and firms . . . may pursue goals (salvation, profits) that they assume to be ideals intrinsically superior to others."[74] These goals help to define what counts as valuable behavior in the association—a definition that may not be accepted in the wider society. In this spirit, Rawls recognizes the legitimacy of both political virtues, which are "shared by citizens and do not depend on any particular comprehensive doctrine," and "virtues falling under various associational ideals," which are the subject of reasonable disagreement among citizens.[75] (Of course, for Rawls and other neutralists, the recognition of the latter is the responsibility of the associations themselves, not the state.) Thus, even if neutralism is incompatible with desert at the state level, it is compatible with desert, according to neutralists themselves, at the associational level. Appeals to desert in the context of business, then, have little to fear from the value objection.

The credit objection is more potent. It begins with the idea that people's putative desert-bases are at least in part the result of natural and social factors beyond their control, and is developed in one of two ways. According to the extreme form of the credit objection, since no one can claim credit for any of their putative desert-bases, no one deserves anything, and desert cannot be used as a criterion for just distribution. Obviously, if it is true that no one deserves anything because they lack the kind of agency required for desert, then this is a truth that holds at the state and business levels. So, if we accept the extreme form of the credit objection, appeals to desert in the context of business, and indeed in all contexts, are illegitimate.

However, as I noted, the extreme form of the credit objection is increasingly unpopular. Most embrace its more moderate form, according to which people's actions and traits are in part, but not in whole, the result of factors beyond their control. At this point, the desert theorist faces a dilemma. Given a coarse-grained conception of desert, requiting it is said to be unfair—people would be rewarded in part for natural and social factors beyond their control. But, given a fine-grained conception of desert, requiting it is said to be impracticable—we cannot separate the part of people's achievements that is due to natural and social factors from the part that is due to their own free choices. As in the case of the value objection, it is questionable whether the moderate form of the credit objection proves what it claims to about theories of justice.[76] But again, let us grant that it does. My claim here is that, while still potent, this objection is significantly less potent in the context of business than in the context of the state.

Consider first the criticism that requiting fine-grained desert is impracticable, because it is very difficult and costly to try to discount the effects of natural and social factors on people's actions and traits. We might agree that this would be very difficult and costly at the state level. It would require government bureaucrats to collect a great deal of sensitive information about people's lives, a process that would involve huge financial and moral costs. At the level of the firm, however, this process would be less difficult and costly. The principal reason is that the key relationships, i.e., between employers and employees, are already in place, and are thought to be, to an extent, morally unproblematic. Instead of requiring the creation of entirely new relationships, then, requiting fine-grained desert would require adjusting and deepening ones that already exist.

With respect to jobs, in the hiring process employees already give employers access to facts about their background, qualifications, and experience. To give an employer the ability to assess fine-grained desert, the employee would need to provide additional facts about his or her background, to give employers a sense of how difficult or easy it was for the employee to acquire his or her qualifications and experience. With respect to compensation, employers already try to distinguish the part of the firm's success (or failure) that is due to employees' contributions from the part that is due to factors beyond their control. For example, some employees (especially executives) are rewarded not simply if their firm's stock price rises, but if it rises relative to the stock prices of comparable firms. The facts collected at the hiring stage could be used to further refine judgments about how difficult or easy it was for the employees to make the contributions they did.[77]

Consider next the criticism that requiting coarse-grained desert is unfair, because how deserving a person is depends in part on factors beyond his or her control. The perception of unfairness at the state level is encouraged, I think, by two ideas. The first is that the state cannot requite many kinds of desert at once. When the state recognizes one kind of desert, it makes a judgment that certain actions and traits are valuable—a judgment that implies that other actions and traits are not.[78] The second idea is that states are difficult to exit. If a person does not do well with respect to his or her state's policy of requiting desert, the person cannot easily improve his or her situation by moving to another state. The result is that a person may be doing badly with respect to his or her state's policy of requiting desert and be unable to do anything about it.

This same result is unlikely to occur, however, at the associational level. Instead of one state with one set of ideas about what is valuable, there are many different firms with many different sets of ideas about what is valuable. There is room, then, to recognize many kinds of desert in the economy overall. More individuals can be seen as deserving, and so more individuals will do well with respect to policies designed to requite desert. Second, and relatedly, firms are easier to leave than states. So, if an individual finds that his or her talents are not appreciated in his or her current firm, the individual can leave and join another one. If, however, he or she does not leave despite doing badly with respect to his or her firm's policy of requiting desert, then we can assume that the individual prefers it to others, and the unfairness is again mitigated.

I do not mean to assert that the credit objection poses *no* problems for appeals to desert in the context of business. My claim is that it poses *less serious* problems in this context than in the context of the state. I do not pretend that employers will be able to assess their employees' fine-grained deserts easily.[79] Doing so will still involve significant financial and moral costs. Nor do I pretend that there is no unfairness in requiting coarse-grained desert in a business. Some individuals will have traits and abilities that are valued by no businesses. Moreover, while firms are *easier* to exit than states, they are not necessarily *easy* to exit. So we cannot always infer from the fact that an employee remains at a firm that he or she endorses its policies.

The upshot of this section is that those who appeal to desert to justify a particular business policy should be, on the whole, less worried by the standard anti-desert arguments than those who appeal to desert to justify a particular state policy. I argued that the value objection does not at all undermine appeals to desert in the context of business. The credit objection in its extreme form does undermine such appeals. But this objection, perhaps as a result of its extreme claims about the nature of human agency, has few supporters. The moderate form of the credit objection also poses problems for appeals to desert in the context of business. But these are less serious problems in the context of business than in the context of the state.

It does not follow from what I have argued that the common business practices of distributing jobs according to qualification and compensation according to contribution are supported by considerations of desert. The foregoing discussion has revealed that there is considerable disagreement about what the precise conditions for desert are. In light of this, we need to examine more carefully whether these common business practices really do requite desert.

6. DO COMMON BUSINESS
PRACTICES REALLY REQUITE DESERT?

Whether or not common business practices regarding the distribution of jobs and compensation requite desert depends, obviously, on what the conditions for desert are. Unfortunately, the disagreement that exists on this subject cannot be resolved here. So we cannot say whether these practices actually do treat people as they deserve. Below I describe what needs to be done to resolve this matter. I note, in particular, that resolving it requires learning more not just about desert, but about common business practices. The claim that firms hire by qualification and compensate according to contribution is true, but vague. My goal in this section is not simply to identify and catalog disputes. Instead, I show how, depending on how these disputes turn out, considerations of desert, rather than supporting the status quo in business, might support unusual or even radical policies.

My claim that there is disagreement about the precise conditions for desert may seem to be in tension with my earlier claim that there is considerable agreement about the nature of desert. It is not. The agreement about desert occurs at relatively high levels of abstraction; the disagreement occurs at lower levels. For example, there is considerable agreement that the credit condition should be accepted. There is disagreement, however, about the form it should take. Even more desert-theorists embrace the value condition. But insofar as they hold different theories of value, they will disagree about what facts can serve as desert-bases in particular cases.

Consider first jobs. We said that employers typically hire people according to their qualifications. To determine whether, in hiring by qualifications, employers are treating people in accordance with their deserts, we first need a more precise account of what facts about employees employers consider to be qualifications. This requires empirical research. Next, we must see which of these facts can serve as desert-bases for jobs. Suppose, for the sake of argument, that employers hire on the basis of native intelligence, education, skills, and experience. Whether these factors qualify as desert-bases depends on our view of desert, and in particular, our interpretation of the credit condition and our view about what is valuable.[80]

While native intelligence is valuable, people cannot claim credit, in any sense, for how intelligent they are. So native intelligence cannot serve as a desert-base on the view of desert we have accepted here.[81] Education, skills, and experience, however, are valuable, and are, at least in part, the result of voluntary actions people perform. Thus, a case can be made that employers do requite desert, understood in a coarse-grained way, when they hire employees on the basis of these factors. Considerations of desert may therefore support the status quo hiring policies in business.

But they may not. If desert is understood in a fine-grained way, then to determine what people deserve we must discount for the effects of natural and social factors on their qualifications. Of course, it may be the case that the person with the best qualifications *pre-discount* is also the person with the best qualifications *post-discount*. That is, the person who has "done the most" may also be the person who has "done the most with what he has." Often, however, these will be different people. As a result, considerations of fine-grained desert may support not the status quo, but an aggressive policy of preferential treatment. A person from a disadvantaged background may have better qualifications given his or her background than a person from a privileged background given his or her background, even if the latter has slightly better qualifications *simpliciter*. To the extent that a program of preferential treatment promotes the hiring of "better" people from disadvantaged backgrounds (i.e., those who have done more with what they have), it may have the effect of requiting people's fine-grained deserts.[82]

Consider next wages. As we noted, an employee's compensation will be in large part a function of the economic value of his or her contribution. However, employers often cannot accurately measure that value directly. Moreover, they have efficiency-based reasons to adopt overall pay structures that have the effect of paying some workers more and some workers less than the economic value of their contributions.[83] As a result, employers—especially in large firms—determine how much to pay their workers by considering facts about their jobs, such as their complexity, importance, and difficulty.[84] Indeed, consulting firms such as Mercer and the Hay Group have devised elaborate job evaluation plans used by numerous organizations that incorporate these and other factors to assess the relative worth of jobs. The first task in determining whether employers' compensation practices requite workers' deserts, then, is to study these plans to see which factors are compensated.

An adequate assessment would also have to consider which, if any, of these factors can serve as desert-bases for wages. The traditional debate among philosophers is about whether the desert-base for wages is effort or contribution.[85] These are not among the factors included in standard job evaluation plans. Presumably, however, some of these factors track what philosophers call "contribution" (e.g., job importance) and others track what they call "effort" (e.g., hours worked). Determining which factors track which element(s) will not be straightforward. It is further complicated by the fact that different philosophers mean different things by "contribution" and "effort." Effort, for example, is understood variously as raw physical exertion, fine-grained contribution,[86] or "everything negative about work," including its dangerousness and unpleasantness.[87] Ultimately, as in the case of jobs, what we think the desert-bases for wages are will reflect our interpretation of the credit condition and our view about what is valuable.[88]

As in the case of jobs, a case can be made that considerations of desert support the status quo compensation policies. As a matter of economic necessity, firms cannot stray too far from the ideal of compensating workers according to their contributions. And contribution is thought by some who understand desert in a coarse-grained way to be a key desert-base for wages.[89] However, considerations of desert have been invoked by others to support very different policies. For example, several philosophers have equated paying workers what they deserve with a doctrine that is widely repudiated by employers, viz., comparable worth.[90] According to this doctrine, workers whose jobs are similar in terms of skill, effort, responsibility, and working conditions should receive similar wages, whether or not the content of their jobs is similar.[91] If comparable worth is supported by considerations of desert, it is supported by a *coarse-grained* conception of it—just a different one than the one used to support the status quo. Fine-grained desert may support a still more radical policy.

7. IF NOT DESERT, THEN MERIT?

I have argued that hiring according to qualification and compensating according to contribution do not necessarily treat people as they deserve. At this point it might be wondered whether there is a better way to conceptualize these practices. Perhaps they can be seen as requiting *merit* as opposed to desert.

A conception of merit endorsed by Louis Pojman supports this suggestion.[92] According to him, desert is a species of merit. For P to merit T in virtue of F, F must be valuable. But for P to deserve T in virtue of F, F must be valuable *and* P must be able to claim credit for F. In other words, merit is desert without the credit condition. As we noted, firms tend to care little about whether people's qualifications and contributions are the result of favorable natural and social factors. What matters is whether they have them or made them, respectively. Thus it is arguable that firms' hiring and compensation policies do requite merit.

The truth of this analysis rests on the truth of Pojman's conception of merit. But this conception is controversial. Sher offers an alternative that is nearly the reverse of Pojman's.[93] While the latter thinks desert is a species of merit, the former thinks merit is a basis of desert. On Sher's view, one can be deserving in virtue of being meritorious, and in other ways as well. According to a third conception of merit, endorsed by Lucas[94] and Roemer,[95] merit is concerned with attributes, while desert is concerned with actions. This view cuts across Pojman's. People are typically responsible for most (but perhaps not all) of their actions, and at least some (but far from all) of their traits. According to a fourth conception, endorsed by Norman Daniels,[96] merit is based not on present attributes but future actions. On his view, P merits a position in virtue of the fact that P will perform best in it.[97] We might use a person's present attributes or past performance to estimate how well he is likely to perform in the future, but strictly speaking the "merit-base" on Daniels's view is future action. A fifth conception of merit is endorsed by Sidgwick.[98] He equates merit and "good" desert.

In light of this, it is far from obvious that the practices of hiring according to qualification and compensating according to contribution requite merit. For all I have said, of course, Pojman's conception may be right, and they do.[99] What is more likely true, however, is that there is no "correct" conception of merit. There are simply different conceptions, tailored to different writers' purposes. In this spirit, we might simply stipulate that firms hire and compensate according to merit, and then consider how this sense of merit relates to desert. But while this may be theoretically convenient, I do not see how it will help to advance the debate about the relevance of desert to questions of job and wage justice.

8. CONCLUSION

The conventional hiring and compensation practices of firms appear to treat people as they deserve. Using recent research on the concept of desert, in this chapter I asked, first, whether they should, and second, whether they do. The arguments political philosophers have used to reject desert as a distributive principle, I argued, have less force in the context of business than in the context of the state. This clears the way for firms' practices to be justified by appealing to considerations of desert. But, I argued, there is disagreement about the conditions for desert, and as a result, it is questionable whether these practices do in fact treat people as they deserve. In fact, I suggested, considerations of desert, instead of supporting the status quo in business, may support policies well outside of the mainstream.

Where do we go from here? The natural inclination, especially among philosophers, will be to try to solve the disagreement about the conditions for desert. I doubt that a complete list of necessary and sufficient conditions for desert can be devised. The boundary of this concept, like many others, is likely to be somewhat vague.[100] At the same time, however, we should not give up hope that some debates about the concept of desert can be resolved. The disagreement about what the desert-bases are for jobs and wages may be one of them.

I believe that some progress can be made using this approach. But I think we can make faster progress using another one. When discussing the sort of questions we have been discussing, it is easy to lose sight of what is important. Conceptual questions, i.e., about the conditions for desert, have some intrinsic value, but their main value, especially for business ethicists, is instrumental. They are valuable because they help us to answer normative questions—in this case, how should jobs and wages be distributed? My suggestion is that we can make progress on these normative questions—even with respect to the considerations typically captured in desert-claims—without taking a stand on the conceptual ones. This is because we can assess the normative significance of the putative desert-bases without deciding whether they are legitimate as bases of *desert*. We can do so using the same arguments that have traditionally been used to establish desert's significance.

Whether businesses (or states) should take into account considerations of desert, or how much weight they should give them, depends on the strength of the arguments for requiting desert. Traditionally, as we saw in section three, it has been claimed that requiting desert is required by respect for persons, or that it has good effects, or that the state of affairs in which people have what they deserve is intrinsically good. My claim is that we can assess the truth of these claims with respect to the putative desert-bases *directly*, putting aside the question of whether these putative desert-bases are legitimate as *desert*-bases. Thus, instead of asking whether, for example, effort or contribution is the desert-base for wages, and then examining the force of respect-based, instrumental value–based, and intrinsic value–based arguments for giving people what they deserve, we can examine the force of these arguments for compensating people according to their efforts and contributions *directly*. For example, we can ask: Will compensating people according to their efforts have good effects? Is this required by respect for persons? Does it have intrinsic value? If the answer to any of these questions is yes, then there is a reason to compensate people according to their efforts. And note that a "yes" answer does not entail that effort is a desert-base for wages. As we noted at the outset, a fact about a person (e.g., that he is hungry) can be a reason for him or her to have some thing (e.g., some food), but not make the person deserving of it. The same result holds in the case of jobs. Instead of asking whether people can deserve jobs in virtue of traits that they can claim only partial credit for, such as having a college education or a certain skill set, and then examining the force of respect-based, instrumental value–based, and intrinsic value–based arguments for giving people what they deserve, we can examine the force of these arguments for hiring people with college educations and certain skill sets directly. For example, we can ask: Does hiring people with college educations have good effects? Is it required by respect for persons? Does it have intrinsic value? Again, a "yes" answer implies that there is a reason to hire people with college educations, without implying that this is a desert-base for jobs.

My point should not be taken too far. I am not arguing that determining the precise conceptual boundaries of desert is unimportant. Doing so may well have important normative implications. I am also not arguing, more radically, that desert is unimportant, and that what really matters are the putative bases of desert, such as effort. A belief in the importance of effort may well *be* a belief in the importance of desert. But, as we have seen, it may not be—or it may be in some circumstances but not others. I have argued that we can make progress on the question of whether, for example, workers should be compensated according to their efforts without solving the classificatory questions about desert that have proved so vexing. We can apply the normative arguments traditionally used to establish the importance of desert to the putative desert-bases themselves. This will help us to make progress on the important normative questions about the just distribution of jobs and wages, even as debate about the precise nature of desert continues.[101]

NOTES

1. I owe this phrase to John Kleinig, "The Concept of Desert," *American Philosophical Quarterly* 8, no. 1 (January 1971): 71–78.

2. This division is not as neat as I imply. Promotions can be conceived of as jobs or as compensation. On this point see Joel Feinberg, *Doing and Deserving* (Princeton, N.J.: Princeton University Press, 1970). For convenience, I put this complication aside.

3. Desert has also played a role in discussions of profits. For arguments that entrepreneurs deserve to keep the profits of their productive enterprises, see N. Scott Arnold, "Why Profits are Deserved," *Ethics* 97, no. 2 (January 1987): 387–402, and Jan Narveson, "Deserving Profits," in *Profits and Morality*, ed. Robin Cowan and Mario J. Rizzo (Chicago: University of Chicago Press, 1995), 48–87. For a criticism of this view, see John Christman, "Entrepreneurs, Profits, and Deserving Market Shares," *Social Philosophy and Policy* 6, no. 1 (Autumn 1988): 1–16. For reasons of space, I put this topic aside.

4. John Rawls, *A Theory of Justice*, rev. ed. (1971; Cambridge, Mass.: Harvard University Press, 1999).

5. Organizational theorists think of distributive justice as concerned exclusively with the justice of outcomes or states of affairs, and procedural justice as concerned exclusively with the justice of procedures or rules. See, for example, George T. Milkovich and Jerry M. Newman, *Compensation*, 7th ed. (New York: McGraw-Hill, 2002), and Robert Folger, "Rethinking Equity Theory: A Referent Cognitions Model," in *Justice in Social Relations*, ed. Hans Werner Bierhoff, Ronald L. Cohen,

and Jerald Greenberg (New York: Plenum, 1986), 145–62. Political philosophers do not think of justice this way. For them, distributive justice is concerned with the distribution of benefits and burdens, and this can be understood to require either certain outcomes or certain procedures.

6. See, for example, Matt Bloom, "The Ethics of Compensation Systems," *Journal of Business Ethics* 52, no. 2 (June 2004): 149–52, and the papers collected in Jerald Greenberg and Russell Cropanzano, *Advances in Organizational Justice* (Stanford, Calif.: Stanford University Press, 2001).

7. Not all of the questions in business ethics are similar to questions in political philosophy. The questions I have mentioned focus on the nature of business organizations. But business ethics also requires thinking about what sorts of decisions managers ought to make when presented with dilemmas in the workplace. For example, should managers do business with clients whose values they find repugnant? I believe that political philosophy is less useful for addressing these questions in business ethics, and I will have nothing to say about such questions here.

8. Robert Dahl offers a parallel case argument for economic democracy. According to him, since democracy is required in the state, and since states and firms are alike, democracy is required in the firm. See Dahl, *A Preface to Economic Democracy* (Berkeley: University of California Press, 1985).

9. Jeffrey Moriarty, "On the Relevance of Political Philosophy to Business Ethics," *Business Ethics Quarterly* 15, no. 3 (July 2005): 453–71.

10. See Robert A. Phillips and Joshua D. Margolis, "Toward an Ethics of Organizations," *Business Ethics Quarterly* 9, no. 4 (October 1999): 619–38.

11. In this section I draw on Jeffrey Moriarty, "Desert," in *Encyclopedia of Business Ethics and Society*, ed. Robert W. Kolb (Thousand Oaks, Calif.: Sage, 2008), 57–75.

12. Feinberg, *Doing and Deserving*, 57.

13. See, for example, Geoffrey Cupit, *Justice as Fittingness* (Oxford, UK: Clarendon Press, 1996).

14. See, for example, David Miller, *Principles of Social Justice* (Cambridge, Mass.: Harvard University Press, 1999).

15. Feinberg, *Doing and Deserving*, 61.

16. David Schmidtz, "How to Deserve," *Political Theory* 30, no. 6 (December 2002): 775.

17. See, for example, Miller, *Principles*.

18. See, for example, Owen McLeod, "Desert and Wages," *Utilitas* 8, no. 2 (July 1996): 205–21.

19. See, for example, Miller, *Principles*, and Kleinig, "Concept of Desert."

20. Robert Young, "Egalitarianism and Personal Desert," *Ethics* 102, no. 2 (January 1992): 339.

21. James Rachels, *Can Ethics Provide Answers?* (Lanham, Md.: Rowman & Littlefield, 1997), 180. See also Miller, *Principles*.

22. Fred Feldman, "Desert: Reconsideration of Some Received Wisdom," *Mind* 104, no. 413 (January 1995): 63–77.

23. See, for example, Feinberg, *Doing and Deserving*, and James Dick, "How to Justify a Distribution of Earnings," *Philosophy and Public Affairs* 4, no. 3 (Spring 1975): 248–72.

24. Feinberg, *Doing and Deserving*, 93.

25. These cases also appear to be incompatible with the value condition. According to it, the value of the desert-base must be the same as the value of the deserved thing. In these cases, the value of the desert-base (viz., hardship) is negative and the value of the deserved thing (viz., compensation) is positive. My explanation below of how these cases are, in fact, compatible with the credit condition will also show how they are compatible with the value condition.

26. David Miller, *Social Justice* (New York: Oxford University Press, 1976), and Saul Smilansky, "Responsibility and Desert: Defending the Connection," *Mind* 105, no. 417 (January 1996): 157–63.

27. Serena Olsaretti, "Distributive Justice and Compensatory Desert," in *Desert and Justice*, ed. Serena Olsaretti (Oxford, UK: Clarendon Press, 2003), 187–204.

28. The credit condition has been challenged in other ways. Sher thinks that the prettiest entrant in the beauty contest deserves first prize, even if she is in no way responsible for her beauty. See George Sher, *Desert* (Princeton, N.J.: Princeton University Press, 1987). Few desert-theorists have tried to explain away this putative counterexample to the credit condition, as they have the putative counterexamples involving compensatory desert. Instead most simply deny that the case Sher describes is a true case of desert. See, for example, Rachels, *Can Ethics*, and Miller, *Principles*. Of course, as in the case of the needy child, they do not deny that the prettiest entrant should win; they simply deny that she deserves to win.

29. Sher, *Desert*, 119.

30. William Galston, *Justice and the Human Good* (Chicago: University of Chicago Press, 1980), 176.

31. See, for example, Milkovich and Newman, *Compensation*. Wages are not the only type of compensation employees receive. Many also receive benefits in the form of medical and life insurance. In theory, an employee's entire compensation package, not just his or her wages, will be a function of the marginal revenue product of the employee's labor. For convenience, however, I will set these other forms of compensation aside and focus on wages only. I will also set aside the distinction between base pay and merit (or performance-based) pay. For a discussion of these issues, see Robert L. Heneman, *Merit Pay: Linking Pay Increases to Performance Ratings* (Reading, Mass.: Addison-Wesley, 1992).

32. As this implies, there may be reasons to pay an employee slightly more or slightly less than his or her marginal revenue product. For example, a more egalitarian—or more hierarchical—overall wage structure in the firm may increase efficiency. On this point see Milkovich and Newman, *Compensation*. Such a wage structure may fail to pay certain employees in accordance with their marginal revenue products.

33. Miller, *Principles*, 184. Other philosophers think that contribution is one but not the only desert-base for wages. See, for example, Joel Feinberg, *Social Philosophy*

(Englewood Cliffs, N.J.: Prentice-Hall, 1973); Thomas Hurka, "Desert: Individualistic and Holistic," in *Desert and Justice*, ed. Serena Olsaretti (Oxford, UK: Clarendon Press, 2003) , 45–68; Young, "Egalitarianism and Personal Desert"; and McLeod, "Desert and Wages."

34. John Stuart Mill, *Utilitarianism*, ed. Roger Crisp (New York: Oxford University Press, 1998), 89. See also Aristotle, *Nicomachean Ethics*, ed. Terence Irwin (Indianapolis: Hackett, 1999), and Henry Sidgwick, *The Methods of Ethics*, 7th ed. (Indianapolis, Ind.: Hackett, 1981).

35. Norman T. Feather, *Values, Achievement, and Justice: Studies in the Psychology of Deservingness* (New York: Kluwer Academic, 1999). See also Miller, *Principles*.

36. J. R. Lucas, *On Justice* (Oxford, UK: Clarendon Press, 1980); and Sher, *Desert*.

37. Sher explicitly adapts this argument to the context of job justice. He says that "when we select among applicants for reasons other than their ability to perform the tasks that define positions, we treat them as passive recipients of largesse or links in causal chains rather than as active contributors to anyone's ends." In doing this, "we violate the requirement that [people] be treated as rational agents." Sher, *Desert*, 126.

38. Rachels, *Can Ethics*, and Schmidtz, "How to Deserve."

39. W. D. Ross, *The Right and the Good*, ed. Philip Stratton-Lake (Oxford, UK: Oxford University Press, 2002); and Miller, *Principles*.

40. Ross, *The Right*, 138.

41. Ross, *The Right*, 138. We might even prefer a world in which the virtuous are happy and the vicious are miserable to a world in which both the virtuous and vicious are happy. This would show that desert "trumps" utility, i.e., it is more important to give people what they deserve than to maximize utility. Ross's argument is intended to establish the weaker claim that requiting desert has *some* value.

42. Interestingly, desert continues to play a role in most contemporary theories of *retributive* justice. Most believe that punishments should be inflicted only on those who deserve them, and that punishment should be in proportion to desert. An increasing number also believe that desert provides a justifying reason for inflicting punishment on an offender. See, for example, Anthony Ellis, "Recent Work on Punishment," *Philosophical Quarterly* 45, no. 179 (April 1995): 225–33.

43. Robert Nozick, *Anarchy, State, and Utopia* (New York: Basic, 1974).

44. Michael J. Sandel, *Liberalism and the Limits of Justice*, 2nd ed. (New York: Cambridge University Press, 1998).

45. G. A. Cohen, "On the Currency of Egalitarian Justice," *Ethics* 99, no. 4 (July 1989): 906–44.

46. Larry Temkin, *Inequality* (New York: Oxford University Press, 1993).

47. See, for example, Charles Larmore, *Patterns of Moral Complexity* (New York: Cambridge University Press, 1987).

48. John Rawls, *Political Liberalism* (New York: Columbia University Press, 1993), 70.

49. Larmore, *Patterns*, 44. Other books by prominent neutralists include Thomas Nagel, *Equality and Partiality* (New York: Oxford University Press, 1991), and Bruce

Ackerman, *Social Justice in the Liberal State* (New Haven, Conn.: Yale University Press, 1980).

50. Steven Wall, "Perfectionism in Politics: A Defense" in *Contemporary Debates in Political Philosophy*, ed. John Christman and Thomas Christiano (New York: Blackwell, forthcoming).

51. Feinberg, *Doing and Deserving*, 61.

52. John Rawls, *Justice as Fairness: A Restatement*, ed. Erin Kelly (Cambridge, Mass.: Harvard University Press, 2001), 73.

53. Some of the policies of a neutralist state might have the effect of requiting desert. For example, promoting economic efficiency might be a permissible aim in a neutralist state, and doing so might have the effect of giving people what they deserve. I see no reason to believe, however, that neutralists and desert-theorists would agree on all policies. Even if they did, significant theoretical disagreements would remain.

54. Rawls, *Theory*, 62.

55. Miller, *Principles*.

56. Aristotle, *Nicomachean Ethics*, 1131a25–27.

57. See, for example, Christopher Lake, *Equality and Responsibility* (New York: Oxford University Press, 2001).

58. Julian Lamont, "The Concept of Desert in Distributive Justice," *Philosophical Quarterly* 44, no. 174 (January 1994): 45–64.

59. Iris Marion Young, *Justice and the Politics of Difference* (Princeton, N.J.: Princeton University Press, 1990), 204.

60. Sandel and Richard Wasserstrom come close to making this claim. Sandel says that the most qualified do not deserve the positions they are qualified for, as their "having the relevant characteristics is in most cases no doing of theirs." Sandel, *Liberalism*, 137. Wasserstrom says that people "do not, for the most part, deserve their qualifications." Wasserstrom, "A Defense of Programs of Preferential Treatment," *National Forum* 58, no. 1 (Winter 1978): 17.

61. See, for example, Stuart Hampshire, "A New Philosophy of the Just Society," *New York Review of Books*, 24 February 1972, 34–39.

62. Several writers, including Sher and Nozick, think Rawls endorses this argument. A minority of writers, including Cohen and Young, think Rawls's objection to desert is not that no one deserves anything, but that we cannot tell what people deserve. In my view, the minority is right. I discuss this type of anti-desert argument below.

63. See, for example, Samuel Scheffler, "Responsibility, Reactive Attitudes, and Liberalism in Philosophy and Politics," *Philosophy and Public Affairs* 21, no. 4 (Autumn 1992): 299–323, and Cupit, *Justice*.

64. Jonathan Wolff, "The Dilemma of Desert," in *Desert and Justice*, ed. Serena Olsaretti (Oxford, UK: Clarendon Press, 2003), 219–32.

65. David Miller, "Deserving Jobs," *Philosophical Quarterly* 42, no. 167 (April 1992): 163.

66. Richard Arneson, "Egalitarianism and the Undeserving Poor," *Journal of Political Philosophy* 5, no. 4 (December 1997): 327–50.

67. Sidgwick, *Methods*, 284.

68. Arneson, "Egalitarianism and the Undeserving."

69. John E. Roemer, *Equality of Opportunity* (Cambridge, Mass.: Harvard University Press, 1998).

70. Arneson, "Egalitarianism and the Undeserving," 349.

71. Rawls, *Theory*, 311.

72. Rawls, *Theory*, 312. See also Sidgwick, *Methods*.

73. For arguments against neutralism, see George Sher, *Beyond Neutrality* (New York: Cambridge University Press, 1997), and Joseph Raz, *The Morality of Freedom* (Oxford, UK: Clarendon Press, 1986). The claim that neutralism is incompatible with desert might also be challenged. It might be argued that a neutralist state could requite some desert-claims, i.e., those that imply value judgments about which there is no reasonable disagreement.

74. Larmore, *Patterns*, 49.

75. Rawls, *Political Liberalism*, 194–95.

76. For criticisms of this argument, see Roemer, *Equality*, and Jeffrey Moriarty, "The Epistemological Argument against Desert," *Utilitas* 17, no. 2 (July 2005): 205–21.

77. This argument might be conceived of as showing not that it is easier for associations to requite fine-grained desert than states, but that it is *just as easy* for states to requite this kind of desert as it is for associations. States can requite this kind of desert by *requiring* that the associations within the state requite it. I agree that, if we think states can require this of associations within their borders, then this suggestion is correct. I have been assuming—more cautiously—that states cannot require this. But if they can, then the moderate form of the credit objection has the same force at the state and associational levels. What I am arguing now is that this force is not great.

78. In fact, I do not think that states need to take a restrictive view about what is valuable when they decide to requite desert. So the perception that it would be unfair for a state to requite desert may be based on a false view of what such a state would be like. If so, then requiting desert at the state level may be no more unfair than requiting it at the associational level.

79. Nor, recall, do I claim that firms will *want* to do this, or *should do* this, all things considered. With respect to (this iteration of) the moderate form of the credit objection, the only issue is whether it is *practicable* for firms to requite (fine-grained) desert.

80. It might be wondered whether there will be disagreement about what is valuable in voluntary associations such as firms. They are typically formed with a specific goal in mind (e.g., making a profit), and, it might be thought, this purpose fully determines what actions are valuable within the association (e.g., selling the firm's products). This is too strong. Disagreement about value within voluntary associations shrinks but does not vanish. For example, all of the members of a firm might think that making a profit is a valuable goal, but there may be disagreement about whether improving the environment (in a way that does not increase the firm's profits) is valuable. Moreover, even in cases where there is agreement about a goal's value, there may be uncertainty as to what actions promote it, and hence count as instrumentally

valuable. For example, some but not all of the members of a firm might think that acquiring a rival will increase the firm's profits.

81. To recall, not all desert-theorists accept the credit condition, in either form. See, for example, Feldman, "Desert: Reconsideration," and Sher, *Desert*.

82. In fact, the issue of deserving jobs is even more complicated than I have indicated. Not everyone thinks that the only basis for deserving a job is one's present qualifications. Miller says that the person who deserves the job is the person who is most likely to perform the job in such a way that he or she deserves the pay associated with it. In a similar move, Schmidtz thinks that a person can deserve a job in virtue of what he or she will do with it. For reasons of space, I set these arguments aside. See Miller, *Principles*, and Schmidtz, "How To Deserve."

83. Milkovich and Newman, *Compensation*, chap. 3.

84. For an analysis of some of these plans, see Karol Soltan, *The Causal Theory of Justice* (Berkeley: University of California Press, 1987).

85. Lamont, "The Concept of Desert."

86. Roemer, *Equality*.

87. Hurka, "Desert: Individualistic." Hurka's interpretation of effort above runs afoul of the credit condition on desert, which rules out hardship as a desert-base. However, as I noted, some writers think that hardship—whether or not it is conceived of as part of effort—is a desert-base for wages.

88. This point is stressed by Wil Waluchow, "Pay Equity: Equal Value to Whom?" *Journal of Business Ethics* 7, no. 3 (March 1988): 185–89.

89. Miller, *Principles*.

90. See, for example, Hurka "Desert: Individualistic," and McLeod, "Desert and Wages."

91. Donald J. Treiman and Heidi I. Hartmann, eds., *Women, Work, and Wages: Equal Pay for Jobs of Equal Value* (Washington, D.C.: National Academy Press, 1981).

92. Louis P. Pojman, "Does Equality Trump Desert?" in *What Do We Deserve? A Reader on Justice and Desert*, ed. Louis P. Pojman and Owen McLeod (New York: Oxford University Press, 1999), 283–97.

93. Sher, *Desert*.

94. J. R. Lucas, *Responsibility* (Oxford, UK: Clarendon Press, 1993).

95. Roemer, *Equality*.

96. Norman Daniels, "Merit and Meritocracy," *Philosophy and Public Affairs* 7, no. 3 (Spring 1978): 206–23.

97. There are two ways to interpret this. We might say P merits job J if and only if P *himself or herself* will perform J best, that is, better than everyone else, or we might say P merits J if and only if P's having J is part of a maximally productive *array* of job assignments. Daniels, "Merit and Meritocracy," endorses the second interpretation, but the first also seems plausible as a conception of merit.

98. Sidgwick, *Methods*.

99. Assuming that firms' policies *do* requite merit—at least in Pojman's sense—it might be asked whether they *should*. This depends on arguments for and against acknowledging merit that are outside the scope of this chapter. However, given the

similarities between (Pojman's conception of) merit and desert, the arguments for (and against) requiting merit are likely to be similar to the arguments for (and against) requiting desert.

100. See also Sher, *Desert*, 199.

101. Thanks to Jeffery Smith for valuable comments on an earlier draft of this chapter.

Chapter Seven

Institutions and Organizations: Communicative Ethics and Business

Jeffery Smith, University of Redlands

In the introduction to this volume I alluded to a distinction between two methodological approaches that seem to permeate the discipline of business ethics. The *institutional* conception is concerned with how to justly organize society's basic institutions; more specifically, it views normative business ethics as a discipline that, first and foremost, asks questions about how the basic political and economic structure of modern society ought to be designed so as to promote moral ends in the operation of business. In this regard, normative business ethics can be thought of as applied moral and political philosophy as it relates to the design of markets and market institutions. The *organizational* conception, in contrast, does not focus our attention on the basic economic and political institutions of society; instead, it recommends that we focus our attention on the management of business organizations and how their operational and governance practices can be developed so as to realize the ends of morality.

Some care needs to be exercised in thinking about this distinction. While there are some business ethicists who strongly advocate one conception over the other, these alternatives are not mutually exclusive, either practically or conceptually.[1] A normative analysis of society's basic political and economic institutions may recommend reforms that directly affect the decisions of managers in business organizations. Market institutions operate according to norms that implicitly and explicitly shape what we expect of managers who exercise discretion in leading firms. Conceptually, too, there is nothing in the logic of the institutional conception that precludes a simultaneous emphasis on organizational design as a way to better realize moral ends. Some have argued that institutional reforms are a necessary although insufficient step toward moral reform in business. What is also needed is a concomitant adjustment in the attitudes and practices of managers who lead business organizations.[2]

147

I begin this chapter with a relatively uncontroversial, yet important starting point: Any reasonable normative theory under consideration by business ethicists needs to be able to account for the institutional and organizational aspects of business. It needs to recognize that the moral dimensions of business involve problems of how we design markets in relation to other political and economic institutions as well as how we cultivate morally grounded managerial and governance practices. Institutional design and organizational practice reinforce one another and are ultimately justified by appeal to related principles.[3] A normative theory that can address both the institutional and organizational dimensions of business will not only integrate moral considerations across different spheres of life, but it will also avoid the mistake of ignoring the interdependence of institutional design and managerial responsibility.

With this observation in mind, it is fitting to explore a theoretical perspective that has received comparatively little attention by business ethicists: communicative or discourse ethics. One of the advantages of communicative ethics, in general, is that it paints a subtle picture of the relationship between society's basic institutions. It provides a framework to evaluate the conduct of business actors externally, in relation to the goals of the market and democratic state, and internally, in relation to the goals of business. In this manner, communicative ethics holds the promise of identifying and linking the institutional and organizational aspects of business ethics in the way that I describe above.

I will begin this chapter with an overview of the work of the German philosopher Jürgen Habermas, who has arguably provided the most systematic presentation of communicative ethics and its relation to dominant questions in moral, political, and legal theory.[4] This will be followed by an examination of the moral responsibilities of businesses, in particular the responsibilities of managers. I will provide both an institutional and organizational perspective on these responsibilities. On the one hand, communicative ethics sets forth norms regarding the operation of business in the context of the political and economic institutions necessary for modern democratic society. On the other hand, I will also argue that business organizations are subject to certain moral constraints in virtue of being a voluntary, cooperative association where managers exercise legally recognized discretion over the terms of economic investment and production. I will conclude with a number of remarks designed to show how these institutional and organizational perspectives offered by communicative ethics are consistent with the overarching aims of Habermas's critical social theory and how they are mutually supportive.[5]

1. MORALITY, ETHICS, AND COMMUNICATIVE ACTION

Communicative ethics begins with a set of distinctively liberal assumptions.[6] First, the norms that govern modern social life differ in their degree of applicability. Moral norms, in the words of Habermas, purport to offer universal prescriptions that bind all individuals, regardless of their cultural affiliation, conceptions of the good, or personal or otherwise limited group interests.[7] Moral norms function as principles that regulate and set the terms of cooperation that are valid for everyone living and working within society's basic legal, political, and economic institutions. The domain of morality is the domain of right or justice. Ethical norms; in contrast, are principles that Habermas believes reflect particular traditions or substantive conceptions of the good life that are not necessarily valid for everyone. Some will subscribe to certain ethical norms; others will subscribe to different, perhaps opposing ethical norms.[8] Whereas moral norms are universal in their applicability to lives of each individual, ethical norms are necessarily limited in their applicability to associations of specific groups or communities.

A second motivating assumption behind communicative ethics parallels the first. In modern societies characterized by a plurality of different cultures and conceptions of the good, the normative basis for regulating the terms of our shared social lives must be premised on principles that everyone can recognize as valid. Accordingly, the organization of social life in modern societies should be grounded on institutional norms that all affected parties can endorse, regardless of their conception of the good life. This strong form of endorsement reflects Habermas's central concern with the *possibility* of social action.[9] Cooperative social life can be sustained only when the activities and aims of modern society's dominant institutions implicitly reflect a consensus on the normative principles that govern how we live with one another.[10]

At the heart of this call for consensual social action is Habermas's idea of communicative action. Communicative action is social action oriented toward mutual understanding and agreement.[11] It stands in contrast to strategic action, which shuns mutual understanding in favor of the manipulation, deception, or instrumental use of others in order to accomplish private ends. The maintenance of society under the modern conditions of pluralism requires that social institutions be ordered so as to preserve communicative rather than strategic action. To organize society simply on strategic grounds will inevitably lead to circumstances where private interests, while convergent from time to time, may lead to conflict.[12] Communicative action implies that there are some needs and interests that individuals collectively share that establish normative principles that regulate the terms of social cooperation. Communicatively structured cooperation, thus, is cooperation that proceeds according to norms that are grounded in reasons that everyone can recognize as regulative for their lives.

It is therefore appropriate to note that a final premise behind communicative ethics is that modern social life can be sustained only under the precondition that we are oriented toward activity that preserves mutual understanding and, ultimately, consensus on the norms that govern the organization of society.[13] This premise is given support by Habermas through a fundamentally pragmatic argument. The way in which individuals interact with one another presupposes a search for mutual understanding and consensus. Individuals implicitly make claims that seek rational acceptance by others: Legislators support laws by offering arguments that affected groups can endorse; political parties reform their platforms in order to gain acceptance by more diverse coalitions; and various civil society organizations mobilize like-minded individuals to bring about changes to an array of professional standards, regulations, and policies. Habermas maintains that a practical examination of these and other forms of social interaction demonstrate not just the willingness of individual actors to find consensus among citizens, but also the implicit commitment to uncover *reasons* to support their calls for social action.[14] To shun this search for mutually acceptable reasons is to shun the very processes that we implicitly *take* to legitimize the institutional arrangements and norms that structure social cooperation.

It should be no surprise that communicative action (so described) frequently breaks down. There are moments when the search for mutually acceptable norms to organize social life fails, either outwardly or inwardly, and we are left with norms that may reflect private or an otherwise more limited set of interests. In these circumstances, Habermas develops a method to repair the communicative fabric of modern society: *discourse*. Habermas extends his pragmatic argument described above to suggest that the search for mutually acceptable reasons implicitly involves the acceptance of public forms of critical dialogue where contested normative claims can be scrutinized by all affected parties in an open discourse where no one is excluded from participation and only the force of the better argument determines whether a particular claim is justified, from the point of view of each party. Thus, while the terms "discourse ethics" and "communicative ethics" are used interchangeably to refer to Habermas's project, institutionalizing discourse is actually a tool whereby communicative action can be restored. Habermas is clear that organizing modern society on the basis of norms that can be rationally endorsed by everyone engaged in discourse is the way in which we can move toward maintaining communicative action in the face of an irreducible plurality of conceptions of the good life. Habermas, thus, maintains that in the face of this irreducible plurality, the pragmatic assumptions behind communicative action imply that institutional arrangements and norms can only claim to be valid when they "meet (or could meet) with the approval of all affected in their capacity *as participants in practical discourse*."[15]

2. COMMUNICATIVE ACTION AND CIVIL SOCIETY (1)

The general picture that is emerging thus far is riddled with complexities that cannot be systematically dealt with in this chapter. These difficulties center on the institutionalization of discourse throughout society and the ways in which moral, ethical, and strategic claims overlap within discourse. I will have something to say on each of these challenges in later sections. It is sufficient to note at this point, however, that Habermas's communicative ethics is an extension of some much larger theoretical insights, many of which were written in his seminal works *Legitimation Crisis* and *The Theory of Communicative Action*. To get a fuller picture of the ways in which communicative ethics remains relevant to theoretical analysis in business ethics, it is necessary to retrace some of the central observations made in these works.

Habermas draws an important distinction between society as a *system* of institutions designed to impose "functional" requirements on individuals and society as a *lifeworld*, composed of institutions that organize life on the basis of "consensually accepted norms."[16] It is more accurate to say that "society as system" and "society as lifeworld" are two perspectives on essentially the same subject; whereas the former views society as a set of institutions that enforce legal requirements through political actions and economic arrangements, the latter views society as composed of associations that interpret and clarify the norms that we collectively think ought to direct political and economic activities. These perspectives give Habermas the theoretical insight to understand two simultaneous phenomena in modern societies: the ever-growing complexity of different subsystems designed to maintain the governmental and economic activities of the modern state, and the rationalization of the lifeworld that continuously prompts us to search for ways to express our shared moral outlook and way of life, despite growing diversity and pluralism.

Habermas's real concern is that a strong, more differentiated set of subsystems have "colonized" aspects of the lifeworld—or, less technically, the legal, political, and economic institutions of the modern state have interfered with the communicative activities of other institutions in civil society.[17] This has had the result of undermining the public process of rationalization that can occur within the freely formed, informal associations that make up civil society.[18] In the absence of this rationalization, the process of identifying the norms that ought to govern modern society is largely determined by the strategic interests that individuals have in maintaining the economic and political structures of the modern state, which may or may not actually reflect our collective aims.

Habermas's proposed alternative involves two central ideas. First, a renewed civil society with a communicative focus holds the potential to effectively identify principles that can, in turn, shape the arrangement of economic, legal, and political institutions. This changes the direction of social influence from the dominance of formal political and economic institutions over civil society to one where civil society exercises influence over the organization of formal institutions.[19] This requires, according to Habermas, that institutions in civil society serve as social spaces to legitimate (or offer supportive reasons) for certain political and economic arrangements. Habermas does not recommend that the formal systems of the modern state dissolve; quite the contrary, the maintenance of the state remains essential for managing large-scale, complex social problems. It is simply that informal associations in civil society can serve an important function of identifying, assessing, and advocating norms that serve to direct and restrain the activities of the state.[20]

Second, the so-called "public" sphere of modern society is not the sole province of the state. The formation of public opinion through communicative activities within civil society, apart from the state, is an integral feature of Habermas's ideal of a more deliberative democratic society that proceeds on the basis of consensus. This theoretical call for deeper forms of democratic interaction is essentially a call for a more robust public examination of the norms and institutional arrangements that govern modern society. Habermas's normative ideal is therefore one where informal associations, in combination with formal political processes, provide the forums in which practical norms governing the organization and operation of society's basic institutions are deliberately scrutinized by all citizens. This includes those norms that have moral, ethical, strategic, and pragmatic significance. Obviously this is not something done in one place, at one time, within one informal association, or through one formal political process; rather, the entire network of formal and informal deliberations forms a tapestry of consensus-building insights that serve to justify a range of social arrangements, political practices, laws, and public policies on the basis of consensus.[21]

3. COMMUNICATIVE ACTION AND CIVIL SOCIETY (2)

The connection between this picture of a renewed, democratic public sphere and communicative ethics is rich and complicated. Although informal associations, in conjunction with the formal processes of the state, should be oriented toward consensus, the ability of any one association or process to specify outcomes that all affected individuals in society can endorse seems difficult to imagine. One need only think, for instance, of the work of labor unions, political action committees, and legislative bodies to remind us that formal institutions and informal associations are fractional and operate in piecemeal and, at times, strategic ways. The corollary to this observation is that public discourse is manifested only imperfectly within actual associations and political processes. Consensus may or may not actually result from efforts that are oriented toward consensus, and the institutionalization of practical discourse described in section one is an empty ideal.

The central tenet of communicative ethics is that valid institutional norms and arrangements are those that have been (or could be) endorsed by all affected parties engaged in discourse. There are some norms that clearly secure the assent (or could secure the assent) of all affected parties. We would expect such principles to broadly reflect the core interests of each citizen, subject to little variation. Examples include, for instance, claims to basic human rights, justice, and welfare. There are other norms, however, that, at best, may secure only the assent of a limited group of individuals with a particular set of interests. Communicative ethics, as I note above, provides a framework for categorizing practical norms into two broad types: those that have universal, moral significance for everyone, and those that have limited, ethical significance for particular communities. Both moral and ethical norms have the ability to coordinate social life and generate mutual understanding. They differ, however, in the scope of coordination and understanding generated.

The realization that actual forms of public discourse in civil and political society are imperfect, combined with the recognition that universal moral norms are (or would be) necessarily general in scope, has prompted Habermas to deal with an apparent tension between communicative ethics and the theory of deliberative democracy outlined in the previous section. The tension is this: How can specific actions by the state, in particular the creation of law, be justified from the moral point of view, when those actions themselves are not fully endorsed by all affected parties engaged in discourse? Put differently, how can actions initiated by the formal institutions of the state ever be morally legitimate when it appears that, at best, their decisions appear to reflect limited ethical, pragmatic, and instrumental considerations rather than universalizable ones?

Thomas McCarthy has suggested that a preliminary answer to this question rests with a distinction that has appeared in Habermas's later work.[22] It is possible to separate the basic structure of society's formal political, economic, and legal institutions from the specific measures or decisions enacted by these institutions. So while there is rarely, if ever, any direct universal endorsement of any particular action taken by the state, there can be universal endorsement of the formal state institutions that create law and public policy. Moral legitimacy can be transferred from the structure of the state and its formal institutions to particular state actions simply in virtue of the fact that the structure of the state and its formal institutions can themselves be legitimated from the moral point of view.

This move is promising. It permits Habermas to maintain his position that the formal institutions of the state are legitimated on the basis of moral norms that everyone, in principle, has (or could have) endorsed. Such institutions are legitimate so long as they are procedurally oriented toward consensus. It also permits Habermas to recognize the complexity involved in instituting discourse at all levels of society. The moral legitimacy of the basic structure of the state and its constitutional formation can be distinguished from the myriad forms of discursive interaction that can occur formally within the state or informally through civil associations. It also remains loyal to Habermas's underlying picture of the public sphere as a complex fabric of related associations that simultaneously address moral, ethical, pragmatic, and instrumental concerns.[23]

One cannot help but be reminded of Habermas's call in earlier writings, however, that specific actions by the state need to be based on reasons that are tested (or testable) by public debate within communicatively oriented communities.

> [I]t follows that we cannot explain the validity claim of norms without recourse to rationally motivated agreement or at least to the conviction that consensus on a recommended norm could be brought about *with reasons*. In that case the model of contracting parties who need know only what an imperative means is inadequate. The appropriate model is rather the communication community [*Kommunikationsgemeinschaft*] of those affected, who as participants in a practical discourse test the validity claims of norms and, to the extent that they accept them with reasons, arrive at the conviction that in the given circumstances the proposed norms are "right."[24]

The later Habermas acknowledges this point in a new and interesting way. He consciously acknowledges that discourse not only results in the formation of shared opinions, but also the formation of a shared will, whereby certain norms are endorsed *even if* they may prove contrary to the opinions of specific individuals.[25] This proves to be an important analytic distinction for Habermas. Practical discourse can result in rational will formation in various ways, not all of which require the substantial rationally motivated agreement (*Einverständnis*) characteristic of universal, moral norms. There are various rationally motivated arrangements (*Vereinbarung*) that aim toward mutual understanding and yet fall short of a deep rationally motivated consensus in which each individual shares the *same* reason to accept a proposed norm or social arrangement. These less demanding agreements are typically formed through acts of negotiation and compromise.[26] Habermas can thus reassert his conviction that the most abstract demands of political morality require rationally motivated agreements regarding the norms that govern the formation of broad political, economic, and legal institutions, while also comfortably accepting the observation that consensus on particular actions by the state rarely materializes.[27]

Habermas also carves out space for what is arguably the most important form of discourse that occurs within modern society: ethical discourse.[28] He explicitly accepts that much of the work designed to secure consensus in society is work that focuses on identifying and clarifying the *values* that define and identify specific groups or communities within society (*Konsens*). There are some values that simply inform certain preferences or aims of a particular social group. These are often subject to the kind of rationally motivated, pragmatic compromises already discussed. There are some values, however, that are so fundamental to the identity of a particular group that they are rarely subject to negotiation and compromise. As such, ethical discourse is focused on a kind of interpretive self-understanding, or an examination of the significance and application of certain values to social arrangements.[29] Habermas recognizes that in a modern, plural society, this form of values clarification is limited to specific groups with specific conceptions of the good life; but he cannot escape the conclusion that the process of ethical discourse within these groups is a basic feature of democratic deliberation. It helps groups within civil society clarify who they are and what institutional changes they will seek to bring about. This, in turn, affects the scope of potential negotiations that occur within other spheres of society and whether there are any conflicts with prevailing political, economic, and legal arrangements.

The project of communicative ethics, then, is sensitive to the core features of modern society. The organization of society's basic political, legal, and economic institutions is morally legitimate only upon the assumption that these institutions are based on principles that reflect the rationally motivated agreements of all individuals, regardless of their group membership or conception of the good life. At the same time, these institutions, while oriented

toward consensus, operate in ways that do not require consensus on all matters on all occasions. Institutional arrangements have the pragmatic feature of
working toward consensus through practices such as negotiation, compromise, voting, administrative appeal, and the like. This forms the basis of legitimate actions by the state, in particular the basis for the legitimate formation of law. Finally, communicative ethics acknowledges not just the
possibility of moral discourse on the universal values that ground the organization of basic political, legal, and economic institutions, but also the need
for ethical discourse on values that are local to particular communities within
civil society.[30]

4. INSTITUTIONAL ASPECTS OF
BUSINESS'S MORAL RESPONSIBILITIES

Businesses are organizations that operate within a broad political, economic,
and legal framework. I began this chapter with a call for us to recognize that
business ethics concerns both the operation of business within this institutional context as well as how we design the institutions to govern the activities of business. The brief overview of communicative ethics that I have offered in the previous sections has two broad implications for how we theorize
the moral responsibilities of businesses and their managers. The first is institutional and the second is organizational.

I begin the institutional perspective with two observations and an inference. First, the market is the institutional home of business. Businesses are
actors in the market, subject to its opportunities and constraints. Without the
market, business would neither exist nor operate effectively. Second, from a
communicative perspective, the formal institutions of the modern state are
morally legitimate to the extent that they are organized according to principles that reflect the interests of every individual. On the assumption that market institutions can be legitimated from the moral point of view, and that the
law is a privileged institution that defines the operation of the market, these
two observations lead us to a rather modest conclusion: Businesses have a
moral responsibility to respect the legal institutions that regulate the terms of
the market. This entails that businesses and their managers have moral responsibilities tied directly to the respect for legal institutions and the decisions rendered by legislative, administrative, and judicial bodies.

In *Between Facts and Norms*, Habermas develops a principle whereby formal political processes have a central (although not exclusive) role to play in
the maintenance of morally legitimate law. According to his so-called principle of democracy, Habermas maintains that laws can claim legitimacy only

when they meet "with the assent (*Zustimmung*) of all citizens in a discursive process of legislation that . . . has been legally constituted."[31] Laws consistent with this principle indicate the freedom of the citizenry to deliberatively endorse the laws to which they will be subjected.[32] The motivation for this principle is found in the very idea of communicative action, i.e., that a norm of social action is valid only on the condition that all of those who are possibly affected by it could find reason to accept its role in regulating social life.[33]

Business managers have two distinct moral responsibilities with regard to the formation of legitimate law, so understood. First, businesses have a responsibility to develop operational strategies that do not contravene the established provisions of legitimately formed law.[34] This follows naturally from the observation that legal requirements carry the force of moral legitimacy when they are developed in accordance with a discursive legislative process oriented toward consensus. As I have suggested above, the domains of morality and democratic law making are distinct; the law involves the public exploration of a broad range of moral, ethical, and pragmatic reasons in the course of examining the validity of a proposed course of action. Habermas, however, still maintains that "legality can produce legitimacy only to the extent that . . . legal discourses are institutionalized in ways made pervious to moral argumentation."[35] This exposes the deep linkage between legitimacy and morality that Habermas derives from the ideal of communicative action. Legal institutions and the particular laws created through their operation are, in a fundamental sense, mechanisms for the integration of moral requirements into norms that are enforced through positive means. This provides a *prima facie* reason for businesses to respect the decisions established through legal channels on matters such as employee and consumer rights, environmental protection, competition and collaboration with other firms, and financial reporting.

Second, as organizations whose operation presupposes a well-developed, legally constituted market system, businesses have a responsibility not to contravene the *necessary conditions* for the ongoing formation of legitimate law. This responsibility extends much deeper than the first.[36]

The implicit principle presupposed by the very idea of communicative action is that societies seeking to autonomously organize cooperative life can do so only on the basis of norms that receive the assent of all affected individuals. Such a society requires the codification of some basic entitlements that maintain the integrity of the democratic law-making process.[37] Thus, Habermas maintains that basic liberties of the citizenry to freedom of speech, association, conscience, and movement are prerequisites to effective public discourse. He also argues that protections against arbitrary and capricious actions by the state are necessary to prevent interruptions to open, public discourse. This requires provisions of equal treatment and due process under the law for individuals who are subject to the control of the state as well as other powerful institutions that can substantially affect the livelihood of individuals. There are two final categories of rights that are essential to the formation of legitimate law: those that protect individuals' entitlement to direct and indirect participation in the law-making process, as well as those that ensure that the minimal welfare conditions necessary for the exercise of all other rights are met.[38]

The important point here is that although the specific operation of business does not necessarily require that these rights be protected, the ongoing operation of a legitimate system of law does. If the market and the operation of business gain legitimacy on the basis of being legally constituted and recognized, then it stands to reason that a moral minimum for any business firm is that it respect these conditions of legitimacy. It is therefore incumbent upon business firms to refrain from activities that undermine the aforementioned rights because they serve as necessary conditions for the development of laws that give business its requisite legitimacy. Such expectations may include, for instance, prohibitions on penalizing employees who are interested in organizing labor unions, respect for the privacy of employees in the workplace, an employer provision of due process before dismissals, assuring an adequate balance of work and nonwork life, careful exercise of discretion in cooperating with the state on matters of national security, and the responsibility not to engage in political activities (e.g., lobbying) that undermine the ability of individuals and communities to effect legislative change.

5. ORGANIZATIONAL ASPECTS OF BUSINESS'S MORAL RESPONSIBILITIES (1)

Organizationally, too, communicative ethics has implications for how we theorize the moral responsibilities of businesses and their managers. This requires that we understand not simply how businesses are part of a larger institutional framework, but how the nature of business relationships necessitates a distinctively communicative account of the firm. This takes us beyond the considerations explicitly raised by Habermas's project.

To begin, consider the ways in which the cooperation among business stakeholders is *internally* directed. The law is certainly one way in which public policy and the limits of the market constrain the operational decisions of management. Within these constraints, however, there is broad latitude for discretion, both by management and the directors that represent shareholders. Indeed many have argued that the strength of a suitably tailored, legally constituted market economy is that operational discretion provides managers with the ability to make decisions that improve a firm's competitive position while respecting the value of social prosperity that justifies the market in the first place. So while the external, legal oversight discussed in the previous section can legitimately regulate the operation of business, it is also accurate to say that agents of the business firm have the freedom to direct it in ways that serve its stakeholders.

Managerial discretion, in particular, involves the use of resources that can positively or negatively affect a broad range of stakeholders. Managers decide when to close a production facility. Managers draft policy regarding hiring, promotion, and termination. Managers execute acquisition plans that carry financial risks. Managers require compliance with work schedules and accounting procedures. Managers decide how and when to fund health care and retirement plans. Management, in short, uses its discretion to carry forth directives that define a business's purpose and strategy by deploying the firm's resources in targeted ways.

This use of discretion in these ways involves the exercise of authority. Managers deploy corporate resources and issue policy directives by exercising the judgment they are granted. But, in the face of certain risks, it is difficult to imagine that stakeholders would willingly accept managerial policies unless there were a compelling set of reasons to do so. These reasons constitute the primary source of managerial authority; in the absence of reasons to support managerial directives, managers lack authority and, at best, execute policy on the basis of economic power or coercion. Discretion therefore implies the exercise of authority and, in turn, the exercise of authority assumes certain standards for its *legitimate* use.[39]

It is fitting at this point to note that the kind of business discretion described above impacts the availability of social goods, e.g., wealth, opportunity, technology, health care, and education. This means that managers do not simply exercise authority over how resources are deployed and what policies are adopted. It follows as well that managers exercise authority over the distribution of these public goods. This makes their discretion even more relevant for a Habermasian approach to business ethics. If legal institutions deliberately design markets to provide business firms with discretion, and business firms voluntarily exercise discretion to provide goods that are deemed important by each citizen, then the legitimacy that would normally be tied to the formal institutions of the state needs to be found within the dispersed authority exercised by business managers. Without the legitimate exercise of authority by managers, it is difficult to see how the market could itself be deemed legitimate from the perspective of each citizen. The legitimate use of managerial authority, thus, demands not simply the ability of managers to effect change in business policy; it demands that business policy be made on the basis of reasons that affected individuals can recognize and endorse.

Managerial authority is something that is derived not simply from the ability of management to facilitate the cooperation necessary for a business to be successful. It is derived from cooperation that proceeds according to internal norms that everyone can endorse.[40] Like the norms prescribing state-level institutional arrangements, however, internal norms for the management of business firms need not require that each and every policy or managerial decision receive rationally motivated agreement from all affected parties. Like states that exercise authority via formal, law-making institutions, business firms can be organized according to broad-based principles that establish the basic entitlements of stakeholders without necessarily requiring that all particular managerial decisions require the examination and endorsement by all affected parties. It is even arguable that many stakeholders have a strong reason to endorse decision-making and governance practices that explicitly avoid the review of lower-level, operational decisions. All parties can acknowledge a strong interest in the benefits obtained through timely decisions and efficient channels of operation.

It is therefore appropriate to describe the moral responsibilities of management derived from the exercise of authoritative discretion as largely procedural in nature.[41] This means that managers have duties to include stakeholder concerns in their decision making and to open avenues of assessment and review of corporate policies; this is important not only for those policies that *direct* stakeholders but also those that *affect* stakeholders. Both of these duties presuppose a willingness to communicate and to seek open channels of communication with stakeholders.

More generally, if the firm is to be managed according to policies that reflect the considered interests of all stakeholders, then it is natural to expect that management should attempt to mitigate policies that adversely impact one stakeholder and provide appropriate compensation where adverse consequences nonetheless result. It also stands to reason that the use of discretion in how to deploy corporate resources is a matter that demands an attentiveness to proportionality; that is, stakeholders should expect a firm's management team to balance the costs and benefits to each group, adjusting for complex considerations like merit, previous costs imposed on other stakeholders, and the ability to seek an overall improvement to the competitive position of the firm.[42] There will be some costs that are simply too high for any stakeholder to reasonably accept in return for his or her contribution. This would preclude actions taken by management that deprive stakeholders of basic human rights or otherwise involve substantial negative consequences to human welfare.

It is also obligatory for management to identify and eliminate conflicts of interest that may arise between the interests of stakeholders and the interests of management. Managers bear the special responsibilities of not only over-seeing and coordinating the productive activity of the business, but also of protecting the interests of other stakeholders. This remains true even in situations where management might have a strong incentive to act contrary to these responsibilities because it serves their own interests. We should expect the legitimate exercise of managerial authority to therefore implement formal methods to prevent such situations from arising.

6. ORGANIZATIONAL ASPECTS OF BUSINESS'S MORAL RESPONSIBILITIES (2)

The strength of these responsibilities is not mitigated by their procedural character. It is consistent with the economic benefits derived from managerial discretion that the aforementioned responsibilities provide managers the flex-ibility to determine how, when, and under what circumstances their policies will be tested against the abstract requirement that management make policy that should be rationally endorsed from the point of view of those who are affected by it. These responsibilities strongly point toward management practices that seek the discursive examination of managerial policy by other stakeholders. This includes a range of possibilities including, but not limited to, ongoing consultation with nongovernmental organizations, collaborative standards development with industry associations, management-labor review of outsourcing practices, employee participation in product development and manufacturing, and greater opportunities for shareholder voice in the nomination of board members.

There are two other compelling reasons why communicative ethics might point toward the broad implementation of discursive practices at the level of the business firm. First, recall that Habermas's theory of democracy maintains a kind of fluid interaction between the formal institutions of the state and the informal associations in civil society. Moral, ethical, pragmatic, and other instrumental matters are reviewed and examined within discourses that take place in multiple locations at multiple times. In an important sense, public opinion and public will are formed through the autonomous activities of civil society organizations.[43] Businesses play a natural role here. Not only do they negotiate, compromise, and cooperate with other associations (like labor unions, industry associations, and nongovernmental organizations) but the interactions that take place between shareholders, managers, employees, suppliers, competitors, and other groups provide opportunities for different individuals to understand the nuances of their social circumstances and to what extent, if any, the formal institutions of the state need to address these circumstances.

Life in business, in short, provides stakeholders with access to "forms and sources of information" that are integral to how they, as citizens, will address formal political institutions.[44] Employees who play a collaborative role in, say, negotiating a firm's new health insurance program will have a much clearer sense of how public policy might be reformed to assist businesses with health-related expenses. Consumer groups will have greater insight into the complexities of international trade agreements after they communicate with multinational businesses about the safety of products manufactured abroad. Institutional investors who take an active interest in corporate governance will be better positioned to advocate for legal reform on matters of board representation. All of these examples illustrate how deliberative interactions at the level of the firm contribute to a robust civil society that surrounds the state's formal institutions to provide sources of information and critique. None of this implies that businesses (or any other civil association) replace the state in addressing large-scale social and economic problems.[45] The Habermasian alternative is that discourse within and between stakeholder groups is an important way to produce reasoned opinions among individual citizens. This occurs not simply within deliberative legislative bodies of the state, but in the informal, day-to-day interactions of citizens who voluntarily structure their lives cooperatively.[46]

I recognize that this picture of business as part of the fabric of civil society is not obviously coherent with various comments made by Habermas.[47] Employing the distinction between society as a "system" and society as "lifeworld," Habermas writes that the market economy is composed of private associations, predicated on labor and commodity exchange, which operate according to a distinctive logic emphasizing efficiency and profit.[48] This early characterization carries over into his later thinking on democratic theory:

> What is meant by "civil society" today, in contrast to the usage in the Marxist tradition, no longer includes the economy as constituted by private law and steered through markets in labor, capital and commodities. Rather, its institutional core comprises those nongovernmental and non-economic connections and voluntary associations that anchor the communication structures of the public sphere in the society component of the lifeworld.[49]

It would be natural to think, on the basis of such comments, that businesses are simply organizational members of the economic system and therefore not part of the "non-economic connections" that "anchor" the communicative aims of civil society. But this inference is difficult to assess. Habermas does not explicitly preclude the possibility that businesses firms *play a role* in opinion and will formation, and there is good reason to believe that they should play a role.[50] A newly constituted civil society that examines the organization and operation of society's dominant political and economic institutions would seem to gain greater strength with the information, insights, and worldviews produced through life in business. More importantly, as the dominant form of social life in modern society, it is natural to look to business as the site for opinion and will formation. Businesses represent a series of private associations that influence relationships in other private spheres of life, including family, labor groups, nonprofit organizations, and schools. So if we follow Habermas and look to private associations outside of business as sources of democratic "legitimations" for the formal institutions of modern society, then it is natural to extend (if only indirectly) the boundaries of civil society to include associations that develop within business.

This naturally brings us to a second, more direct reason to accept the notion that business organizations play a substantial role in furthering communicative action: Productive business relationships can be best sustained when they are communicatively oriented, rather than predicated merely on strategic motives.

It is commonly thought that relationships between business stakeholders are inherently strategic. Some business ethicists, for instance, have constructed normative frameworks premised on the notion that businesses are most accurately described as a nexus of contracts, formed on the basis of the mutual satisfaction of self-interest.[51] Even those who do not adopt such a thoroughgoing economic conception of the business firm have emphasized the extent to which stakeholders are, first and foremost, instrumentally rational actors that only contingently seek cooperative arrangements. Communicative ethics provides an alternative to this picture. Cooperation is made more secure through consensus-seeking practices.

Like social arrangements found in other spheres of society, cooperative action within business firms takes various forms. Sometimes cooperation is implicit in that individuals and groups share an interest in particular policy with little, or any, examination. In these cases it is fair to characterize the cooperation engendered as a simple convergence of interests through happenstance.[52] The reasons that any one individual or group may have to implicitly endorse a policy are reasons that others may or may not consciously share; however, to the extent that other individuals and groups have *some* reason for supporting the policy, there can be said to be a kind of agreement on the norms that guide the management of the firm.

In different situations the examination of managerial policy is more explicit, often prompted by concerns or objections raised by stakeholders. This kind of scrutiny can (and is often designed to) lead to negotiated agreements that represent a kind of shared understanding of how cooperative activity can be maintained in the face of conflict. The clearest illustrations of such negotiated compromises are collective bargaining contracts between unions and management. These negotiated agreements move stakeholders closer to situations where each party has a reason to support a particular policy or course of action; more importantly, negotiated compromises are essentially cooperative because the outcome reflects action norms that everyone can endorse, even if grounded partially in their own interest satisfaction. Compromise also forces parties to adjust and reexamine their positions and address objections leveled by other parties. The dialogic character of negotiated compromise, thus, remains quite distinct from the self-interested contracting imagined by economic models of the firm.

Cooperation is also strengthened when there is greater convergence on the values that define the purpose of the business's activity. Discursive efforts that refine a mission statement or engage stakeholders to solve public problems are examples of managerial efforts to interpret what a company's values mean, and how they should shape operational decisions. Business ethicists have observed that business firms are moral communities with shared resources, shared leadership, and most importantly, shared values.[53] Communities function well when core values authentically direct their management and governance; accordingly, it has proven important for businesses to set aside moments for the critical examination of shared *ethical* values that provide interpretations of the underlying goals and purposes that unite a community of stakeholders.[54]

It is possible, as well, that stakeholders come to the realization that universal *moral* norms regulate the terms of a firm's operation. Recent cases involving the operation of multinational corporations in Asia illustrate this point nicely. Consumer groups, nongovernmental organizations, and labor groups have played a significant role in challenging the supply chain practices of many multinational firms in the garment and shoe industry. This prompted companies such as Adidas-Salomon to assert their commitment to human rights; in particular, Adidas-Salomon developed an entirely new set of "Standards of Engagement" for their international supply chain in order to eliminate forced overtime, child labor, and poor environmental conditions.[55] This move represented not simply the recognition of the criticisms raised by critical stakeholders. It also required that Adidas-Salomon reorient its operations and implement specific reporting and assessment practices to enforce its commitment to human rights in the form of more stringent standards. Adidas-Salomon ultimately altered its operations so as to better address the interests of all stakeholders and facilitate a new level of cooperation with consumers, employees, and local communities, based upon new operational norms with decidedly moral significance.

These different forms of cooperation underscore how there is not a bright line between the motives behind the pursuit of individual (or group) interest and communicative action. Just as Habermas outlines broad differences between rationally motivated agreements built upon shared reasons, rationally negotiated arrangements built upon convergent reasons, and agreements that express a common set of ethical convictions, there are a range of different managerial practices that can garner different forms of consensus. Stakeholders clearly assert their limited interests in the formation of contracts and negotiated settlements. This, however, implies neither that strategic action is *constitutive* of all business relationships, nor that communicative action cannot be served through social arrangements that are built from the identification of common interest that may not have been previously identified. Although the empirical evidence is not entirely clear on this point, work in the area of stakeholder dialogue effectively underscores the mutual advantages that can result from discourse focused on the search for common interests. The dialogic interaction of corporate constituencies can facilitate consideration, trust, flexibility, and agenda-setting power.[56] This, in turn, tends to promote not only ongoing, broad-based examination of shared values, but also a willingness to refine more specific policies to promote conflict resolution.[57] This has the beneficial effect of limiting coordination problems, enhancing private interest satisfaction among stakeholder groups, and most importantly, opening up greater opportunities for stakeholders to identify with the interests of other groups.[58] A normative framework that views business firms as only composed of simple, instrumental contracts belies the complexity and interdependent nature of business problems and the potential for multilateral solutions.[59]

To review: There are two general points that underscore how businesses can be properly thought of as organizations that play a significant role in facilitating communicative action. On the one hand, businesses are associations that serve the broader aims of a democratic civil society. They are the site of rational opinion and will formation in addition to providing opportunities for citizens to gain an understanding of the public issues addressed by the formal institutions of the state. In this regard, the social relationships that make up life within business firms provide intellectual opportunities for individuals to critically examine the status quo and explore options for public policy and legal reform. The greater the opportunities that stakeholders have for discursive interaction with one another, the more likely it is that such intellectual insights will be robust and well informed. On the other hand, business firms themselves successfully coordinate social action among stakeholders when their management teams seek different forms of rationally motivated consensus. Habermas provides us with an outline of how consensus can emerge within plural, democratic societies. A parallel set of considerations leads us to the conclusion that consensus-oriented management, whether through moral discovery, compromise, negotiation, or ethical reflection, can produce firms that enhance socialization, social integration, and the realization of underlying shared interests.

7. UNITING INSTITUTIONAL AND ORGANIZATIONAL BUSINESS ETHICS

The advantage that communicative ethics has for the field of business ethics is that it resists any sharp division between the moral requirements created by the arrangement of political and economic institutions and the moral requirements arising out of the exercise of discretion by business managers. Habermas's picture of modern society distributes the site for the legitimation of practical norms among a broad range of formal institutions and informal associations. Thus, the divide between institutional and organizational requirements begins to blur once we accept the basic notion that businesses are simply part of the larger social fabric where we seek to organize social life consensually, on the basis of shared reasons.

I have argued that communicative ethics provides the normative groundwork for business ethics on a number of fronts. First, to the extent that businesses are market actors, business managers have a responsibility to engage in activities that are consistent with a legally constituted market. This implies that managers have direct responsibilities not simply to obey the law, but also to support the conditions necessary for the development of legitimate law. Second, businesses organizations are explicitly designed under the law to exercise discretion on matters related to the production and distribution of public goods. Since such discretion presupposes the exercise of authority, it stands to reason that managerial authority stands in need of legitimation. This demands that corporate stakeholders not merely have good reasons to accept and follow managerial policy, but that the grounds that support such policy be capable of being endorsed by those who are affected by it. To preserve the greatest level of managerial discretion possible, I argue that the legitimate exercise of managerial authority should be largely procedural in nature, calling for management to implement practices that encourage the ongoing consideration and review of the interests of each stakeholder group. The moral responsibilities of managers are therefore tied to promoting critical dialogue and discursive interaction with affected stakeholder groups. Finally, and arguably most importantly, the social activity of business is integral to fostering effective communicative action throughout modern society, both in other informal associations and within formal political institutions. Stakeholder interactions create opportunities for individual citizens to problematize laws and policies as well as to gain additional intellectual insight into the reasons that support existing political and economic arrangements. Critical, dialogic interactions between stakeholders, in short, are instrumental in promoting the development of a well-informed citizenry that can examine the terms of social cooperation at all levels of society. This call for an integration of business life and political action expresses a more basic Habermasian point that cooperation is facilitated on simultaneous levels throughout civil society. This remains true even for business, despite the tendency to narrowly conceive of it as an association predicated on the pursuit of mutual advantage.

This chapter serves, at best, as a preview of how communicative ethics can provide a normative framework to tackle basic issues addressed by business ethicists. These issues include, but are not necessarily limited to, corporate responsibilities to local communities, employee rights and responsibilities, corporate governance, duties toward consumers and customers, and the relationship between moral responsibility and the law. It is therefore fitting that any future work in the area of communicative ethics and business begin to separate specific ethical problems in order to provide the necessary details of the larger theoretical picture. As I have suggested, this work has yet to be done, but it nonetheless demands our attention.

NOTES

1. For a position that favors what I am calling the institutional approach, see John Boatright, "Does Business Ethics Rest on a Mistake?" *Business Ethics Quarterly* 9, no. 4 (1999): 583–91, and "Business Ethics and the Theory of the Firm," *American Business Law Journal* 34 (1996): 217–38. For a comprehensive example of the organizational approach to normative business ethics, see Kenneth Goodpaster, *Conscience and Corporate Culture* (Malden, Mass.: Blackwell, 2007).

2. Jeffery Smith, "Moral Markets and Moral Managers Revisited," *Journal of Business Ethics* 61 (2005): 129–41.

3. Christopher McMahon, "The Political Theory of Organizations and Business Ethics," *Philosophy and Public Affairs* 24 (1995): 292–313.

4. Central works of Habermas referenced throughout this discussion include *Moral Consciousness and Communicative Action*, trans. Christian Lenhardt and Shierry Nicholsen (Cambridge, Mass.: MIT Press, 1990); *Justification and Application: Remarks on Discourse Ethics*, trans. Ciaran Cronin (Cambridge, Mass.: MIT Press, 1993); "On the Cognitive Content of Morality," *Proceedings of the Aristotelian Society*

96 (1996): 331–37; *Legitimation Crisis*, trans. Thomas McCarthy (Boston: Beacon, 1975); *Between Facts and Norms: Contributions to a Discourse Theory of Law and Democracy*, trans. William Rehg (Cambridge, Mass.: MIT Press, 1996); *Communication and the Evolution of Society*, trans. Thomas McCarthy (Boston: Beacon Press, 1984); and *The Theory of Communicative Action*, vol. 2, *Lifeworld and System: A Critique of Functionalist Reason*, trans. Thomas McCarthy (Boston: Beacon Press, 1987).

5. For simplicity's sake, I will generally refer to Habermas's project as "communicative ethics"; however, I recognize that this does not do full justice to the ethical, political, and legal dimensions of Habermas's comprehensive philosophy. Communicative ethics is arguably only one feature of an integrated, comprehensive critical social theory.

6. Readers will immediately see parallels between the work of Habermas and John Rawls. For detailed discussion of the similarities and differences between these two authors, see Habermas, "Reconciliation on the Public Use of Reason: Remarks on John Rawls' Political Liberalism," *Journal of Philosophy* 92, no. 3 (1995): 109–31, and Rawls, "Political Liberalism: A Reply to Habermas," *Journal of Philosophy* 92, no. 3 (1995): 132–80. For a critical review of this debate see Christopher McMahon, "Why There Is No Issue between Rawls and Habermas," *Journal of Philosophy* 99, no. 3 (2002): 111–29.

7. Habermas, *Justification and Application*, 24.

8. Habermas, *Justification and Application*, 59.

9. Kenneth Baynes, *The Normative Grounds of Social Criticism: Kant, Rawls, and Habermas* (Albany: SUNY Press, 1992), 81.

10. Habermas, *Moral Consciousness and Communicative Action*, 58.

11. Habermas, *Communication and the Evolution of Society*, 286. See also Baynes, *Normative Grounds*, 79–88.

12. Habermas asserts, for instance, that "[a] norm has a binding character—therein consists its validity. . . . But if only empirical motives (such as inclinations, interest and fear of sanctions) sustain the agreement, it is impossible to see why a party to the contract should continue to feel bound to the norms when his original motives change." *Legitimation Crisis*, 104.

13. Habermas, *Legitimation Crisis*, 108, and *Moral Consciousness and Communicative Action*, 102.

14. Habermas, *Moral Consciousness and Communicative Action*, 49–68.

15. Habermas, *Moral Consciousness and Communicative Action*, 66 (Habermas's italics).

16. Baynes, *Normative Grounds of Social Criticism*, 174. See also Kenneth Baynes, "Rational Reconstruction and Social Criticism: Habermas's Model of Interpretive Social Science," *Philosophical Forum* 21 (1989): 122–45. Habermas originally makes this distinction in *Theory of Communicative Action: Lifeworld and System*, 113–98.

17. Habermas, *Legitimation Crisis*, 41–50, and *Theory of Communicative Action: Lifeworld and System*, 355.

18. Baynes, *Normative Grounds of Social Criticism*, 174–78.

19. Habermas, *Theory of Communicative Action: Lifeworld and System*, 328. He writes: "The rationalization of the lifeworld makes possible, on the one hand, the differentiation of autonomous subsystems and opens up, at the same time, the utopian horizon of civil society in which the formally organized spheres of action of the bourgeois (economy and state apparatus) constitute the foundations for the post traditional lifeworld of l'homme (private sphere) and citoyen (public sphere)."

20. I owe this characterization to Kenneth Baynes and his reference to Habermas's essay "The New Obscurity: The Crisis of the Welfare State and the Exhaustion of Utopian Energies," in *The New Conservatism*, trans. Shierry Weber Nicholsen (Cambridge, Mass.: MIT Press, 1989), 63–65.

21. Habermas, *Between Facts and Norms*, 366–73.

22. Thomas McCarthy, "Legitimacy and Diversity: Dialectical Reflections on Analytical Distinctions," *Cardozo Law Review* 17, nos. 4–5 (March 1996): 1083–1125. See also Thomas McCarthy, "Practical Discourse: On the Relation of Morality to Politics," in *Ideals and Illusions: On Reconstruction and Deconstruction in Contemporary Critical Theory* (Cambridge, Mass.: MIT Press, 1991), 182–85.

23. William Rehg, *Insight and Solidarity: The Discourse Ethics of Jürgen Habermas* (Berkeley: University of California Press, 1994), 211–49.

24. Habermas, *Legitimation Crisis*, 105.

25. See McCarthy, "Legitimacy and Diversity," 1096–97.

26. Habermas, *Justification and Application*, 60. I use McCarthy's translations of the German words "Einverständnis" and "Vereinbarung." Later I also borrow his description of the term "Konsens." See his "Legitimacy and Diversity," 1099.

27. Habermas, *Between Facts and Norms*, 140–42.

28. Habermas, *Justification and Application*, 11–12 and 23–24. See McCarthy, "Legitimacy and Diversity," 1104–5 for a detailed discussion of this point.

29. Habermas, *Justification and Application*, 23, and *Between Facts and Norms*, 108–9.

30. Habermas, *Between Facts and Norms*, 154–56.

31. Habermas, *Between Facts and Norms*, 110.

32. Habermas, *Between Facts and Norms*, 118–31. See also Habermas, "Law and Morality," *Tanner Lectures on Human Values* 8 (1988): 217–79, and Darryl Reed, "Stakeholder Management Theory: A Critical Theory Perspective," *Business Ethics Quarterly* 9, no. 3 (1999): 453–83.

33. Habermas, *Between Facts and Norms*, 107.

34. Darryl Reed, "Three Realms of Corporate Social Responsibility: Distinguishing Legitimacy, Morality, and Ethics," *Journal of Business Ethics* 21, no. 1 (1999), 23–53.

35. Habermas, "Law and Morality," 243–44.

36. Reed, "Three Realms," 27.

37. Habermas, *Between Facts and Norms*, 122–26.

38. For an informative discussion of these entitlements see Kenneth Baynes, "Democracy and the Rechtstaat: Habermas's *Faktizitaet und Geltung*," in *The Cambridge Companion to Habermas*, ed. Stephen White (New York: Cambridge University Press, 1994), 201–32.

39. This parallels a common idea found in modern political thought that the exercise of authority by the state requires that individual citizens have sufficient reason to abide by the state's directives. For a comprehensive analysis of the role of managerial authority and business ethics, see Christopher McMahon, *Authority and Democracy: A General Theory of Government and Management* (Princeton, N.J.: Princeton University Press, 1994).

40. I infer this conclusion from an observation made by Nien-hê Hsieh, "Managers, Workers, and Authority," *Journal of Business Ethics* 71, no. 4 (2007): 347–57. Christopher McMahon argues that managerial authority is derived from the fact that each individual member of the firm has reason to prefer a system of manager-led cooperation. He refers to this type of authority as "C-authority." See *Authority and Democracy*, 102–26 and 231–57. My account of authority departs from McMahon's in two key respects. First, part of what makes authority legitimate is that the content of managerial policy can be endorsed, i.e., the reasons behind managerial policy should be reasons that are either acceptable by all parties or the result of decision-making processes that are endorsed by all. Second, authority is legitimated to the extent that those affected by managerial policy can endorse it, not simply those who are directed by it.

41. These responsibilities follow those outlined by the Clarkson Centre for Business Ethics in its "Principles of Stakeholder Management," *Business Ethics Quarterly* 12, no. 2 (2002): 257–64. The procedural nature of these principles permits various theoretical justifications.

42. For a discussion of merit as a standard for the just treatment of stakeholders, see Robert Phillips, *Stakeholder Theory and Organizational Ethics* (San Francisco: Berrett-Koehler, 2003).

43. Habermas, *Between Facts and Norms*, 371.

44. Baynes, *Normative Grounds of Social Criticism*, 180.

45. Baynes, *Normative Grounds of Social Criticism*, 179. For an interesting comparison to this claim in an international context, see Andreas Scherer, Guido Palazzo, and Dorothée Baumann, "Global Rules and Private Actors: Toward a New Role of the Transnational Corporation in Global Governance," *Business Ethics Quarterly* 16, no. 4 (2006): 505–32, and Andreas Scherer and Guido Palazzo, "Toward a Political Conception of Corporate Social Responsibility: Business and Society Seen from a Habermasian Perspective," *Academy of Management Review* 32, no. 4 (2007): 1096–1120.

46. At the same time, recall that Habermas warns us that the market and formal institutions of the state tend to "colonize" civil society by displacing rational will formation with instrumental ends like profit and power. This engenders a certain level of pessimism about the possibility of businesses successfully promoting communicative action in the way that I have just described. If business organizations should play a role in rational opinion and will formation, then either there is a strong reason to protect forms of discursive interaction from the colonizing influences of society's formal institutions or business managers need to recognize the operational importance of discourse.

47. I thank Wim Dubbink and Bert van de Ven for calling this point to my attention.

48. Habermas, *Communication and the Evolution of Society*, 178–82.

49. Habermas, *Between Facts and Norms*, 366–67.

50. Kenneth Baynes, for example, maintains that businesses are autonomous associations that can reflectively examine the terms and conditions of the market. *Normative Grounds of Social Criticism*, 179. See Habermas, "The New Obscurity," 63–64.

51. Boatright, "Business Ethics and the Theory of the Firm," 219–22.

52. Jeffery Smith, "A Précis of a Communicative Theory of the Firm," *Business Ethics: A European Review* 13, no. 4 (2004): 323.

53. Norman Bowie, "The Firm as a Moral Community," in *Morality, Rationality, and Efficiency: New Perspectives on Socio-Economics*, ed. Richard Coughlin (Armonk, N.Y.: M. E. Sharpe, 1991), 169–83.

54. For an example, see Kenneth Goodpaster's examination of Medtronic, Inc. in his *Conscience and Corporate Culture*, 150–75.

55. I draw my understanding of this case from Laura Hartman, Richard Wokutch, and J. Lawrence French, "Adidas-Salomon: Child Labor and Health and Safety Initiatives in Vietnam and Brazil," in *Rising above Sweatshops: Innovative Approaches to Global Labor Challenges*, ed. Laura Hartman, Denis Arnold, and Richard Wokutch (Westport: Praeger, 2003), 191–248.

56. Jem Bendell, "Talking for Change? Reflections on Effective Stakeholder Dialogue," in *Unfolding Stakeholder Thinking*, vol. 2, ed. Jorg Andriof, Sandra Waddock, Bryan Husted, and Sutherland Rahman (Sheffield, UK: Greenleaf, 2003), 53–69.

57. Jonathan Cohen, "State of the Union: NGO-Business Partnership Stakeholders," in *Unfolding Stakeholder Thinking*, vol. 2, ed. Jorg Andriof et al. (Sheffield, UK: Greenleaf, 2003), 106–27.

58. Andrew Crane and Sharon Livesey, "Are You Talking to Me? Stakeholder Communication and the Risks and Rewards of Dialogue," in *Unfolding Stakeholder Thinking*, vol. 2, ed. Jorg Andriof et al. (Sheffield, UK: Greenleaf, 2003), 39–52. Research on trust within organizations also underscores the strong connection between trust-building behavior and mutual advantage. Jay Barney and Mark Hansen, "Trustworthiness as a Source of Competitive Advantage," *Strategic Management Journal* 15 (1994): 175–91; Ralph Chami and Connel Fullerkamp, "Trust and Efficiency," *Journal of Banking and Finance* 26 (2002): 1785–1809; Philip Bromiley and Larry Cummings, "Organizations with Trust," in *Research in Negotiation*, ed. R. J. Lewicki, B. H. Sheppard, and R. Bies (Greenwich, Conn.: JAI Press, 1995), 219–47.

59. Jerry Calton and Lawrence Lad, "Social Contracting as a Trust-Building Process of Network Governance," *Business Ethics Quarterly* 5 (1995): 271–95. For a more comprehensive treatment of this point, see my "Précis of a Communicative Theory of the Firm."

Chapter Eight

On the Need for Theory in Business Ethics

Mitchell R. Haney, University of North Florida

As is the case with much of the short history of modern applied ethics, business ethics has largely unfolded as bringing to bear tools and resources of modern ethical theories to the moral quandaries within the practice of business. Without a doubt, modern ethical theories such as rights theory, deontology, utilitarianism, and even sophisticated forms of egoism have motivated those interested in the moral complexities of business to deepen their awareness and understanding. The question that this chapter seeks to explore is whether or not it is time to outgrow a certain strain of the application of ethical theory—as it has been conceived in much of modern philosophy—and to embrace an anti-theoretical perspective in our endeavor to tackle diverse issues in the ethics of business.[1] Here I will argue that it is quite plausible that modern ethical theory as it has been characteristically understood fails to provide a plausible account of the nature of moral value as well as fails to prescribe appropriate models for mature moral decision making for business ethics. As a result, business ethicists should continue their trend away from modern ethical theory and toward various proposals endorsed by anti-theorists in ethics.

Following a detailed discussion of the commitments of modern ethical theory, I will argue for the above conclusion by rendering a series of plausibility arguments. It is my conviction, given the nature of the debates, that settling the theory versus anti-theory controversy is not only out of the bounds of this simple paper, but it may—at bottom—not be resolvable at all.[2] Such arguments will try to amass the salient reasons against modern ethical theory, as well as those reasons which lend credence to anti-theoretical ethical positions. I will conclude with a brief exposition of what I take to be the upshot of embracing ethical anti-theory for the future of business ethics as a philosophical endeavor.

1. MODERN ETHICAL THEORY

Questions about the adequacy of modern ethical theory are nothing new. At least since Elizabeth Anscombe's watershed paper "Modern Moral Philosophy" in 1958, many have explicitly challenged the picture of ethics as it has been conceived within modern ethical theory. We do not have the time to rehearse all the misgivings philosophers have had about modern ethical theory, but in order to demonstrate the general implausibility of such theorizing we need to understand the family of notions that are regularly but tacitly held to be conditions to adequately capturing morality.

Modern ethical theory, whether in the hands of a Kantian, a utilitarian, or a rights theorist, tends to aspire to two goals for any ethical theory. First, an adequate theory should be able to explain what features of the world make various actions morally right or wrong, as well as character traits and states of affairs morally good or evil. Let us call this the "explicability thesis" (ET). So, for instance, the moral hedonist holds that pleasure is morally good and pain is morally evil, and it is on the basis of whether or not an action produces overall pleasure or pain that it is morally right or wrong. Second, an adequate ethical theory should be able to prescribe a tractable procedure for conscious moral deliberation. Let us call this the "decision-procedure thesis" (DT).[3] These two goals are orthogonal insofar as the achievement of one does not issue in the achievement of the other and, strictly speaking, one need not seek to fulfill both ET and DT. However, many modern ethical theorists have had the ambition to achieve both of these goals, and many have held that the principles they defend capture the grounds of moral value as well as being adequate guides for rational moral deliberation. We will not assume that the failure of modern ethical theory to produce a system adequately fulfilling one of these goals yields a failure of modern ethical theorizing overall. However, the aspirations to fulfill ET and DT are conditioned by some deeper assumptions that anti-theorists have found wanting.

At the heart of modern ethical theory's hopes to fulfill both ET and DT is the thought that we can adequately capture the conditions for correct application of moral concepts within moral principles. A moral principle, as has been conceived since Kant, is a biconditional generalization that ties a list of non-moral features, thought to be individually necessary and jointly sufficient, to the application of a moral concept (e.g., morally right, wrong, good, or bad at the most general level and respectful, wrongful harm, helpful, prosperous, etc., at more specific levels).[4] It is also thought to be the case that the list of features in the application conditions of the biconditional must be projectable across a limitless number of cases; for instance, a classical utilitarian holds that an act is morally right if and only if the act produces more happiness over unhappiness for all affected. Finally, it is required that the nonmoral features tied to the moral concepts will always have the same moral valencies (e.g., right-making, wrong-making, etc.). Again, to illustrate, the classical utilitarian holds that happiness is always a right-making feature and unhappiness a wrong-making feature. The idea that morality can be captured or adequately reasoned about in terms of such general moral principles has come to be called in the literature "generalism."[5] And such generalism has been a tacit condition in the aim to fulfill, at the very least, ET, if not DT as well.

We can observe generalism emerging in business ethics within any number of discussions of moral business practice and policy. We can observe the assumption in arguments over whether or not failure to offer reasons for the termination of an employee is—without exception—an act of moral disrespect or if requiring such explanations would be immoral on the grounds that it would always limit human freedom. Regardless of the stance taken in the employment-at-will debate, we witness ethicists projecting features underlying "disrespectful behavior" or underlying "inappropriate limits on human freedom" across a broad range of cases in employment practice. Generalism creeps into most ethical discussions (within and without of business ethics), because it is a prominent assumption of all modern ethical theorizing; principles are premised upon the notion that certain types or categories of action have moral characteristics, and thereby offer reasons for or against certain behavior, across a broad range of situations.

In addition to the assumptions that we can capture the truth conditions for all moral concepts, and that such truth conditions are projectable across a wide array of cases, is an aspiration that such conditions be relatively simple. The hope to fulfill ET as well as DT seems to motivate many theorists to project that morality be relatively simple in its content. As is explained to all first-year philosophy students, we assume that the simplest explanation is most likely to be true. Occam's razor has long been a tool of theoreticians in the sciences. Simplicity, in turn, has come to be an embedded virtue of all theorizing, including ethical theorizing. How does this impact our interests here?

First, so as not to be too hasty with modern ethical theorizing, embracing generalism as a condition for fulfilling the explicability thesis is in and of itself compatible with morality still being so complex as to escape the understanding of finite cognitive creatures such as ourselves. As such, it is possible to aim at ET under the conditions of generalism, but fail to yield a normative theory simple enough as to be practicable for the decision-procedure thesis. However, such a form of ethical theory has not been terribly palatable to many theoreticians because of their hope to not only have us fulfill ET but DT as well.[6] In order for there to be a tractable procedure for moral deliberation, it must assume that morality is accessible to limited cognitive creatures such as ourselves. It is not agreeable to many ethical theorists that morality only be accessible to minds that approach omniscience. Thus, it is argued that since "ought implies can,"[7] we must be able to capture DT in a reasonably compact set of principles or procedures. Given this position, theorists hope that morality be relatively simple—that it be cognizable and communicable in a rather undemanding list of the conditions for the appropriate application of moral concepts embedded within principles.[8]

Though a demand for simplicity constrains the level of complexity that could still be permitted under conditions of generalism, simplicity may not be incompatible with the morality being grounded in multiple features held to be valuable. Moral pluralism holds that the moral value of actions, character traits, and so forth are rooted in more than one feature of our world. For example, some pluralists hold that the rightness and wrongness of actions is determined by both valuable consequences and procedural fairness. As an instance, Freeman's expression of "stakeholder theory" exhibits commitment to a pluralistic system that holds equality and respect for autonomy as the paramount features needed in deciding what acts and policies we should choose in the world of business.[9] This is not the only form of moral pluralism available or the only form utilized in business ethics; in fact, more often than not, business ethicists tend to commit themselves to some form of pluralistic ethics that aims to balance the moral demands of respecting individuals and the best consequences for all affected. Nevertheless, a demand for simplicity inexorably favors any view that appears to capture morality with fewer features and an easier decision-procedure over any view that has more features or a more difficult process for reasonable moral thinking. In fact, the condition for simplicity has tended to drive theorists' hopes for a defensible form of moral monism—i.e., the position that all morality can be explained and/or understood to be rooted in one morally relevant feature in the world. This vision of proper ethical theory has certainly been the case in much modern ethical theory in general. To a limited extent, such simplicity exhibits itself in business ethics as practitioners either extend one of these monistic theories to business (such as in Kantian deontology or utilitarianism) or seek to systematize the ethics of business in its own right under a single explanatory and guiding principle (such as in libertarian or stakeholder thinking that attempts to build an endogenous ethical theory of business).

The current state of ethical theorizing in the subfield of business ethics is not easily captured, as the field has grown much more diversified. However, it seems that business ethicists, along with many other applied ethicists, have tended to acknowledge the messiness of real life and how ethical theory can sometimes distort the complexities of that life. Nevertheless, the aspirations to explain moral value as well as to provide useful guidance pervade much of the work being done in the ethics of business. There are still signs that ethicists aspire to achieve the fulfillment of ET and DT for the ethics of business, and that these aspirations usually bring with them the conditions of generalism and simplicity. Unfortunately, it is ill advised to nurture such aspirations. Before I move to show the implausibility of modern ethical theory for business ethics, I want to acknowledge the work in business ethics that has been and continues to be done under its influence.

2. BUSINESS ETHICS AND MODERN ETHICAL THEORY

Although ethical issues of business have been acknowledged for as long as we have been reflective about our commercial transactions, the advent of normative theorizing being applied to such issues is quite recent. I am not one for tracking baptismal moments, but literature devoted to ethical theorizing with a purposeful eye to aiding and evaluating business practice clearly came into its own in the 1980s. For such a short history, business ethics, as a normative discipline, quickly became quite sophisticated in its normative views. Many of the criticisms of our canonical ethical theories often do not hold against the more thoughtful accounts of such views now defended by many business ethicists. Consider a few instances. Norman Bowie's defense of Kantian deontology is quite sophisticated; thus, his understanding of Kantianism steers clear of typical concerns over empty formalism and absolutism that are associated with less refined Kantian views. Andrew Gustafson has brought a more humanistic and less calculative utilitarianism to bear on the ethics of business. The works of Tibor Machan and Ian Maitland each constructively add to the development of Smithian liberalism and extend it beyond the slogans found in simplistic readings of Milton Friedman.[10] And Robert Solomon deftly extended the full tradition of virtue ethics to the life of business.[11] The full range of normative theories are represented as well as skillfully developed in the area of business ethics, and their contributions have been immeasurable in their ability to make us think about and review our own perspectives on various particular ethical issues as well as the moral value of business in general. In spite of the relative sophistication and interest of contemporary ethical theory, the power of such theories to fulfill ET and DT is sufficiently problematic as to motivate rejecting ethical theory in favor of some anti-theoretical approaches to business ethics.

3. MORAL PLURALISM IN BUSINESS ETHICS

Modern ethical theory congealed with Sidgwick's *Methods of Ethics*.[12] It is the first influential work that consciously envisioned the need to capture morality in a simple set of projectable features and recognized that there were competing theories that hearkened to diverse nonmoral features as necessary and sufficient for the application of moral concepts. Sidgwick felt the sting of not being able to find the feature or features sufficient to eliminate all competitors in the ethical theory game. He was left with being unable to adequately determine whether or not utilitarianism or egoism best explained morality and which yielded the best moral decision-procedure. However, this apparent failure to definitively settle on the best theory did not dissuade others from accepting Sidgwick's assumptions concerning what would constitute the proper structure of any adequate ethical theory. Sidgwick set the stage for ethical theorizing in the twentieth century.

In spite of Sidgwick's and the rest of modern ethical theory's failure to fulfill uncontentiously both ET and DT, ethical theorizing has been amazingly resilient. This is due to the fact that insofar as we pursue a theory that aspires to explain and/or to guide us, the conditions of generalism and simplicity tacitly come with the pursuit. In fact, McKeever and Ridge correctly diagnose that ethical theorists do tend to assume the constraints of generalism to be something akin to transcendental principles, i.e., the very conditions for thinking about morality. It is difficult for theorists to conceive of moral reasoning without the strictures of generalism, as well as simplicity, precisely insofar as theorists believe morality to be as systematic as other phenomena over which thinkers have created theories. However, the strictures of generalism and drive for simplicity may be more of a kind of intellectual hopefulness than they are binding requirements. The hope of systematizing morality keeps the project of ethical theorizing alive, in spite of its continual failure to produce a theory that has clearly and uncontentiously explained the bases of moral value (ET) and/or provided tractable and determinate moral guides (DT). As McKeever and Ridge quite rightly argue, the mere fact that we have yet to find an ethical theory that reasonably fulfills both ET and DT does not—by itself—necessitate the conclusion that we should abandon the theoretical project.[13] Just as moral disagreement does not necessitate moral relativism, a continued lack of closure on the project of ethical theory does not necessitate that the project is doomed in perpetuity. Past failure under relentless trials by "the best and the brightest" in conjunction with other theoretical, empirical, and practical considerations does, I think, make our aspirations toward such ethical theorizing much less reasonable.[14] We will return to this line of thinking below, but let us consider some more intricate moral theories that have arisen in the realm of business ethics.

Many business ethicists have taken approving attitudes toward various forms of nonrelativistic moral pluralism because of the shortfalls (both theoretical and practical) of modern ethical theories of a monist variety. These monist theories aimed to fulfill ET and/or DT with a single morally relevant feature (e.g., respect for persons) and/or a single supreme moral principle (e.g., the categorical imperative). It is such theories that appear to have failed to achieve the aspirations of modern ethical theory, according to many ethical theorists. Thus, a significant number of theorists—inside and outside of business ethics—have come to explicitly defend some form of the view that the final moral value of actions, characters, and policies is determined by some range of moral values rather than by a single moral value.[15] This is what is known by the general name "moral pluralism."

Given that moral pluralism has become ubiquitous in business ethics circles, where many have more or less agreed that justice, consequences, care, and self-interest are generally among those features of our experience that are morally relevant to the ethical evaluation of acts, policies, and character, it is safe to say that the simplicity of moral monism has been jettisoned as being too simple to capture the limitless variety of cases we encounter in our moral lives. What this indicates is that the push for simplicity has been overridden by the desire for a kind of descriptive and intuitive accuracy in our attempts to capture justified applications of our assortment of moral concepts. If this is right, then we need not spend the time to run through the standard worries about the inadequacy of the traditional forms of moral monism (e.g., classical utilitarianism, Kant's ethics, classical egoism, certain varieties of monistic libertarianism, etc.). Suffice it to say that those who engage the ethics of business have embraced W. D. Ross's sentiment (even if they do not ultimately accept his form of moral pluralism or his moral intuitionism) that we would rather have our reflections on the nature of moral normativity to be accurate than to be simple.[16]

However, among moral pluralists we find a range of views. Some of these views are pluralistic about moral value but argue for explicit ways in which some values always trump other values when they compete. For instance, a somewhat popular general model that one finds defended at various levels of sophistication is one that prescribes the following moral principle: An act is right if and only if it maximizes good consequences (however such a good is naturally explained) for all affected except when such an act violates the rights or autonomy of a person(s).[17] This is an expression of a form of moral pluralism that one may call "hierarchical moral pluralism." Such a view argues that the appropriate application of moral rightness (and wrongness) supervenes[18] irreducibly on more than one nonmoral feature, but it holds that one feature will always trump the other in cases of conflict. In *Theory of Justice*, Rawls defended a form of hierarchical pluralism in his "difference principle," when he argued that inequality in the distribution of primary goods is only justified in cases where the unequal distribution is to the best advantage of the least well-off.[19] Such forms of moral pluralism have been quite popular, because they do a relatively better job than their monistic counterparts in capturing the complexities of moral life, while remaining as simple as possible. These moral pluralists are more sensitive to the ways in which morality resists uncomplicated moral principles sought by ethical monists, but they still aspire to generalism and/or comparative simplicity as conditions for explaining morality and providing moral guidance in their views. Thus, such moral pluralists are still moral theorists in the modern ethical tradition.

The other popular form of moral pluralism that has arisen in business ethics is more like that of W. D. Ross. It is a nonhierarchical moral pluralism, whereby there is some list of nonmoral features that when present are relevant to the proper application of moral concepts, and these features will compete or collude to determine the final moral value of a given act, policy, or practice. However, there exists no rule or principle for adjudicating conflicts between right-making and wrong-making features. Rather than prescribe secondary moral principles for adjudicated conflicts in real cases, Ross and others hold that settling such conflicts is a matter of experienced moral judgment and not algorithmic. For instance, John Dienhart elaborates a complex form of moral pluralism, as a set of moral values that apply at the level of the institutions of business. Utilizing Werhane's pluralistic reading of Adam Smith alongside Aristotle's account of the virtues, Dienhart explores how justice, care, happiness, and self-interest are moral values that are all interpreted within individual and institutional contexts, and that the interpretation of these values sets the interpretive horizon for moral deliberation. In the end, moral deliberation cannot be adequately captured in a complete and structured cognitive process. Instead, moral pluralism demands "interpretational openness," that although any moral judgment is constrained by our rudimentary conceptions of justice, care, happiness, and self-interest, our judgment should not allow the values to be interpretively reduced to a singular set of necessary and sufficient conditions for the application and adjudication of the values. Such a reduction would treat all individuals, institutions, and situations as if they are alike, but (as Aristotle acknowledges) the final judgment of the moral value of an act, policy, or character trait lies in the particular.[20] The themes we find characteristic of nonhierarchical moral pluralism are abundant in business ethics.

Robert Frederick nicely describes one impetus for a kind of nonhierarchical pluralism in business ethics.[21] In his account, he calls it "pluralistic relativism." The attraction to a set of features that are morally relevant but none are supreme is that it promises to be an ethical view that has the virtues (but not the vices) of both ethical absolutism and ethical relativism. In short, he thinks that nonhierarchical pluralism aspires to be an ethical view that acknowledges the flexibility of ethical demands without being too permissive in its flexibility. Frederick sympathizes with the aspirations of such a view, but he failed to see at the time that anyone had yet generated a view with enough substance to supplant the more traditional views one finds under moral absolutism and moral relativism. However, in the same volume, Sandra Rosenthal and Rogene Bucholz elaborate various types of nonhierarchical pluralism under the heading of pragmatism. For Rosenthal and Bucholz, the first key feature that pragmatism has to offer normative theory is its "implicit moral pluralism with all the problems this involves."[22] They then define moral pluralism the following way:

> There is no one unifying, monistic principle from which lesser principles can be derived. According to moral pluralism, the right act is the one which is subsumed under the proper balance of rules or principles or theories, but in none of these theories can there be guidance in deciding when to use a particular theory, for each theory is self-enclosed or absolute: no principle or rule can provide any guidance for the moral reasoning that underlies the choice among the various principles or rules. The basis for this choice . . . , the very foundation for moral decision-making, remains mysterious and outside the realm of philosophical illumination.[23]

It appears that for Rosenthal and Bucholz there is neither a supreme principle that explains all of morality (ET) nor is there any such single principle that could be used to reasonably determine what we should choose when we have conflicts between other moral values (DT). As such, they urge that pragmatism is pluralist at the level of both moral explanation and moral guidance. They go on to argue that any adequate ethical view must have theoretical coherence at some point, but they urge that the coherence of pragmatism's pluralism is to be found in its nonmoral commitments about human nature rather than within its ethical standards. Rosenthal and Bucholz go farther than most in attempting to adequately capture a form of moral pluralism that is thoroughly pluralistic about both what explains the moral value of acts, characters, and so on, and for decision-making guidance as well. What generally follows in their account is that values such as justice, care, good consequences for the whole, and even self-interest naturally emerge from human interactions with each other and their environment. None of these values is explicable by any of the others and there is no way to project how we should substantively judge all cases of conflict before they occur. Instead, pragmatists have a method of openness that sees moral reasoning as an activity that is "concrete, imaginative, attunement to situational complexities."[24] Now, this may appear to be mysterious, but most nonhierarchical moral pluralists urge that normative moral judgment should not be explicated in any algorithmic manner.[25]

Given that moral pluralism of either a hierarchical or a nonhierarchical variety is so prominent in the business ethics literature, it seems that moral pluralism must be the foil (rather than traditional forms of moral monism) if one aims to question the value of ethical theorizing in general. So, anti-theorists ask, if moral pluralist views are ethical theories, then how well do they do in fulfilling ET and DT?

4. ANTI-THEORY IN BUSINESS ETHICS

Anti-theorists' primary challenger comes in the form of moral pluralism. As such, they must show the implausibility of the position, and to do so they must speak to both its hierarchical and nonhierarchical varieties. Hierarchical forms of pluralism still suffer from a deep tendency to yield strongly counterintuitive consequences because when two (or more) irreducible moral values conflict, these pluralists *a priori* prescribe which of the competing values will trump its competitors. Thus, such forms of pluralism rule out ahead of time any values being overridden in reverse from its prescribed hierarchy.

Consider a form of mitigated consequentialism that states that an act or policy is morally right if and only if it maximizes good consequences for all affected except in cases where the act or policy violates the rights or autonomy of persons. Now consider the following case: At the conclusion of World War II, the United States faced the need to employ returning servicemen and to create a non-wartime economy as active as the wartime economy.[26] If the U.S. government, in conjunction with American manufacturers, did not do this as swiftly as possible, then the United States would most certainly fall into a postwar depression. The rub, however, was that many Americans who remembered the prewar depression were of somewhat limited means. They distrusted the use of loans and credit and were disposed to save their money rather than spend it. It is the case that corporate America (with the blessings of the FCC) used the new medium of television to shift American attitudes about spending their money on new "luxury" items as well as using credit to purchase such items. The major manufacturers moved situation-comedy writers to develop plots in which the characters struggle with the decision to spend their hard-earned cash to purchase a luxury item, such as a dishwasher, as well as struggle with whether to buy such on store credit. In all cases the plots wrap up with the characters deciding to make the purchase, finding that they are so much happier because of their new item, and finding that buying on credit did not destroy their financial lives.

This is but one way in which corporate America converted Americans into consumers and saved the United States from spiraling into a postwar depression. It catalyzed consumer buying habits that made the United States into the leading economic power for the rest of the twentieth century. Now if it is the case that this use of television yielded the greatest possible consequences for all affected, it did so at the expense of violating viewers' autonomy. They were manipulated (some will argue) into desiring luxury items and cajoled into believing that it was economically feasible to buy them on credit. Manufacturers and television writers accomplished this knowing that Americans would likely do so because they would identify with characters in their situation comedies. Our mitigated consequentialist would condemn these policies and actions as immoral because—under their principle—there is no quantity or quality of consequences of an action that can overrule the wrongness of violating the autonomy of persons. We all know of other hypothetical cases in which the consequences of our actions intuitively overrule the violation of autonomy and, as such, hierarchical moral pluralism appears not to be in a much better position than moral monism as far as its ability to adequately explain the complexities of moral value and/or moral evaluation in a generalized manner.

Given the above, hierarchical moral pluralism still appears to aspire to generality and simplicity, because it still pursues the explanation of morality by features that can be projected across innumerable cases and have specific moral valences. Given the types of examples above, such views still fail to adequately fulfill ET, and this is due to the implausibility of the generality and simplicity conditions conjoined to ET. Given such weaknesses, I will spend no more time critiquing versions of hierarchical pluralism. This leaves us with the idea that the strongest contender for an adequate moral theory must be forms of nonhierarchical moral pluralism. The rest of this section will attempt to deepen our understanding of this view within the ethics of business and conclude by raising questions about its theoretical and practical adequacy (although many of these criticisms apply *mutatis mutandis* to all forms of ethical theorizing that maintain generalism as a condition to fulfilling either the explanatory or guidance aspirations of ethical theory).

How does nonhierarchical moral pluralism fare in relationship to the theoretical aims of ET and DT? First, it should be noted that this form of pluralism abandons hope to fulfill the typical aspirations of DT. Insofar as nonhierarchical moral pluralism commits itself to the idea that—at bottom—moral reasoning "remains mysterious and outside the realm of philosophical illumination,"[27] it abandons the aim of DT and distances itself from this aspiration of modern ethical theory. At this juncture it is a bit hyperbolic to say that one must think of moral reasoning as beyond philosophical inquiry in order to be a nonhierarchical moral pluralist; one could be such a moral pluralist and utilize what cognitive psychologists have learned of reliable human decision making to preserve the claim that moral judgment is largely not rule based or algorithmic in nature.[28]

For the purpose of simplicity, let us use Ross's view as a paradigm case of nonhierarchical moral pluralism and its attempt to fulfill the explanatory aspiration (ET) of ethical theory. He holds that there is a limited range of features relevant to the moral value of acts, policies, and character, but no feature in that range is morally superior to any other. Thus, what might be most morally salient in one case may not be so in another. However, in that range of features, Ross holds that the nonmoral features associated with veracity, beneficence, fidelity, and so on, are such that wherever and whenever they are present, they are morally relevant. In addition, Ross holds that when they are present they will be morally relevant in the same way, e.g., truthfulness is always a right-making feature in a situation. In our earlier terminology, these features are projectable across all cases and always have the same moral valence. Thus, Ross continues to hold that in his list of morally relevant features all fulfill the conditions of generalism. As such, Ross envisions a way of explaining the nature of moral value in his list of morally relevant features such that the moral value of any act, policy, or character will be explained by the presence, absence, and configuration of features from this and only this list.[29]

Most forms of nonhierarchical moral pluralism adhere to generalism in this form. But, as Jonathan Dancy has continued to effectively argue, even generalism in this form holds that whenever a feature from a list of morally relevant features is present, then it is morally relevant and morally relevant in a certain way (even though it may be overridden by another morally relevant feature in any given situation). For instance, the protection of self-interest is a morally relevant feature and a right-making feature and, as such, it must be part of what makes an action morally right even though it might be overridden by the well-being of others in a given circumstance. In no case could self-interest not be morally relevant or a wrong-making feature. In Dancy's terminology, the generalism that continues to be maintained by nonhierarchical moral pluralists forbids the possibilities of "silencing" or "reversal" of morally relevant features.[30] However, there is a strong intuition that features we believe to be morally relevant and relevant in certain ways can silence or reverse their moral valence. For instance, although fulfilling self-interest is morally relevant in many business situations where others' interests are not in jeopardy, it appears that fulfilling it at the significant expense to others at the very least silences self-interest (e.g., it is not morally relevant in such cases) or reverses its valence (e.g., fulfilling self-interest at the expense of others is a wrong-making feature). Or, to recall our earlier example of the use of situation comedies to effect peoples' consumer behavior, autonomy is often said to be a hallmark morally relevant feature insofar as it is always morally relevant and always a right-making feature. However, if the absolute protection of said autonomy would cause more or less universal suffering through a severe economic depression, then it could be reasoned that protecting individual autonomy would be morally silenced or the act of protecting it would reverse its valence to being a wrong-making feature in that situation. As such, even central features to morality, such as self-interest and autonomy, can be reasonably understood as features that can be silenced or reversed. In the cases outlined so far, it may appear that the well-being of the majority is the sole moral feature that trumps all others; thus, what I have demonstrated is not the plausibility of any anti-theoretical position but the plausibility of consequentialism. However, even the well-being of the many may be silenced or reversed.

Suppose that the manipulation involved in the use of situation comedies were to lead to the destruction of individual autonomy (e.g., where the freedom to act or not on one's desires were removed altogether). In this case, the power of advertising would be tantamount to the implantation of a control device in each person's head (and he or she could not do anything but go out and buy a specific brand of automobile). If this were the case, then it would appear that, regardless of protecting the majority from suffering, protecting persons' autonomy would at least trump and possibly silence the moral relevance of mass suffering from an economic depression.[31]

So, what's the upshot of such examples? If generalism, as it has been adhered to in modern ethical theory, is correct, then such silencing and reversals of valence should be normative impossibilities. At the very least, such examples should appear to be deeply counterintuitive. However, the few brief examples thus far—and one could expand the list—show that it is not normatively implausible to think that features which play prominently in business ethics are subject to these common moral phenomena.[32] Critics of the kind of anti-theoretical considerations presented above will often turn our attention to the apparent generality necessary for reasons as such in order to *prove* that moral theory is correct to embrace generalism. The argument aims to show that reasons (of any and all varieties) can only have normative power if they can be subsumed under broader general truths or claims (e.g., laws, principles, norms, etc.). Thus, critics claim that generalism is a necessary feature of reasoning as such, moral reasoning included. Generalism is a transcendental regulative norm governing all moral reasoning, and what the examples above prove is not that we abandon ethical theory, but that we lack the right articulation of moral principles.[33]

On this view it is often argued that, since we must maintain generalism and we want moral principles that capture the intuitive complexities of moral life, the moral principles must become more complex and, as such, build into the application conditions for moral values all the relevant exceptions.[34] Thus, they would hold that an appropriate moral principle may be formulated like the following: An act is morally right if and only if it fulfills self-interest, except in cases where it undermines the well-being, or rights, or autonomy, or X, of others. Thus, generalists of this variety want to maintain, at the very least, some form of moral pluralism, because they argue that there is a more general theoretical consideration that necessitates that moral principles cannot be abandoned on pain of irrationality. As such, they are willing to embrace much more complex moral principles in order to maintain generalism.

There are four basic responses to this line of reasoning—two theoretical and two practical. First, paralleling concerns that J. L. Mackie raised about rule utilitarianism, it seems that adding the complexity of exceptions to the moral principles we are prescribed to live by, once all the exceptions are included, tell us no more than what act utilitarianism would have prescribed in the first place.[35] As a result, a sophisticated rule utilitarianism's account of a moral rule would be an unnecessary epicycle to our understanding of the appropriate conditions for the application of moral rightness. Analogously, once we include in the appropriately sophisticated moral principles all the relevant exceptions (i.e., covering all the conditions in which the antecedent morally relevant feature is trumped, silenced, or reversed in its value) then the principle plays no more role in our understanding than what would be assessed by any anti-theorist who focused directly on the morally relevant features particular to each given situation. In other words, such principles abandon all hope to fulfill the aspiration of generality. Hence, it seems theoretically plausible that once any theorist attempts to make generalism fit our moral intuitions concerning the flexibility of morally relevant features in our moral experience, then the generalism he or she seeks to defend collapses back into an anti-theoretical form of moral particularism.

Second, there is also a more direct defense of moral theory. This is to claim that generalism is a necessary regulative ideal on all moral reasoning. The idea is that we cannot reason without some form of moral principles committed to generalism, due to the fact that moral reasons can only be captured as reasons because of their relationship to a moral principle that projects some feature as relevant across cases and relevant in certain ways (even if the principle is quite complex). The anti-theorist response to this line of reasoning is that this argument shows more about what we think is necessary for theoretical systematization than what is necessary for practical reasoning in the real world. What the argument for the need for general principles demonstrates is actually more about what philosophers—driven by the dream of a final theory—think is necessary for moral reasons than about the actual practices of reasonable human beings in real moral situations. On the one hand, the claim that moral reasons must be subsumable under moral principles in order to be moral reasons at all seems to reflect more the Socratic prejudices of philosophers than the effective cognitive and behavioral habits of most reasonable human beings. The typically reliable, non-rule-based moral judgment of most human beings speaks against the need of moral reasons to rely on moral principles to be guiding reasons at all. Thus, the failure to capture a tractable decision-procedure (DT) stands as some evidence against this transcendental move. On the other hand, if this is solely about explaining morality (ET) and theorists are correct that generalism is a regulative constraint on any explanation of moral value, then any account of moral value without appeal to general moral rules or principles must be deeply incoherent. As I will suggest shortly, however, it is not incoherent to explain morality without appeal to the types of moral generalizations that hold features to be morally relevant in all cases and to have the same moral valence. If this is correct, then generalism is not a regulative principle to explaining moral value.

In tandem with the above theoretical concerns, there is a pair of simple practical objections to the preceding defense of ethical theory. The first is that if generalism is a necessary regulative ideal for any adequate moral reasoning, then it is incumbent upon theorists to provide a defensible set of moral principles that fulfill ET and/or DT. Much of the defense of moral theory in this debate operates at the level of metatheory rather than normative theory. This is to say that much of the discussion has been a theoretical defense of theory as such rather than attempting to provide an ethical theory that adequately explains moral value and/or guides moral reasoning. However, if generalism is necessary to morality, then the final proof is in whether or not theorists can provide the set of moral principles that are adequately general and simple for fulfilling ET, if not DT as well. And the adequacy of said principles is judged—in part—on whether they concur with our intuition that morally relevant features can be silenced or reversed in individual cases. Most of those who defend the need for principles are typically silent as to the content that the moral principles should take; it often seems that defenders of ethical theory in this debate tend to fall into the position that it is a matter of principle that we need principles, and they become mute when asked for the content of such principles.[36] The response is that the proof of the power of principles to explain and guide is in finding moral principles that adequately explain morality and guide moral decision making. But, as most anti-theorists will point out, what partially motivates the plausibility of their view has been the history of theorists' being unable to provide substantive, defensible moral principles that fulfill the demand of simplicity and, especially, the demand of generalism. Thus, anti-theorists are moved to think about morality in the absence of moral principles.

When moral theorists provide what appears to be adequate content for their moral principles, then—as indicated above—these will tend to be moral principles that contain exceptions or are of the *prima facie* variety. The hitch with such moral principles is that they will either fail to adequately capture the flexibility of morality or be so complex as to be intractable and, thus, useless. As to the first problem, they can fail to capture the nuances of morality because they still reflect the theoretical hope that the conditions of the application of moral values are universally projectable. They therefore succumb to the numerous counterexamples that indicate the contextual flexibility of morality. If they attempt to capture all the flexibility within principles that expect to capture the necessary and sufficient conditions of application for the moral concepts, then the moral principles will lose the intended generality while meeting an explanatory function. Moreover, the complexity of such moral principles would be too complex to be adequately comprehended or used by beings like us, and thus be inadequate to guiding moral reasoning. It appears plausible (although not conclusive) that modern ethical theorists' adherence to generalism and simplicity that conditions the hopes of fulfilling ET and DT is misguided. The lesson for business ethicists is that it is plausible that we should abandon our explicit or tacit acceptance of modern ethical theory and continue the movement toward more anti-theoretical ethical approaches, which we have tended toward as we have already embraced types of nonhierarchical forms of moral pluralism in the first place. The remainder of this investigation aims to outline an anti-theoretical vision applicable to business ethics.

5. IMPLICATIONS FOR BUSINESS ETHICS

Part of the impetus for discussing the plausibility of anti-theory for business ethics arose from a discussion to which I was a party. There were a few of us—all philosophers—at a business ethics conference discussing how we taught our business ethics courses. I was astonished that quite independently but uniformly we each admitted (and with some hesitancy by some as if it might be a philosophical heresy) that the more we taught the course, the less time we devoted to teaching ethical theories. Instead, we each admitted that the focus of our courses had become more devoted to teaching critical thinking skills—e.g., identifying relevant facts, common relevant values, and so forth—and developing skills for providing thoughtful justifications for moral decisions. We acknowledged that we elicited such skills from our students even in the absence of their formally learning the range of moral principles elucidated and defended by generalists. Directly or indirectly we all admitted that knowing ethical theories was not necessary to understanding morality and to making sensible moral decisions. This, along with all said above, raises the question What is to be done in business ethics in the absence of modern ethical theory?

There is still plenty that can be carried over from modern ethical theory, but it will be carried over without its more problematic trappings. I hope that I have shown that it is plausible that the assumptions of generalism and simplicity as necessary parts to fulfilling ET and DT are the more problematic elements of modern ethical theorizing. If this is plausible, then we need to have an idea of how we can engage in interesting and useful thinking about morality without these assumptions. I think we can, and in many ways, we already do so in our daily moral practices. It is not that we must eschew moral generalities per se, it is that we must eschew the rigidity we think moral generalities must have in order to adequately explain moral values and guide moral decision making. In short, we need to abandon the idea that moral generalities contain features that are universally projectable and always projectable in the same way. And, as I noted above, if this story is coherent, as I believe it to be, then generalism cannot be a regulative ideal for moral thinking.

Dancy makes a useful distinction between "invariable" and "invariant" morally relevant features.[37] Insofar as the generalism of modern ethical theory holds that the features listed in a moral principle must always be morally relevant and relevant in the same way, it is committed to the claim that morally relevant features are invariable, i.e., they are *never* irrelevant and *never* have a different moral valence. However, this is precisely part of what makes the assumption of generalism so problematic for modern ethical theorists. We need not think that morally relevant features (e.g., avoidance of suffering, autonomy, honesty, etc.) are invariable in order to ensure their moral relevance. They may be, according to Dancy, "invariant" moral features. An invariant morally relevant feature is one that in our experience tends not to be silenced or reversed, but it does not hold that there is no situation in which that feature can be (or has been) silenced or reversed.[38] According to certain anti-theorists like Dancy, this is the genuine function of moral principles and rules. They are a kind of heuristic tool to remind us of those features that—in the breadth and length of human experience—have tended to remain more often morally relevant and relevant in certain ways across cases, and without extending such a claim to the position that they could *never* be irrelevant or relevant in a different way. Thus, moral principles and rules—properly conceived—are ways of communicating, capturing, and utilizing the most general moral knowledge we have without committing ourselves to the theoretical prejudices captured by the conditions of generalism and simplicity.

At this point, one may say that this is merely a matter of what it is that we mean by "ethical theory." I agree that this is part of the matter. Whether we call a systematization of morality that bases itself on the assumptions of generalism and simplicity or the anti-generalist variety described here an "ethical theory" is of no matter to me. What is most important is to understand that when we articulate and think about morally relevant features, such as duties, rights, autonomy, self-interest, character, and so forth, we are considering features that are, at most, morally invariant rather than morally invariable. Although this makes the process of considering the nature of morality and proper moral decision making much messier than even the going views of nonhierarchical pluralism, it mirrors the complexity of morality as such.

In business ethics, many have already welcomed the idea that morality is more complex than any modern ethical theories have been able to adequately capture. If it is the case that in teaching and researching issues in business ethics, specialists have already distanced themselves from modern ethical theories, then they have already moved a significant way toward anti-theoretical positions in ethics. Moreover, if it is plausible that generalism and simplicity are the assumptions of ethical theorizing that make modern ethical theory problematic to successfully engaging in teaching and discussing ethical issues in business, then, as I have tried to show here, business ethicists should consciously embrace the abandonment of the kinds of moral principles and systematization that are the hallmarks of modern ethical theorizing (even as they arise in nonhierarchical forms of moral pluralism). I think that this is the kind of approach to understanding the nature of morality and moral decision making that fits best with discussions and practices that already occur in the research of business ethics, as well as with the critical-thinking emphasis that has been arising in the teaching of business ethics. An anti-theoretical approach of the kind outlined here provides some level of adequate explication of morality and some parameters in moral decision making without sacrificing the complexity of moral life as it is lived and experienced, including the life of business.

In many ways the teaching, thinking, and writing by many business ethicists betray a certain trust of the generalism and simplicity found in classical modern ethical theory. However, at the same time, they still speak of general applicable moral values. The only point to emphasize here is that in utilizing general moral values business ethicists consciously steer away from the generalism that still lurks in many forms of nonhierarchical moral pluralism that weds itself to the invariability of morally relevant features, and explicitly embrace the weaker form of generalism that only commits itself to the invariance of many morally relevant features. This shift in attitude and emphasis will help steer business ethics away from certain kinds of debates that may be driven more by theoretical hopes than by the practical needs of persons in and affected by business, and it will keep those of us tackling the complexities of morality in business honest about the limits of our Socratic proclivities.

NOTES

1. Anti-theorists in any field typically recognize that they are not calling for us to be nontheoretical per se, but they call for us to eschew a certain conception of theorizing that dominates a field of study. In our case, I will question a prominent picture of how we are to reflectively understand moral value and/or moral decision making.

2. Paul Moser has argued in the realm of epistemic normativity that there are no "non-question-begging" arguments for opposing sides in epistemology. All sides utilize intuition-pumping examples that favor their own views. I think that this is paralleled in ethical theorizing. Thus, the best that can be done is to imagine which vision of the nature of morality seems most plausible given our moral experience and other theoretical convictions that we hope to fit into an empirically and metaphysically adequate conception of life as we know it. See *Philosophy after Objectivity: Making Sense in Perspective* (New York: Oxford University Press, 1993).

3. For more on these assumptions, see Mark Timmons, *Moral Theory: An Introduction* (Lanham, Md.: Rowman & Littlefield, 2002), and Sean McKeever and Michael Ridge, *Principled Ethics: Generalism as a Regulative Ideal* (New York: Oxford University Press, 2006).

4. McKeever and Ridge, *Principled Ethics*, do an excellent job elucidating this conception of moral principles.

5. See, in particular, Jonathan Dancy, *Ethics without Principles* (New York: Oxford University Press, 2004).

6. I would suggest that although Occam's razor has always been a tool for sorting competing theories, a shift has occurred in much modern ethical theorizing (and possibly even scientific theorizing), in which simplicity of explanation has moved from a comparative virtue between competing theories to an assumption or regulative principle about the nature of morality itself. See Nancy Cartwright, *How the Laws of Physics Lie* (New York: Oxford University Press, 1983).

7. Most ethicists hold that in order to require or forbid any activity, it must be an activity that we are capable of performing.

8. Bernard Gert's work is an excellent example of a sophisticated but conscious demand for simplicity. See *Morality: Its Nature and Justification* (New York: Oxford University Press, 2005).

9. R. Edward Freeman, *Strategic Management: A Stakeholder Approach* (Boston: Pitman, 1984).

10. Norman Bowie, *Business Ethics: A Kantian Perspective* (Malden, Mass.: Blackwell, 1999); Andrew Gustafson, "Utilitarianism and Business Ethics," in *Ethical Issues in Business: A Philosophical Approach*, ed. Thomas Donaldson, Patricia Hogue Werhane, and Joseph Van Zandt (Upper Saddle River, N.J.: Prentice Hall,

2008); Tibor Machan, *Business Ethics in the Global Market* (Stanford, Calif.: Hoover, 1999); and Ian Maitland, "The Human Face of Self-Interest," *Journal of Business Ethics* 38, no. 1 (June 2002): 3–17.

11. Although it is debatable whether or not virtue theorists hold to the conception of ethical theories attempting to cash out the necessary and sufficient conditions for the proper application of moral concepts in nonmoral terms, some who ally themselves with virtue ethics may do so, and others may not insofar as they prefer to explicate morality with thick moral concepts that find the moral and nonmoral features to be inextricably intertwined. See Robert Solomon, *Ethics and Excellence: Cooperation and Integrity in Business* (New York: Oxford University Press, 1992), and *It's Good Business: Ethics and Free Enterprise for the New Millennium* (Lanham, Md.: Rowman & Littlefield, 1997). See also Edwin Hartman, *Organizational Ethics and the Good Life* (New York: Oxford University Press, 1996), and Marvin Brown, *Corporate Integrity: Rethinking Organizational Ethics and Leadership* (New York: Cambridge University Press, 2005).

12. See Bernard Williams, *Making Sense of Humanity and Other Philosophical Papers, 1982–1993* (New York: Cambridge University Press, 1995), and Margaret Walker, "Where Do Moral Theories Come From?" *Philosophical Forum* 26 (1995): 242–57. Each argues that Sidgwick's *Methods* is the watershed moment for modern ethical theorizing.

13. In fact, I find myself in the odd tension that any "anti-theorist" finds himself or herself. I am arguing in a theoretical manner for the inadequacy of ethical theory. However, it is not really theory as such that is the problem, but a certain popular and limited version of the point and proper structure of ethical theorizing that is brought into question here.

14. The same, I think, could be concluded about other disciplines that aspire to dream of a "final theory" in the face of a recalcitrant set of phenomena. On such in physics, see Cartwright, *How the Laws of Physics Lie*.

15. See John Dienhart, *Business, Institutions, and Ethics: A Text with Cases and Readings* (New York: Oxford University Press, 2000); Patricia Werhane, *Moral Imagination and Management Decision-Making* (New York: Oxford University Press, 1999); and, outside of business ethics, see Mark Johnson, *Moral Imagination: Implications of Cognitive Science for Ethics* (Chicago: University of Chicago Press, 1993); John Kekes, *The Morality of Pluralism* (Princeton, N.J.: Princeton University Press, 1993); Timmons, *Moral Theory*; and Robert Audi, *Practical Reasoning and Ethical Decision* (New York: Routledge, 2006).

16. For a classical statement of moral pluralism see W. D. Ross, *The Right and the Good*, ed. Philip Stratton-Lake (1930; Oxford, UK: Oxford University Press, 2002). For a contemporary defense of such a view see Robert Audi, *The Good in the Right: A Theory of Intuition and Intrinsic Value* (Princeton, N.J.: Princeton University Press, 2004).

17. James Rachels, *The Elements of Moral Philosophy*, 2nd ed. (New York: McGraw-Hill, 1993).

18. By "supervenes" I mean nothing metaphysically robust. I merely mean that there is a consistency constraint that if one asserts that features X, Y, and Z are fun-

damentally relevant to right action in one case, then, on pain of irrationality, they are relevant in all cases. What is dubbed a supervenience relation here, R. M. Hare calls universal prescriptivism in his own work. See *Essays in Ethical Theory* (New York: Oxford University Press, 1989).

19. See John Rawls, *A Theory of Justice* (1971; Cambridge, Mass.: Harvard University Press, 1999).

20. In addition to Dienhart, *Business, Institutions, and Ethics*, a similar sentiment has been expressed by Solomon, *Ethics and Excellence*; Hartman, *Organizational Ethics and the Good Life*; and Brown, *Corporate Integrity*.

21. Robert Frederick, ed., *A Companion to Business Ethics* (Malden, Mass.: Blackwell, 1999).

22. Sandra Rosenthal and Rogene Bucholz, "Toward New Directions in Business Ethics: Some Pragmatic Pathways," in *A Companion to Business Ethics*, ed. Robert Frederick (Malden, Mass.: Blackwell, 1999), 112.

23. Rosenthal and Bucholz, "Toward New Directions," 113.

24. Rosenthal and Bucholz, "Toward New Directions," 112.

25. Thus nonhierarchical moral pluralists would reject Michael Jensen's call for developing simple single objectives for business managers, because of the fact that they can be algorithmically captured and the results quantitatively measured. See "Value Maximization, Stakeholder Theory, and the Corporate Objective Function," *Business Ethics Quarterly* 12, no. 2 (April 2002): 235.

26. Peter French, *Corporate Ethics* (Fort Worth, Tex.: Harcourt Brace, 1995).

27. Rosenthal and Bucholz, "Toward New Directions."

28. For a nice discussion of how modern cognitive science may illuminate non-algorithmic accounts of moral decision making, see Larry May, Marilyn Friedman, and Andy Clark, eds., *Mind and Morals* (Cambridge, Mass.: MIT Press, 1996).

29. For more in-depth analysis of Ross's generalism, see Jonathan Dancy, *Moral Reasons* (Oxford, UK: Blackwell, 1993).

30. Dancy, *Moral Reasons*.

31. Another feature that many suppose to be always morally relevant and relevant in the same way is the feature of human life (i.e., being alive). However, many intuitively see how being alive could be silenced or reversed in cases where the quality of life is such as to make it an evil or silenced by the suffering to be avoided. Hence, even with a morally relevant feature as important as life, we may find the plausibility of silencing and reversal.

32. For other examples, see Dancy, *Moral Reasons*, and David McNaughton, *Moral Vision: An Introduction to Ethics* (New York: Basil Blackwell, 1988).

33. See McKeever and Ridge, *Principled Ethics*.

34. Another alternative is of the following character: Alan Donagan, *The Theory of Morality* (Chicago: University of Chicago Press, 1977); Onora O'Neill, *Towards Justice and Virtue: A Constructive Account of Practical Reasoning* (New York: Cambridge University Press, 1996); and Audi, *The Good in the Right* have all suggested that the values captured in moral principles (usually of the supremely general variety such as the respect for persons) are not usefully definable in necessary and sufficient application conditions and, thus, they are context sensitive and open to interpretation

in moral decision making. The anti-theorist would welcome this type of move, because either one could easily question to what extent these kinds of principles do any work in explaining morality in ways sought by generalists, or one could claim that these theorists must be admitting to a kind of theory that abandons generalism.

35. See J. L. Mackie, *Ethics: Inventing Right and Wrong* (New York: Penguin Books, 1977).

36. See McKeever and Ridge, *Principled Ethics.*

37. Dancy, *Ethics without Principles.*

38. I think of Dancy's thought here as being much like the new riddle of induction: Although in our experience all emeralds we've experienced to date have been green, this cannot rule out that they are grue. The same could be said of morally relevant features: Although, in our experience, some act X has always been morally right, we cannot rule out a time at which it is silenced or reversed.

Chapter Nine

Values and Capitalism

Christopher Michaelson, University of St. Thomas

The defining terms of contemporary business ethics set up a conflict between two forms of value, economic and ethical. "Business ethics," "business and society," "social issues in management," "corporate financial performance vs. corporate social performance," "stakeholders vs. stockholders," "corporate responsibility," and "corporate citizenship," among other terms, each, fundamentally, pair an ethical interest with an economic modifier (or vice versa).[1] This tension is set forth in the work of contemporary free market economists, like Milton Friedman, to which the contemporary field of business ethics is a response. Free market economists, broadly speaking, suggest that economic value is the only form of value that matters (or the primary form of value in terms of which other forms of value can be measured), and in their work, business ethics tends to have the status of an uninvited guest that needs swiftly to be shown the door. Friedman, in his often-quoted "The Social Responsibility of Business Is to Increase Its Profits,"[2] seeks as much as possible to obviate the conflict by suggesting that the principal ethical duty of managers is to increase profit in support of owners' economic interests. His opponents, also to speak in broad terms, contend that certain ethical obligations are uncompromising and that legitimate economic activity must balance economic and ethical value. The point where they meet, which also is the fundamental point of conflict, is where alleged market imperfections warrant consideration of a moderating force to correct for the imbalance between economic and ethical value. It is on this point where the business ethics debate focuses—whether seeking to weigh relative values, to achieve confluence between them, or to define the tolerance for variation without upsetting the balance. The debate is characterized by its defining terms, notwithstanding the breadth and importance of each topic to the human good, as a two-dimensional debate.

But why should we place disproportionate emphasis upon ethics as a unique form of value, competing for attention with economic interest in free market capitalism? In practice, our judgments about the value of economic activity, even our ethical judgments, betray sensitivity to and awareness of aesthetic value. For example, in the familiar tradeoff between quantity and quality of production, the former is typically measured according to economic indicators (e.g., units of production, dollar value), whereas the latter can as easily be cast as an aesthetic issue (e.g., craftsmanship, absence of quality defects) or as an ethical issue (e.g., product safety, value to the customer). Moreover, in the course of product design and production, tradeoffs are routinely contemplated that involve a delicate balance between economic, aesthetic, and ethical interests. For instance, think of the automobile industry's standard of three-pointed seat-belts as safer than two-pointed but more aesthetically palatable and less (economically) costly to the consumer than the six-pointed type that race car drivers wear, or the debates between skyscraper architects and engineers over the relative placement of emergency stairwells and elevator shafts in consideration of quantity of square footage and the quality of continuous interior space.

One way to answer the question that I pose in the previous paragraph is that "we should not," and to suggest that aesthetic value belongs in a different conversation than the one about business ethics, which we could call "business aesthetics." If we were to settle for that answer, I think we would quickly reach the conclusion, needing only the examples above, that to isolate consideration of economic and aesthetic value from other forms of value (particularly ethical) would be to leave out an important part of the conversation. That is to say that the tradeoffs and balances to be achieved between economic and aesthetic value have important ethical implications that cannot be ignored. Likewise for economic and ethical conflicts that have aesthetic implications and even aesthetic and ethical conflicts with economic implications. The path, therefore, that this chapter explores is how our ethical judgments about business might be influenced by the consideration of aesthetic value as a form of value related but not reducible to economic or ethical value.

We might also ask why aesthetics warrants special attention as an alternative form of value that deserves consideration in the ethics and economics debate. After all, there are many possible taxonomies of value, none of them universally accepted, and many other "pluralistic" accounts of value that assert that value judgments are complex and not reducible to one common unit of measure.[3] The reasons for this chapter's emphasis on aesthetic value are that, first, in contemporary philosophical value theory, ethics and aesthetics are the principal value classifications; second, and perhaps not coincidentally, aesthetic value has established tensions with questions of both economic and ethical value that suggest that it is often neither possible nor desirable to isolate or even distinguish them from one another.

Aesthetic value has not been given formal attention within the standard terms of a business ethics debate that has gone on informally for millennia (see, for example, Confucius' teachings on the hierarchy of professions, or Aristotle's discomfort with usury). This debate has its contemporary roots in the Friedmanesque property conception of the firm, which is a product of Western markets and corporate ownership structures and does not seem to make space for formal consideration of aesthetic value. In another sense, however, this interest in the "beauty of capitalism," as we are prone to say when it works well, is not at all new. In *The Wealth of Nations*, Adam Smith's delight at the eighteen-step pin manufacturing process (a process that has elicited disapproval from ethicists[4]) is reminiscent of his contemporary David Hume's analogy of nature and a clock, in which Hume infers the existence of a divine being from the systematic functioning of nature. Both philosophers in these passages are primarily awed by the order of the world left alone, though whereas Hume was apprehending the natural world around us, Smith was apprehending the world of human industry and inferring the existence of an invisible hand. Indeed, there is something beautifully abstract about the ideal of confluence between market supply and demand, of human needs being satisfied by market forces, of innovation and creativity transforming today's wants into tomorrow's solutions, of a self-regulating system balancing the interests of producers and consumers in synchronicity with the interests of the sources and destinations of their productivity and consumption around them—a harmony which, Mark Taylor asserts, Smith transported from aesthetics for economics.[5] Our awe at the beauty of capitalism implies a sort of pleasure analogous to our experience of the natural world or of a well-tempered clavier, the sort of pleasure that in contemporary theory and society is often associated with an aesthetic point of view. From this point of view, it is not a mistake that Smith frequently refers to "manufacture" and "art" in the same sentence or as mutual substitutes, nor that the object of efficient capitalism is "opulence" and "luxury" that has value beyond its economic quotient.

1. THE CASE OF THE THREE GORGES DAM

The two-dimensional debate between ethics and economics has much in common with a two-dimensional debate between aesthetics and economics. In this latter debate, aesthetics theorists (accompanied by starving artists) blame

inefficient market forces for failing to price the products of aesthetic endeavor commensurate with their intrinsic value. Whereas the object of ethical
endeavor is typically characterized as "the good," the object of aesthetic endeavor is typically characterized as "the beautiful." Just as the good often
seems to have an economic price that sadly needs to be paid if one has the
moral strength to pursue it for its own sake, so the beautiful often must be its
own reward, since its instrumental value is often not commensurate with its
beauty. This claim that the market fails to price beauty efficiently can be extended further to nature, insofar as its value to commercial enterprise due to
its resource abundance (oil, minerals, timber, water, etc.) is often a source of
tension between industrialists and preservationists. The self-interest that is often blamed for business ethics failure also clouds aesthetic judgment when
there is measurable economic benefit from clear-cutting ancient forests,
drilling through glaciers, and prospecting amid inconveniently located coral
reefs. The argument for the preservation of the natural environment has emphasized ethical obligation to animals and to future generations of human beings, but there also is an argument that nature, irrespective of the moral rights
of its living, feeling organisms, has rights to its own pristine serenity simply
because it is nature, which has value irrespective of other considerations in
view of its natural beauty.

Take, for example, the case of the Three Gorges Dam in the Yangtze River
Valley, a project that exemplifies rational economic deliberation to many of
its promoters and detractors alike. The dam, which was to be completed more
than fifty years after the idea was first endorsed by Mao Zedong in 1958, was
designed to create unprecedented hydroelectric power generation capacity[6]
for the world's most populous country, whose economic growth and associated energy demand are perhaps the most exciting and concerning economic
story of the twenty-first century. Although a product of the world's oldest
continuous civilization, critics of the Three Gorges Dam project have characterized it as a vain project driven by new money—that is, the bias of the nou-
veau riche for anything that is new at the expense of objects of long-standing
value not of their own creation. In other words, critics of the project cast it in
the familiar terms of short-term (economic) versus long-term (ethical) value.

The most obvious benefit of constructing the dam is the economic value of
more power generation to service more individual and industrial consumers
who are propelling further economic growth. The most obvious cost of the
project is often framed primarily as an ethical concern: the displacement of
more than one million Yangtze River Valley residents whose homes and land
would be forever submerged under a reservoir filled with billions of cubic
meters of water. It is alleged that in the minds of generations of Chinese
politicians who have supported the project, there is enthusiasm for the cause

of economic growth and insensitivity to the lives of the displaced residents, many of whom have protested that their material compensation is inadequate or that there could be no such thing as adequate material compensation. In the minds of critics, this apparently utilitarian calculation does not compute. The problem with rational economic deliberation, to these ethicists, is that its goods are incommensurable with ethical goods with which economic goods compete.

In fact, the debate over the Three Gorges Dam is much more complex than the two-dimensional debate between the economic value of power generation gained and the ethical value of ways of life lost. In general, decisions about environmental management rarely pose a simple, two-dimensional dilemma between ethics and economics; rather, each of multiple alternative solutions typically has complex implications for ethics, economics, and other stakeholder preferences.[7] In this case, that complexity includes the fact that, ethical costs notwithstanding, there are significant ethical benefits to be gained as a result of building the dam. These include safer river navigation, better protection against catastrophic floods (such as the one in 1954 that was the original catalyst for the idea), and reduced pollution (hydropower is a far cleaner energy source than coal, which in China, as elsewhere, is one of the primary concerns of those seeking to mitigate the environmental and social costs of climate change). Are the rational economic actors who approved the dam simply insensitive to that which cannot be measured in economic terms? Perhaps not; it is possible that they just choose to emphasize the ethical benefits over the ethical costs. Sometimes economic value can be argued to be ethical, as in the case of a nation seeking to lift hundreds of millions of its citizens from relative poverty to a new middle class, from a pyramid to a pear-shaped economy.

This kind of vision or achievement can also be argued to be beautiful. Aesthetic disinterestedness, which has been the dominant notion characterizing the prevailing aesthetic attitude in contemporary Western philosophy, is indifferent to the sort of desire that motivates economic measures of value which ethical measures of value are supposed to constrain. Disinterestedness is the condition of being free from interests that would impair one's status as a fair and impartial judge of artistic and natural value, and is fundamental to the dominant contemporary theory and practice of aesthetic judgment. It is the reason why we applaud between symphony movements while not milling about as they are played. It is also behind the practice of hanging paintings in the quietude of eggshell museum walls so as to eliminate extraneous influences on our perception, much as a contemporary ethical point of view involves retreating to careful consideration of the facts irrespective of one's personal interest in those facts. An extreme version of disinterestedness has been the basis for the "art for art's sake" movement that asserts that art is an end in itself, which if pure must not be pursued or judged in view of any other ends. In this sense, disinterestedness is the aesthetic analogue of moral impartiality, which has been held—not without controversy, but most commonly in business ethics theory and practice—to be fundamental to sound ethical judgment in contemporary ethical theory.

One sort of disinterested pleasure that we could take in the Three Gorges Dam is the same kind of pleasure that market economists seem to derive from the smooth intersection of supply and demand. From this perspective, we might be awed by the audacious courage of politicians willing to take on the resistance of millions of residents for the alleged broader benefit of society and the environment. Although courage is often taken to be a moral virtue, the vision and coordination required to accomplish such a courageous feat might well be perceived to be beautiful in its own way. Moreover, we might be astonished by the ability and precision of workers and machinery literally to move mountains, to take on one of the world's great rivers, taming and controlling it for human use. The utility of the river is not at all disinterested, but the logistical ballet of machinery and humanity required to vacate and then reinvent the Three Gorges site can be observed, disinterestedly, evoking wonder. One can easily argue that the officials responsible for the Three Gorges Dam have a highly refined aesthetic sensibility, that a proper object of economic activity can be the pursuit of the beautiful. "Proponents of the Three Gorges Dam, most notably the Chinese government, claim that, like the Great Wall of China, the Three Gorges will become the Great Dam of China—a symbol of human achievement and a source of national pride."[8] Indeed, aesthetics has often noted a tension between the ethical obligation of human beings to leave nature undisturbed and the aesthetic significance of our ability to shape our natural surroundings to serve our practical, symbolic, and aesthetic ends. When the United States was proving its prowess as an economic leader in the twentieth century, it aggressively sought to symbolize that prowess in the form of its skyscrapers; this led to the famous legend of the architect of the Chrysler Building, who hid the spire in the elevator shaft in order to outwit his competition in the race for the title of world's tallest only to be supplanted a year later with the completion of the Empire State Building. Since the end of the twentieth century, it has been Asian cities that have competed for the world's tallest building, demonstrating the continuing importance of aesthetic symbolism as an indicator of economic dominance.

As with the complexity of the ethical debate over the Three Gorges Dam, it is possible to argue for and against the project on aesthetic grounds. Whereas the ethical debate over the flooding of the Three Gorges highlights concern for the present and future lives that are being disrupted by the project, the aesthetic case against the project focuses on concern for the destruction of natural and cultural relics. The dam irreversibly and fundamentally transforms the appearance of the majestic Three Gorges—in fact, submerging those gorges under water—replacing them with a majesty of its own. But it is a different aesthetic that sees beauty in a gigantic human construction project instead of a product of geological evolution. This part of the aesthetic case against the dam argues against change, particularly avoidable human alteration of the natural environment, while another part of the aesthetic case argues against destruction, particularly, avoidable present destruction of past human achievement. In addition to the contemporary dwellings that are being lost, "the rising waters of the Yangtze . . . have also submerged more than 1,000 sites containing millennia-old cultural relics."[9] Although the origins of formal aesthetic theory, like those of ethical theory, have sought to identify a unitary object of endeavor (beauty or goodness), practical aesthetic reasoning, like practical ethics, has had to deal with the reality that there are competing notions of what is beautiful or good.

2. THE CASE OF GAUGUIN

When so-called economic rationality is deemed irrational by ethical theorists, often the charge is that it has failed to account for the value of long-term ethical considerations. This charge can be as easily levied against economic rationality by aesthetics theorists, with an interesting twist. Rather than always arguing that aesthetic value is undervalued by the market, they are more prone to suggest that the imperfect market we live with ascribes excessive volatility to the real value of art objects, particularly in the case of the human-made type. Martha Woodmansee[10] traces the formation of the aesthetic attitude in Western thought as a reaction to social change in the eighteenth century that "witnessed momentous changes in the production, distribution, and consumption of art." As the middle class expanded and the practice of elite patronage diminished, more artists came to depend on or be victimized by market demand as an imperfect economic measure of aesthetic value. Consumers' collective willingness to pay for something is not always, and perhaps is not often, a fair measure of its noneconomic value. Often, art objects are undervalued, but sometimes they are grossly overvalued. Consider, for example, the exceptional but familiar story of the artist whose genius is not fully appreciated by the market until his life is over, after which the limited supply of his production fetches auction prices as nearly irrational as the executive compensation the contemporary market throws at star chief executives. The main difference between their respective geniuses is their varying degrees of perceived quantifiability, though it has not been demonstrably proven that executive compensation is any more science than guesswork or, for that matter, art. In the tension here between art and science, qualitative measurement and quantitative measurement, we see again a familiar parallel in the tension between ethics and economics and the relative futility of applying accurate quantitative measures to ethical value over the long run.

One artist who would have benefited had he been able to trade during his lifetime in a futures market for his paintings was Paul Gauguin. In his story, we see even more vividly the perceived tradeoff that leads to our romanticized cliché of the starving artist who works for no money but for the love of his creation. This cliché is not unlike that of the religious servant, such as Mother Teresa or St. Francis of Assisi, who toils in deference to a greater good without regard for personal material interest (although we are likely to harbor a more compromised admiration for Gauguin than for a saint). The Gauguin legend, for effect, depicts as stark a contrast as possible between what we can term the "Market Gauguin"—a stockbroker who trudges to and from work, day after day, grudgingly supporting a wife and their children in a comfortable, upper-middle-class lifestyle—and the "Savage Gauguin"—the wild-eyed, burgeoning artist who one day breaks ranks with conformity and abandons his family for the South Seas, where he has barely enough discipline and energy between his laziness and sexual exploits to build a portfolio that contemporary critics contend ranks him as one of the founders of Modernism.[11] The Market Gauguin, competent enough at his vocation that he can envision a perfectly materially comfortable and most ordinary life ahead of him ("and therefore the most terrible," as Tolstoy would say), begins to take up his painting hobby in the evenings until it possesses him to become the Savage Gauguin. This is how the transformation is depicted in fictionalized representations of Gauguin's life by W. Somerset Maugham (*The Moon and Sixpence*), Mario Vargas Llosa (*The Way to Paradise*), and, for ethical analysis, Bernard Williams ("Moral Luck"), while such reputable biographers as Sweetman and Goldwater have tried in sympathy to depict Gauguin as more rational, less savage. Whereas the legend characterizes the Market Gauguin as a theretofore responsible family man who gives up on his other-regarding obligations to pursue self-interest, leaving both his family and himself economically destitute, his biographers demur. They paint a picture of a Gauguin torn between his tortured sense of responsibility to family and his love of painting, a genius artist who might otherwise have wasted away in the market had he not left it to become a savage, a father who intended to care through his second career for his family, driven to rage by a market that did not reward him and enable him to support his family, until it was too late.

The Gauguin story demonstrates the possibility that aesthetic and ethical value are sometimes incommensurable, as may be ethical and economic value. Let us set aside for our purposes the question of whether aesthetic and ethical value can be reduced to one or the other, and more specifically the question of whether Gauguin was morally irresponsible. (This question has garnered significant attention from ethical theorists and aesthetic theorists alike, many of them exploring whether Gauguin's ethical biography matters in the appraisal of his aesthetic production.[12]) The question of aesthetic and ethical dissonance would not arise if not first for the matter of aesthetic and economic dissonance which, arguably, forced Gauguin to choose—between professions, between locations, and, ultimately, between his family and his passion for painting. Had Gauguin not had to become a star artist in his own time in order to morally justify his career choice, had he rather been able to earn a respectable living in a European studio, enough to fund research excursions to the South Seas with reasonable assurance of being able to afford the way back again, he might not have been faced with the moral choices he made.

The best evidence of market imperfection when it comes to aesthetic production is the very market volatility that leads us disinterestedly to regard Gauguin's paintings on museum walls today, many decades after his death in destitution. Were it not for the fact that aesthetic production, seemingly victimized most of the time by undervaluation, was some of the time overvalued, the claim of market imperfection might have the tenor of bitterness. But market volatility for aesthetic objects points at least to a timing problem. Just as there is a timing problem in getting today's chief executives, whose average tenure is less than ten years, to solve such ethical problems as climate change, the time horizon of which is measured in decades and centuries, so there is a timing problem in rewarding today's artists commensurate with the aesthetic value of their work when considered judgment of that value may not be reliable until after their lifetimes have long passed by.

Certainly, Gauguin hoped that the market would recognize the value of his work in his lifetime, but he did not expect the market to do so. He was not, in the classic sense, a rational economic actor; he was willing to forgo economic rewards for aesthetic rewards if he had to choose, though of course he would have preferred not to have had to choose. Economic rationality, driven by material self-interest, is supposed to explain collective behavior, while reserving that there may be outliers such as Gauguin who resist the general tide, who are unsatisfied by market forces but who continue to act as they do even with ample evidence that their lack of material satisfaction will know no relief unless they acquiesce. Most of them will acquiesce, proving the predictive capacity of economic rationality to explain human behavior in terms of economic self-interest. While economic rationality therefore makes an exception for the peculiar minority whose interests are not predictable primarily in economic terms, it does not have a clear answer for why the market as a collective organism exhibits irrationally volatile behavior in its attempt to price aesthetic production in economic terms.

Not that Gauguin was not self-interested; by most legendary accounts, he was not only self-interested but appallingly so, abandoning his family in Europe and then fathering children in his new home for whom he did not provide any care. Gauguin's self-interest was even material in that sense of being physical, but he cared less for the material comforts that were aided by economic well-being than for the savage pleasures that give his paintings that characteristically primitive appearance. Gauguin might be a rare character in history, but he is less rare than the stereotypical economic man or moral saint who are driven singly or even primarily by one form of value. He was quite common in experiencing human conflicts of values that ultimately led him to what Martha Nussbaum calls "tragic conflict,"[13] regarding which it is impossible to satisfy either one of two (or more) competing, legitimate forms of value without making a tragic sacrifice of the other(s). As much as Gauguin can be construed to be the paradigm of self-interest, he is also in another sense paradigmatically disinterested, uniquely driven by aesthetic ends, unconcerned with the material impact on his economic and physical well-being as long as he was producing aesthetic value.

3. AESTHETICS AND CAPITALIST VALUES

Until this point, this chapter has set forth two main points through the Three Gorges Dam and Gauguin examples. The Three Gorges Dam example demonstrates how aesthetic value emerges as an alternative form of value that may be seen by differently interested parties to compete or concur with ethical and economic value in decisions how scarce resources should be allocated. This example also illustrates the common challenges in defending aesthetic and ethical value, which resist direct quantification, against economic arguments. While the Three Gorges Dam example suggests that different perspectives on aesthetic and ethical value do not always lead us to the same preferences, the Gauguin example more starkly demonstrates that there are cases in which aesthetic and ethical value may be seen to compete with one another. In the standard interpretation of the Gauguin example, in fact, Gauguin's renunciation of his economic obligations to his family constituted an ethical failure that rendered considerable aesthetic benefits unto humanity in general.

These examples may demonstrate how aesthetics might complicate the two-dimensional debate between ethics and economics, but the important question is whether aesthetics constructively contributes to a broader debate about what is valuable in business and in human life. Although it has been argued by Western theorists that art that is of any value is necessarily moral (by the late Tolstoy renouncing the production of the early Tolstoy), that art cultivates moral sensitivity (by Aristotle as interpreted by Nussbaum), and that beauty is a symbol of morality (by Kant as interpreted by Guyer), the Three Gorges Dam and Gauguin examples show that it is by no means a consensus view that aesthetic value necessarily supports ethical value. Not only is the proper aesthetic conclusion a matter of contention among aesthetics theorists, but there is also debate about whether there is such a thing that can be distinguished as an aesthetic attitude or point of view[14]—that is, whether disinterestedness is possible, and if it is, whether aesthetic disinterestedness is something unique and deserving of our attention. We might ask, therefore, how things might have turned out differently, with the Three Gorges Dam and Gauguin, with a different aesthetic point of view.

The first answer we are forced to consider is the possibility that they might not have turned out differently at all. Take, for example, the Three Gorges Dam, and the objective of mastering nature. We might take this objective to have aesthetic value insofar as corralling the wild river for human use inspires an appreciation that transcends the instrumental value that human beings gain from the project. The ability to manipulate the world around us in ways that are not immediately apparent to the observer of the finished product has awed human beings throughout history; as much as we admire such ancient structures as the Great Pyramids, the Easter Island statues, and the Great Wall for their aesthetic appearance, we study them further to understand how those who erected them overcame the practical challenges posed by natural obstacles. Like the Three Gorges Dam, all of these examples had unglamorous goals characteristic of large public infrastructure projects. The combination of technological inventiveness and human will necessary to construct them is analogous to the qualities required to support our contemporary obsession with the skyscraper, and the status conferred upon the city or country where the tallest ones reside.

But recall the terms of the aesthetic debate over the Three Gorges Dam— whether the symbolic aesthetic value that the dam shares with other large-scale construction efforts is of greater value than, and therefore warranting the sacrifice of, competing forms of aesthetic value. Those competing forms include the natural (environmental) aesthetic value that preexisted the project, along with the aesthetic value of the cultural relics that have been submerged. We know that a vigorous global public debate has taken place on this question, but we do not know how seriously the policy makers who made the decision to proceed with destruction have taken the alternatives. Moreover, we would be hard pressed to quantify how much weight aesthetic symbolism has played in the overall case for the dam, considering that it has been far from the only justification for the project. It is reasonable to wonder, in a case like this where there is so much practically to gain or lose, whether disinterested attention is even possible or desirable—a key point of aesthetic skeptics who question the possibility of an aesthetic attitude. We might contend, rather, that instead of being a reflection of disinterested attention, that aesthetic preferences reflect the interests of those who have them—an individual, a group, or a society. Notably, the foremost critics of the Three Gorges Dam have been those whose material interests are most directly affected by the project—those who were displaced, an important but hardly disinterested constituency. They have been joined by those on the outside looking in from more technologically and economically developed markets whose societies underwent similar debates in years past (whether about hydroelectric power, coal-fired energy, or the continuing debate about drilling for fossil fuels in the Arctic). In this case, the preferences expressed by the political elites responsible for the decision to go forward with the project reflect values of policy makers that emphasize technological access, material productivity, and symbolic achievement—ethical, economic, and aesthetic values.

Another answer to the question of whether a different aesthetic attitude could have made a difference therefore emphasizes the value of aesthetics as an antidote to pure economic rationality. An aesthetic point of view opens up the possibility that reclaiming supposedly primitive, "savage" values should instead be considered cultural progress. From this perspective, we might examine the relative priority of values—economic, ethical, and aesthetic—and find decision makers' world views worthy of reexamination. Here, Gauguin finds an ally in those ancient Chinese landscapes admired by traditionalist elders for whom the triumvirate of painting, poetry, and calligraphy were the highest forms of activity. From this extreme, in which aesthetic values predominate, the economic benefits of the Three Gorges Dam are harder to defend, posing those difficult ethical questions about the trade-offs of power generation for preservation. We cannot imagine a policy stance in which natural and cultural relics are altogether inviolable, for this would prohibit human activity completely. It is possible, though, to imagine a policy against destruction on as massive a scale as that which has taken place in the Three Gorges, in which the hills and gorges might instead have been set aside as parkland and in which historic status might have been conferred upon the existing and past neighborhoods. However, such changes in policy stance are not made without consequences; the prioritization of economic productivity above ethical displacement of human lives and aesthetic preservationist values would have sweeping consequences for a country's growth ambitions. Can we even imagine how things might have been different if Gauguin had another path than the extreme solution he found to his professional frustration? Any alternative would have had catastrophic consequences for his legacy as an artist, and we would be left to reconstruct a century-plus of Modernism without his influence. The husband and father that his family regained in this scenario would hardly resemble at all the Gauguin we have come to know through the legend. Because of the sacrifice that Gauguin inflicted upon his family, our contemporary museums are blessed with his depiction through Western-trained eyes of the peaceful existence of the South Seas "savage."

It is intellectually convenient to cast these examples as debates between capitalist and conservationist values in the case of the dam and selfish and selfless values in the case of Gauguin. But in fact these debates are not about a static set of capitalist economic values in tension with ethics; rather, they are about differing views on what values, in what proportions, expressing what preferences, belong in the market. Exploring these values, beyond the two-dimensional tension between economics and ethics that they pose, is particularly important in a twenty-first century that is poised to see Asian economies ascend to a position of economic dominance enjoyed by North American and European economies for the past several centuries. It is important for us to recognize this change as portending not only a change in the relative balance of economic fortunes but also of cultural influence. What impact will this change have on the relative priority of values that compose what the world's most economically dominant societies prescribe to be good living? How will tomorrow's dominant economic actors pressure today's leaders to conform to their view of how much work, what kind of work, and what sorts of other priorities matter? What reflects more advanced capitalist values—the ability to harness the savage river, and one's inner savage, to produce the goods that are economically necessary to materially support one's people, and one's family—or the ability to appreciate that the beauty in the seemingly savage might reflect a more advanced sensibility about values than our comparatively simple economic and ethical constructs allow, giving us pause about our dependence upon economic measures of performance that seem to be the source of so much ethical tension? Do Gauguin's paintings seem to communicate from the developed economic power to the emerging market, that you should not aspire to be more like me, but rather I should aspire to be more like you?

NOTES

1. Although economic value is seen to be fundamental to the practical existence of the free market, in the parlance of business ethics—which was developed by ethicists, not economists—economic adjectives more often tend to modify ethical nouns. Even

with the so-called "triple bottom line," social and environmental objectives are grouped as "ethical" in contrast to the third category of economic objectives.

2. Milton Friedman, "The Social Responsibility of Business Is to Increase Its Profits," *New York Times Magazine*, 13 September 1970.

3. On values pluralism, see, for example, Isaiah Berlin, *Concepts and Categories* (London: Hogarth, 1978); Bernard Williams, *Ethics and the Limits of Philosophy* (Cambridge, Mass.: Harvard University Press, 1985); Martha Nussbaum, *Love's Knowledge: Essays on Philosophy and Literature* (New York: Oxford University Press, 1990); and Elizabeth Anderson, *Value in Ethics and Economics* (Cambridge, Mass.: Harvard University Press, 1993). More specifically on the connection between aesthetics and ethics, see Marcia Muelder Eaton, *Merit, Aesthetic and Ethical* (New York: Oxford University Press, 2001), and Jerrold Levinson, ed., *Aesthetics and Ethics: Essays at the Intersection* (New York: Cambridge University Press, 1998).

4. See, for example, Judith Schwartz, "Meaningful Work," *Ethics* 92, no. 4 (July 1982): 634–46.

5. Mark C. Taylor, *Confidence Games: Money and Markets in a World without Redemption* (Chicago: University of Chicago Press, 2004).

6. Dai Qing and Lawrence R. Sullivan, "The Three Gorges Dam and China's Energy Dilemma," *Journal of International Affairs* 53, no. 1 (Fall 1999): 56–57.

7. Mark Sagoff, "Do Non-Native Species Threaten the Environment?" *Journal of Agricultural and Environmental Ethics* 18 (2005): 215–36.

8. Manik Suri, "A River in Peril: The Waters Rise at Three Gorges," *Harvard International Review* 25, no. 3 (Fall 2003): 10.

9. Suri, "River in Peril," 11.

10. Martha Woodmansee, *The Author, Art, and the Market: Rereading the History of Aesthetics* (New York: Columbia University Press, 1994), 22.

11. Arthur Danto, "Paul Gauguin," in *Encounters and Reflections: Art in the Historical Present* (New York: Farrar, Straus and Giroux, 1990), 187.

12. For example, Michael Slote, *Goods and Virtues* (Oxford, UK: Clarendon Press, 1983); Owen Flanagan, "Admirable Immorality and Admirable Imperfection," *Journal of Philosophy* 83 (1986): 41–60; and Marcia Baron, "On Admirable Immorality," *Ethics* 96 (1986): 557–66.

13. Martha Nussbaum, *The Fragility of Goodness* (New York: Cambridge University Press, 1986), 25.

14. See, for example, George Dickie's retort ("All Aesthetic Attitude Theories Fail: The Myth of the Aesthetic Attitude") to Jerome Stolnitz ("The Aesthetic Attitude") and the Kantian aesthetic tradition in George Dickie, Richard Sclafani, and Ronald Roblin, eds., *Aesthetics: A Critical Anthology* (New York: St. Martin's Press, 1989).

Bibliography

Ackerman, Bruce. *Social Justice in the Liberal State*. New Haven, Conn.: Yale University Press, 1980.

Aguilera, Ruth, and Gregory Jackson. "The Cross-National Diversity of Corporate Governance: Dimensions and Determinants." *Academy of Management Review* 28 (June 2003): 447–65.

Akaah, I., and E. Riordan. "Judgments of Professionals about Ethical Issues in Marketing Research: A Replication and Extension." *Journal of Marketing Research* 26, no. 1 (1989): 112–20.

Akerlof, George, and Janet Yellen, eds. *Efficiency Wage Models of the Labor Market*. New York: Cambridge University Press, 1986.

Anderson, Elizabeth. *Value in Ethics and Economics*. Cambridge, Mass.: Harvard University Press, 1993.

Andriof, Jorg, Sandra Waddock, Bryan Husted, and Sutherland Rahman, eds. *Unfolding Stakeholder Thinking*. Vols. 1 and 2. Sheffield, UK: Greenleaf, 2003.

Anshen, Melvin. *Corporate Strategies for Social Performance*. London: MacMillan, 1980.

Aristotle. *Nicomachean Ethics*. Edited by Terence Irwin. Indianapolis, Ind.: Hackett, 1999.

Arneson, Richard. "Egalitarianism and the Undeserving Poor." *Journal of Political Philosophy* 5, no. 4 (December 1997): 327–50.

Arnold, Denis G. *The Ethics of Global Business*. Malden, Mass.: Blackwell, forthcoming.

Arnold, N. Scott. "Why Profits Are Deserved." *Ethics* 97, no. 2 (January 1987): 387–402.

Audi, Robert. *The Good in the Right: A Theory of Intuition and Intrinsic Value*. Princeton, N.J.: Princeton University Press, 2004.

——. *Moral Value and Human Diversity*. New York: Oxford University Press, 2007.

——. *Practical Reasoning and Ethical Decision*. New York: Routledge, 2006.

Barney, Jay, and Mark Hansen. "Trustworthiness as a Source of Competitive Advantage." *Strategic Management Journal* 15 (1994): 175–91.

Baron, Marcia. "On Admirable Immorality." *Ethics* 96 (1986): 557–66.

Barry, Brian. *Justice as Impartiality.* Oxford, UK: Clarendon, 1995.

———. *Theories of Justice.* London: Harvester-Wheatsheaf, 1989.

Baumhart, R. "Problems in Review: How Ethical Are Businessmen?" *Harvard Business Review* 39, no. 4 (1961): 6–9.

Bayles, Michael D. "Moral Theory and Application." *Social Theory and Practice* 10 (1984): 97–120.

Baynes, Kenneth. "Democracy and the Rechtstaat: Habermas's *Faktizitaet und Geltung*." In *The Cambridge Companion to Habermas*, edited by Stephen White, 201–32. New York: Cambridge University Press, 1994.

———. *The Normative Grounds of Social Criticism: Kant, Rawls, and Habermas.* Albany: SUNY Press, 1992.

———. "Rational Reconstruction and Social Criticism: Habermas's Model of Interpretive Social Science." *Philosophical Forum* 21 (1989): 122–45.

Beadle, R. "The Misappropriation of MacIntyre." *Reason in Practice* 2, no. 2 (2002): 45–54.

Beadle, R., and G. Moore. "MacIntyre on Virtue and Organization." *Organization Studies* 27, no. 3 (2006): 323–40.

Beauchamp, Tom, and Norman Bowie. *Ethical Theory and Business.* 6th ed. Upper Saddle River, N.J.: Prentice Hall, 2001.

Berlin, Isaiah. *Concepts and Categories.* London: Hogarth, 1978.

Blair, Margaret M. *Ownership and Control: Rethinking Corporate Governance for the Twenty-First Century.* Washington, D.C.: Brookings, 1995.

Blair, Margaret M., and Thomas Kochan, eds. *The New Relationship: Human Capital in the American Corporation.* Washington, D.C.: Brookings, 2000.

Blair, Margaret M., and Lynn Stout. "A Team Production Theory of Corporate Law." *Virginia Law Review* 84 (March 1999): 247–328.

Bloom, Matt. "The Ethics of Compensation Systems." *Journal of Business Ethics* 52, no. 2 (June 2004): 149–52.

Boatright, John R. "Business Ethics and the Theory of the Firm." *American Business Law Journal* 34 (1996): 217–38.

———. "Does Business Ethics Rest on a Mistake?" *Business Ethics Quarterly* 9, no. 4 (1999): 583–91.

———. *Ethics in Finance.* Malden, Mass.: Blackwell, 1999.

———. "What's Wrong—and What's Right—with Stakeholder Theory." *Journal of Private Enterprise* 21, no. 2 (2006): 106–30.

Boucher, David, and Paul Kelly, eds. *The Social Contract from Hobbes to Rawls.* London: Routledge, 1994.

Bowie, Norman E. *The Blackwell Guide to Business Ethics.* Malden, Mass.: Blackwell, 2002.

———. *Business Ethics: A Kantian Perspective.* Malden, Mass.: Blackwell, 1999.

———. "The Firm as a Moral Community." In *Morality, Rationality, and Efficiency: New Perspectives on Socio-Economics*, edited by Richard Coughlin, 169–83. Armonk, N.Y.: M. E. Sharpe, 1991.

Brenkert, George G. "Marketing to Inner-City Blacks: PowerMaster and Moral Responsibility." *Business Ethics Quarterly* 8, no. 1 (1998): 1–18.

Brenner, S., and E. Molander. "Is the Ethics of Business Changing?" *Harvard Business Review* 55, no. 1 (1977): 57–71.

Bromiley, Philip, and Larry Cummings. "Organizations with Trust." In *Research in Negotiation*, edited by R. J. Lewicki, B. H. Sheppard, and R. Bies, 219–47. Greenwich, Conn.: JAI Press, 1995.

Brown, Marvin T. *Corporate Integrity: Rethinking Organizational Ethics and Leadership*. New York: Cambridge University Press, 2005.

Calton, Jerry, and Lawrence Lad. "Social Contracting as a Trust-Building Process of Network Governance." *Business Ethics Quarterly* 5 (1995): 271–95.

Cartwright, Nancy. *How the Laws of Physics Lie*. New York: Oxford University Press, 1983.

Chami, Ralph, and Connel Fullerkamp. "Trust and Efficiency." *Journal of Banking and Finance* 26 (2002): 1785–1809.

Child, James, and Alexei Marcoux. "Freeman and Evan: Stakeholder Theory in the Original Position." *Business Ethics Quarterly* 9, no. 2 (1999): 207–23.

Christman, John. "Entrepreneurs, Profits, and Deserving Market Shares." *Social Philosophy and Policy* 6, no. 1 (Autumn 1988): 1–16.

Clark, Barry, and Herbert Gintis. "Rawlsian Justice and Economic Systems." *Philosophy and Public Affairs* 7, no. 4 (1978): 302–25.

Clarkson Centre for Business Ethics. "Principles of Stakeholder Management." *Business Ethics Quarterly* 12, no. 2 (2002): 257–64.

Coase, Ronald. "The Nature of the Firm." *Economica* 4, no. 16 (1937): 386–405.

Cohen, G. A. *If You're an Egalitarian, How Come You're So Rich?* Cambridge, Mass.: Harvard University Press, 2000.

——. "Incentives, Inequality, and Community." In *The Tanner Lectures on Human Values*. Vol. 13, edited by Grethe Peterson, 265–329. Salt Lake City: University of Utah Press, 1992.

——. "On the Currency of Egalitarian Justice." *Ethics* 99, no. 4 (July 1989): 906–44.

——. "The Pareto Argument for Inequality." *Social Philosophy and Policy* 12, no. 1 (1995): 160–85.

——. "Where the Action Is: On the Site of Distributive Justice." *Philosophy and Public Affairs* 26, no. 1 (1997): 3–30.

Cohen, Joshua. "The Economic Basis for Deliberative Democracy." *Social Philosophy and Policy* 6, no. 2 (1989): 25–50.

——. "Taking People As They Are?" *Philosophy and Public Affairs* 30, no. 4 (2001): 361–86.

Cupit, Geoffrey. *Justice as Fittingness*. Oxford, UK: Clarendon Press, 1996.

Cyert, Richard M., and James March. *A Behavioral Theory of the Firm*. 2nd ed. 1963; Oxford, UK: Blackwell, 1992.

D'Agostino, Fred. *Free Public Reason: Making It Up As We Go*. New York: Oxford University Press, 1996.

Dahl, Robert. *A Preface to Economic Democracy*. Berkeley: University of California Press, 1985.

Dancy, Jonathan. *Ethics without Principles*. New York: Oxford University Press, 2004.

———. *Moral Reasons*. Oxford, UK: Blackwell, 1993.

Daniels, Norman. "Merit and Meritocracy." *Philosophy and Public Affairs* 7, no. 3 (Spring 1978): 206–23.

———, ed. *Reading Rawls: Critical Studies on Rawls's* A Theory of Justice. Stanford, Calif.: Stanford University Press, 1989.

Danto, Arthur. "Paul Gauguin." In *Encounters and Reflections: Art in the Historical Present*. New York: Farrar, Straus & Giroux, 1990.

DesJardins, Joseph. "Virtues and Business Ethics." In *An Introduction to Business Ethics*, edited by G. Chryssides and J. Kaler, 136–42. London: Chapman and Hall, 1993.

Dick, James. "How to Justify a Distribution of Earnings." *Philosophy and Public Affairs* 4, no. 3 (Spring 1975): 248–72.

Dickie, George, Richard Sclafani, and Ronald Roblin, eds. *Aesthetics: A Critical Anthology*. New York: St. Martin's, 1989.

Dienhart, John. *Business, Institutions, and Ethics: A Text with Cases and Readings*. New York: Oxford University Press, 2000.

DiMaggio, P., and W. Powell. "The Iron Cage Revisited: Institutional Isomorphism and Collective Rationality in Organizational Fields." *American Sociological Review* 48, no. 2 (1983): 147–60.

Dobson, J. "The Feminist Firm: A Comment." *Business Ethics Quarterly* 6, no. 2 (1996): 227–32.

———. "MacIntyre's Position on Business: A Response to Wicks." *Business Ethics Quarterly* 7, no. 4 (1997): 125–32.

Dodd, E. "For Whom Are Corporate Managers Trustees?" *Harvard Law Review* 45, no. 7 (1932): 1145–63.

Donagan, Alan. *The Theory of Morality*. Chicago: University of Chicago Press, 1977.

Donaldson, Thomas. *Corporations and Morality*. Englewood Cliffs, N.J.: Prentice Hall, 1982.

———. *The Ethics of International Business*. New York: Oxford University Press, 1989.

Donaldson, Thomas, and Thomas W. Dunfee. "Précis for *Ties That Bind*." *Business and Society Review* 105 (2000): 436–43.

———. "Securing the Ties That Bind: A Response to Commentators." *Business and Society Review* 105 (2000): 480–92.

———. *Ties That Bind: A Social Contracts Approach to Business Ethics*. Cambridge, Mass.: Harvard Business School Press, 1999.

Donaldson, Thomas, Patricia Werhane, and Joseph Van Zandt. *Ethical Issues in Business: A Philosophical Approach*. 8th ed. Upper Saddle River, N.J.: Prentice Hall, 2008.

Donnely, Jack. "Human Rights and Asian Values: A Defense of 'Western' Universalism." In *The East Asian Challenge for Human Rights*, edited by Joanne R. Bauer and Daniel A. Bell, 60–87. New York: Cambridge University Press, 1999.

Doris, J. *Lack of Character: Personality and Moral Behaviour*. New York: Cambridge University Press, 2002.

Drucker, Peter. *The Practice of Management*. London: Heinemann, 1956.

Dunfee, Thomas. "Do Firms with Unique Competencies for Rescuing Victims of Human Catastrophes Have Special Obligations?" *Business Ethics Quarterly* 16 (2005): 185–210.

———. "Extant Social Contracts." *Business Ethics Quarterly* 1 (1991): 23–52.

Dunfee, Thomas, and Thomas Donaldson. "Book Review Dialogue: Tightening the Ties That Bind; Defending a Contractarian Approach to Business Ethics." *American Business Law Journal* 37 (2000): 579–85.

Dworkin, Gerald. *The Theory and Practice of Autonomy*. New York: Cambridge University Press, 1988.

Dworkin, Ronald. *Taking Rights Seriously*. Cambridge, Mass.: Harvard University Press, 1978.

Eaton, Marcia M. *Merit, Aesthetic and Ethical*. New York: Oxford University Press, 2001.

Ellis, Anthony. "Recent Work on Punishment." *Philosophical Quarterly* 45, no. 179 (April 1995): 225–33.

Estlund, David. "Liberalism, Equality, and Fraternity in Cohen's Critique of Rawls." *Journal of Political Philosophy* 6, no. 1 (1998): 99–112.

Evan, William M., and R. Edward Freeman. "A Stakeholder Theory of the Modern Corporation: Kantian Capitalism." In *Ethical Theory and Business*, 4th ed., edited by Tom L. Beauchamp and Norman E. Bowie, 97–106. Upper Saddle River, N.J.: Prentice Hall, 1993.

Feather, Norman T. *Values, Achievement, and Justice: Studies in the Psychology of Deservingness*. New York: Kluwer Academic, 1999.

Feinberg, Joel. *Doing and Deserving*. Princeton, N.J.: Princeton University Press, 1970.

———. *Social Philosophy*. Englewood Cliffs, N.J.: Prentice Hall, 1973.

Feldman, Fred. "Desert: Reconsideration of Some Received Wisdom." *Mind* 104, no. 413 (January 1995): 63–77.

Fishkin, James S., and Peter Laslett, eds. *Debating Deliberative Democracy*. Malden, Mass.: Blackwell Publishing, 2003.

Flanagan, Owen. "Admirable Immorality and Admirable Imperfection." *Journal of Philosophy* 83 (1986): 41–60.

Folger, Robert. "Rethinking Equity Theory: A Referent Cognitions Model." In *Justice in Social Relations*, edited by Hans Werner Bierhoff, Ronald L. Cohen, and Jerald Greenberg, 145–62. New York: Plenum, 1986.

Foot, Philippa. *Virtues and Vices and Other Essays in Moral Philosophy*. Oxford, UK: Blackwell, 1978.

Frankfurt, Harry. *The Importance of What We Care About*. New York: Cambridge University Press, 1988.

Frederick, Robert, ed. *A Companion to Business Ethics*. Malden, Mass.: Blackwell, 1999.

Freeman, R. Edward. "The Politics of Stakeholder Theory: Some Future Directions." *Business Ethics Quarterly* 4, no. 4 (1994): 409–21.

———. "A Stakeholder Theory of the Modern Corporation." In *Perspectives in Business Ethics*, edited by L. P. Hartman. New York: McGraw-Hill, 2002.

———. *Strategic Management: A Stakeholder Approach*. Boston: Pitman, 1984.

Freeman, R. Edward, and William M. Evan. "Corporate Governance: A Stakeholder Interpretation." *Journal of Behavioral Economics* 19, no. 4 (1990): 337–59.

Freeman, Samuel, ed. *The Cambridge Companion to Rawls*. New York: Cambridge University Press, 2003.

———. *Justice and the Social Contract: Essays on Rawlsian Political Philosophy*. New York: Oxford University Press, 2007.

———. *Social Philosophy*. Englewood Cliffs: Prentice Hall, 1973.

French, Peter A. *Corporate Ethics*. Fort Worth, Tex.: Harcourt Brace, 1995.

Friedman, Milton. "The Social Responsibility of Business Is to Increase Its Profits." *New York Times Magazine*, 13 September 1970, 122–25.

Galston, William. *Justice and the Human Good*. Chicago: University of Chicago Press, 1980.

Garrouste, Pierre, and Stéphane Saussier. "Looking for a Theory of the Firm: Future Challenges." *Journal of Economic Behavior and Organization* 58, no. 2 (2005): 178–99.

Gaus, Gerald F. *Justificatory Liberalism: An Essay on Epistemology and Political Theory*. New York: Oxford University Press, 1996.

———. *Value and Justification: The Foundations of Liberal Theory*. New York: Cambridge University Press, 1990.

Gauthier, David. *Morals by Agreement*. Oxford, UK: Clarendon Press, 1986.

———. "Public Reason." *Social Philosophy and Policy* 12 (1995): 19–42.

Gert, Bernard. *Common Morality: Deciding What to Do*. New York: Oxford University Press, 2004.

———. *Morality: Its Nature and Justification*. New York: Oxford University Press, 2005.

Gewirth, Alan. *Human Rights: Essays on Justification and Applications*. Chicago: University of Chicago Press, 1982.

Goldman, Robert. *Gauguin*. New York: Harry N. Abrams, 1957.

Goodpaster, Kenneth. "Business Ethics and Stakeholder Analysis." *Business Ethics Quarterly* 1, no. 1 (1991): 53–73.

———. *Conscience and Corporate Culture*. Malden, Mass.: Blackwell, 2007.

Goodpaster, Kenneth, and John Matthews. "Can a Corporation Have a Conscience?" *Harvard Business Review* 60, no. 1 (1982): 132–41.

Gough, J. W. *The Social Contract*. Oxford, UK: Clarendon Press, 1957.

Greenberg, Jerald, and Russell Cropanzano. *Advances in Organizational Justice*. Stanford, Calif.: Stanford University Press, 2001.

Gustafson, Andrew. "Utilitarianism and Business Ethics." In *Ethical Issues in Business: A Philosophical Approach*, edited by Thomas Donaldson, Patricia Werhane, and Joseph Van Zandt. Upper Saddle River, N.J.: Prentice Hall, 2008.

Guyer, Paul. *Kant and the Experience of Freedom*. New York: Cambridge University Press, 1996.

Habermas, Jürgen. *Between Facts and Norms: Contributions to a Discourse Theory of Law and Democracy*, translated by William Rehg. Cambridge, Mass.: MIT Press, 1996.

———. *Communication and the Evolution of Society*, translated by Thomas McCarthy. Boston: Beacon Press, 1984.

———. *Justification and Application: Remarks on Discourse Ethics*, translated by Ciaran Cronin. Cambridge, Mass.: MIT Press, 1993.

———. "Law and Morality." *Tanner Lectures on Human Values* 8 (1988): 217–79.

———. *Legitimation Crisis*, translated by Thomas McCarthy. Boston: Beacon, 1975.

———. *Moral Consciousness and Communicative Action*, translated by Christian Lenhardt and Shierry Weber Nicholsen. Cambridge, Mass.: MIT Press, 1990.

———. "The New Obscurity: The Crisis of the Welfare State and the Exhaustion of Utopian Energies." In *The New Conservatism*, translated by Shierry Weber Nicholsen. Cambridge, Mass.: MIT Press, 1989.

———. "On the Cognitive Content of Morality." *Proceedings of the Aristotelian Society* 96 (1996): 331–37.

———. "Reconciliation on the Public Use of Reason: Remarks on John Rawls' Political Liberalism," *Journal of Philosophy* 92, no. 3 (1995): 109–31.

———. *The Theory of Communicative Action*. Vol. 2, *Lifeworld and System: A Critique of Functionalist Reason*, translated by Thomas McCarthy. Boston: Beacon Press, 1987.

Hampshire, Stuart. "A New Philosophy of the Just Society." *New York Review of Books*, 24 February 1972, 34–39.

Hampton, Jean. "Contract and Consent." In *A Companion to Contemporary Political Philosophy,* edited by Robert E. Goodin and Philip Pettit, 379–93. Oxford, UK: Blackwell, 1993.

———. *Hobbes and the Social Contract Tradition*. New York: Cambridge University Press, 1986.

———. *Political Philosophy*. Boulder, Colo.: Westview Press, 1997.

Hare, R. M. *Essays in Ethical Theory*. New York: Oxford University Press, 1989.

Harman, Gilbert. "No Character or Personality." *Business Ethics Quarterly* 13, no. 1 (2003): 87–94.

Hartman, Edwin M. "Moral Philosophy, Political Philosophy, and Organizational Ethics: A Response to Phillips and Margolis." *Business Ethics Quarterly* 11, no. 4 (2001): 643–87.

———. *Organizational Ethics and the Good Life*. New York: Oxford University Press, 1996.

Hartman, Laura P., William Shaw, and Rodney Stevenson. "Exploring the Ethics and Economics of Global Labor Standards: A Challenge to Integrated Social Contract Theory." *Business Ethics Quarterly* 13 (2003): 193–220.

Hartman, Laura P., Richard Wokutch, and J. Lawrence French. "Adidas-Salomon: Child Labor and Health and Safety Initiatives in Vietnam and Brazil." In *Rising above Sweatshops: Innovative Approaches to Global Labor Challenges*, edited by Laura Hartman, Denis Arnold, and Richard Wokutch, 191–248. Westport: Praeger, 2003.

Hausman, Daniel, and Michael McPherson. *Economic Analysis, Moral Philosophy, and Public Policy.* 2nd ed. New York: Cambridge University Press, 2006.

Heath, Joseph. "Business Ethics without Stakeholders." *Business Ethics Quarterly* 16, no. 4 (2006): 533–57.

Hendry, John. "Missing the Target: Normative Stakeholder Theory and the Corporate Governance Debate." *Business Ethics Quarterly* 11, no. 1 (2001): 159–76.

Heneman, Robert L. *Merit Pay: Linking Pay Increases to Performance Ratings* (Reading, Mass.: Addison-Wesley, 1992).

Herman, Barbara. *The Practice of Moral Judgment.* Cambridge, Mass.: Harvard University Press, 1996.

Hessen, Robert. *In Defense of the Corporation.* Stanford, Calif.: Hoover, 1979.

Hill, Thomas. *Dignity and Practical Reason in Kant's Moral Theory.* Ithaca, N.Y.: Cornell University Press, 1992.

Holtman, Sarah. "Three Strategies for Theorizing about Justice." *American Philosophical Quarterly* 40 (2003): 77–90.

Hooker, Brad, and Margaret Little, eds. *Moral Particularism.* New York: Oxford University Press, 2001.

Horvath, Charles. "Excellence v. Effectiveness: MacIntyre's Critique of Business." *Business Ethics Quarterly* 5, no. 3 (1995): 499–532.

Hsieh, Nien-hê. "Justice in Production." *Journal of Political Philosophy*, forthcoming.

———. "Managers, Workers, and Authority." *Journal of Business Ethics* 71, no. 4 (2007): 347–57.

———. "The Obligations of Transnational Corporations: Rawlsian Justice and the Duty of Assistance." *Business Ethics Quarterly* 14 (2004): 643–61.

———. "Property Rights in Crisis: Managers and Rescue." In *Ethics and the Pharmaceutical Industry in the Twenty-First Century*, edited by Michael Santoro and Thomas Gorrie, 379–85. New York: Cambridge University Press, 2005.

———. "Rawlsian Justice and Workplace Republicanism." *Social Theory and Practice* 31, no. 1 (2005): 115–42.

Hurka, Thomas. "Desert: Individualistic and Holistic." In *Desert and Justice*, edited by Serena Olsaretti, 45–68. Oxford, UK: Clarendon Press, 2003.

Husted, Brian. "A Critique of the Empirical Methods of Integrative Social Contracts Theory." *Journal of Business Ethics* 20 (1999): 227–35.

Inoue, Tatsuo. "Liberal Democracy and Asian Orientalism." In *The East Asian Challenge for Human Rights*, edited by Joanne R. Bauer and Daniel A. Bell, 27–59. New York: Cambridge University Press, 1999.

Jackall, Robert. *Moral Mazes.* New York: Oxford University Press, 1988.

Jensen, Michael C. "Value Maximization, Stakeholder Theory, and the Corporate Objective Function." *Business Ethics Quarterly* 12, no. 2 (April 2002): 235–56.

Johnson, Mark. *Moral Imagination: Implications of Cognitive Science for Ethics.* Chicago: University of Chicago Press, 1993.

Jones, Thomas. "Instrumental Stakeholder Theory: A Synthesis of Ethics and Economics." *Academy of Management Review* 20, no. 2 (1995): 404–37.

Jones, Thomas, and Andrew Wicks. "Convergent Stakeholder Theory." *Academy of Management Review* 24, no. 2 (1999): 206–21.

Kagan, Shelly. *Normative Ethics.* Boulder, Colo.: Westview, 1997.

Kant, Immanuel. *Groundwork of the Metaphysics of Morals*, edited by Mary Gregor. New York: Cambridge University Press, 1998.

——. *Metaphysics of Morals*, edited by Mary Gregor. New York: Cambridge University Press, 1996.

Keeley, Michael. *A Social-Contract Theory of Organizations.* Notre Dame, Ind.: University of Notre Dame Press, 1988.

Kekes, John. *The Morality of Pluralism.* Princeton, N.J.: Princeton University Press, 1993.

Kirzner, Israel. *Competition and Entrepreneurship.* Chicago: University of Chicago Press, 1973.

Klein, S. "Is a Moral Organization Possible?" *Business and Professional Ethics Journal* 7, no. 1 (1988): 51–73.

Kleinig, John. "The Concept of Desert." *American Philosophical Quarterly* 8, no. 1 (January 1971): 71–78.

Koehn, Daryl. "A Role for Virtue Ethics in the Analysis of Business Practice." *Business Ethics Quarterly* 5, no. 3 (1995): 531–39.

——. "The Role of Virtue Ethics in the Analysis of Business Practice." Paper presented at the annual conference of the Society for Business Ethics, Atlanta, Georgia, 1993.

——. "Virtue Ethics, the Firm and Moral Psychology." *Business Ethics Quarterly* 8, no. 3 (1998): 497–513.

Krouse, Richard, and Michael McPherson. "Capitalism, 'Property-Owning Democracy' and the Welfare State." In *Democracy and the Welfare State*, edited by Amy Gutmann, 81–105. Princeton, N.J.: Princeton University Press, 1988.

Kymlicka, Will. *Contemporary Political Philosophy.* 2nd ed. New York: Oxford University Press, 2002.

——. "The Social Contract Tradition." In *A Companion to Ethics,* edited by Peter Singer, 186–204. Oxford, UK: Basil Blackwell, 1991.

Lake, Christopher. *Equality and Responsibility.* New York: Oxford University Press, 2001.

Lamont, Julian. "The Concept of Desert in Distributive Justice." *Philosophical Quarterly* 44, no. 174 (January 1994): 45–64.

Larmore, Charles. *Patterns of Moral Complexity.* New York: Cambridge University Press, 1987.

Lessnoff, Michael. *Social Contract.* London: Macmillan, 1986.

Levinson, Jerrold, ed. *Aesthetics and Ethics: Essays at the Intersection.* New York: Cambridge University Press, 1998.

Lomasky, Loren. *Persons, Rights, and the Moral Community.* New York: Oxford University Press, 1987.

Lucas, J. R. *On Justice.* Oxford, UK: Clarendon Press, 1980.

——. *Responsibility*. Oxford, UK: Clarendon Press, 1993.

Machan, Tibor R. *Business Ethics in the Global Market*. Stanford, Calif.: Hoover, 1999.

——. *Commerce and Morality*. Totowa, N.J.: Rowman & Littlefield, 1988.

MacIntyre, Alasdair. *After Virtue*. 2nd ed. London: Duckworth, 1985.

——. "Against Utilitarianism." In *Aims in Education*, edited by S. Wiseman, 1–23. Manchester, UK: University of Manchester Press, 1964.

——. "Corporate Modernity and Moral Judgment: Are They Mutually Exclusive?" In *Ethics and Problems of the Twenty-First Century*, edited by Kenneth Goodpaster and K. Sayre, 122–33. Notre Dame, Ind.: University of Notre Dame Press, 1979.

——. *Marxism and Christianity*. London: Duckworth, 1995.

——. "A Partial Response to My Critics." In *After MacIntyre*, edited by J. Horton and S. Mendus, 282–304. Cambridge, UK: Polity Press, 1994.

——. "Social Structures and Their Threats to Moral Agency." *Philosophy* 7, no. 4 (1999): 311–29.

——. Utilitarianism and Cost Benefit Analysis." In *Values in the Electric Power Industry*, edited by K. Sayre, 217–37. Notre Dame, Ind.: University of Notre Dame Press, 1977.

Mackie, J. L. *Ethics: Inventing Right and Wrong*. New York: Penguin, 1977.

Maitland, Ian. "The Human Face of Self-Interest." *Journal of Business Ethics* 38, no. 1 (June 2002): 3–17.

——. "Priceless Goods: How Should Life-Saving Drugs Be Priced?" *Business Ethics Quarterly* 12, no. 4 (2002): 451–80.

——. "Rights in the Workplace: A Nozickian Argument." *Journal of Business Ethics* 8, no. 12 (December 1989): 951–54.

March, James, and Herbert Simon. *Organizations*. 2nd ed. Oxford, UK: Blackwell, 1993.

Marens, R. "Burying the Past: The Neglected Legacy of Business Ethics from the Postwar Years." Paper presented at the Society for Business Ethics Annual Meeting, August 2006.

Margolis, Joshua D., and Robert A. Phillips. "Toward an Ethics of Organizations." *Business Ethics Quarterly* 9, no. 4 (1999): 619–38.

Maugham, W. Somerset. *The Moon and Sixpence*. London: Heinemann, 1919.

May, Larry, Marilyn Friedman, and Andy Clark, eds. *Mind and Morals: Essays on Cognitive Science and Ethics*. Cambridge, Mass.: MIT Press, 1996.

Mayer, Don, and Anita Cava. "Social Contract Theory and Gender Discrimination." *Business Ethics Quarterly* 5 (1995): 257–70.

McCarthy, Thomas. *Ideals and Illusions: On Reconstruction and Deconstruction in Contemporary Critical Theory*. Cambridge, Mass.: MIT Press, 1991.

——. "Legitimacy and Diversity: Dialectical Reflections on Analytical Distinctions," *Cardozo Law Review* 17, nos. 4–5 (March 1996): 1083–1125.

McClelland, J. S. *A History of Western Political Thought*. London: Routledge, 1996.

McKeever, Sean, and Michael Ridge. *Principled Ethics: Generalism as a Regulative Ideal*. New York: Oxford University Press, 2006.

McLeod, Owen. "Desert and Wages." *Utilitas* 8, no. 2 (July 1996): 205–21.

McMahon, Christopher. *Authority and Democracy: A General Theory of Government and Management*. Princeton, N.J.: Princeton University Press, 1994.

——. "The Political Theory of Organizations and Business Ethics." *Philosophy and Public Affairs* 24 (1995): 292–313.

——. "Why There Is No Issue between Rawls and Habermas." *Journal of Philosophy* 99, no. 3 (2002): 111–29.

McNaughton, David. *Moral Vision: An Introduction to Ethics*. New York: Basil Blackwell, 1988.

Melden, A. I. *Rights and Persons*. Berkeley: University of California Press, 1977.

Michael, Michael L. "Business Ethics: The Law of Rules." *Business Ethics Quarterly* 16, no. 4 (2006): 475–504.

Michaelman, Frank. "Rawls on Constitutionalism and Constitutional Law." In *The Cambridge Companion to Rawls*, edited by Samuel Freeman. New York: Cambridge University Press, 2003.

Milkovich, George T., and Jerry M. Newman. *Compensation*. 7th ed. New York: McGraw-Hill, 2002.

Mill, John Stuart. *Utilitarianism*, edited by Roger Crisp. New York: Oxford University Press, 1998.

Miller, David. "Deserving Jobs." *Philosophical Quarterly* 42, no. 167 (April 1992): 161–81.

——. *Market, State, and Community: Theoretical Foundations of Market Socialism*. Oxford, UK: Clarendon Press, 1989.

——. *Principles of Social Justice*. Cambridge, Mass.: Harvard University Press, 1999.

——. *Social Justice*. New York: Oxford University Press, 1976.

Moberg, Dennis. "Management as Judges in Employee Disputes: An Occasion for Moral Imagination." *Business Ethics Quarterly* 13, no. 4 (2003): 454–77.

Moore, Geoff. "Corporate Character: Modern Virtue Ethics and the Virtuous Corporation." *Business Ethics Quarterly* 15, no. 4 (2005): 659–85.

——. "Humanizing Business: A Modern Virtue Ethics Approach." *Business Ethics Quarterly* 15, no. 2 (2005): 237–55.

——. "On the Implications of the Practice-Institution Distinction: MacIntyre and the Application of Modern Virtue Ethics to Business." *Business Ethics Quarterly* 12, no. 1 (2002): 19–32.

Moore, Geoff, and R. Beadle. "In Search of Organizational Virtue in Business: Agents, Goods, Practices, Institutions and Environments." *Organization Studies* 27, no. 3 (2006): 369–89.

Morgan, Gareth. *Images of Organization*. Thousand Oaks, Calif.: Sage, 1997.

Moriarty, Jeffrey. "Desert." In *Encyclopedia of Business Ethics and Society*, edited by Robert W. Kolb. Thousand Oaks, Calif.: Sage, forthcoming.

——. "The Epistemological Argument against Desert." *Utilitas* 17, no. 2 (July 2005): 205–21.

——. "On the Relevance of Political Philosophy to Business Ethics." *Business Ethics Quarterly* 15, no. 3 (July 2005): 453–71.

Morse, J. "The Missing Link between Virtue Theory and Business Ethics." *Journal of Applied Philosophy* 16, no. 1 (1999): 47–58.

Moser, Paul K. *Philosophy after Objectivity: Making Sense in Perspective.* New York: Oxford University Press, 1993.

Nagel, Thomas. *Equality and Partiality.* New York: Oxford University Press, 1991.

———. "Rawls and Liberalism." In *The Cambridge Companion to Rawls*, edited by Samuel Freeman, 62–85. New York: Cambridge University Press, 2003.

Narveson, Jan. "Democracy and Economic Rights." *Social Philosophy and Policy* 9 (1992): 29–61.

———. "Deserving Profits." In *Profits and Morality*, edited by Robin Cowan and Mario J. Rizzo, 48–87. Chicago: University of Chicago Press, 1995.

Nelson, R., and S. Gopalan. "Do Organizational Cultures Replicate National Cultures? Isomorphism, Rejection and Reciprocal Opposition in the Corporate Values of Three Countries." *Organization Studies* 24, no. 7 (2003): 1115–51.

Nozick, Robert. *Anarchy, State, and Utopia.* New York: Basic, 1974.

Nussbaum, Martha. *The Fragility of Goodness.* New York: Cambridge University Press, 1986.

———. *Love's Knowledge: Essays on Philosophy and Literature.* New York: Oxford University Press, 1990.

———. "Rawls and Feminism." In *The Cambridge Companion to Rawls*, edited by Samuel Freeman, 62–85. New York: Cambridge University Press, 2003.

———. *Women and Human Development.* New York: Cambridge University Press, 2001.

Olsaretti, Serena. "Distributive Justice and Compensatory Desert." In *Desert and Justice*, edited by Serena Olsaretti, 187–204. Oxford, UK: Clarendon Press, 2003.

Olson, Mancur. *The Logic of Collective Action.* Cambridge, Mass.: Harvard University Press, 1965.

O'Neill, Onora. "Agents of Justice." In *Global Justice*, edited by Thomas Pogge, 188–202. Oxford, UK: Blackwell, 2001.

———. *Bounds of Justice.* New York: Cambridge University Press, 2000.

———. *Towards Justice and Virtue: A Constructive Account of Practical Reasoning.* New York: Cambridge University Press, 1996.

Orlitzky, Marc, Frank Schmidt, and Sara Rynes. "Corporate Social and Financial Performance: A Meta-analysis." *Organization Studies* 24, no. 3 (2003): 403–41.

Pateman, Carole. *Participation and Democratic Theory.* New York: Cambridge University Press, 1970.

Peffer, Rodney. "Towards a More Adequate Rawlsian Theory of Social Justice." *Pacific Philosophical Quarterly* 75, no. 3–4 (1994): 251–71.

Petersen, Verner C. *Beyond Rules in Society and Business.* Northampton, UK: Edward Elgar, 2002.

Pettit, Philip. *Republicanism: A Theory of Freedom and Government.* New York: Oxford University Press, 1997.

Phillips, Robert A. *Stakeholder Theory and Organizational Ethics.* San Francisco: Berrett-Koehler, 2003.

Phillips, Robert A., and Joshua D. Margolis. "Toward an Ethics of Organizations." *Business Ethics Quarterly* 9, no. 4 (October 1999): 619–38.

Plato. *The Republic*. Harmondsworth, UK: Penguin, 1982.

Pogge, Thomas. "On the Site of Distributive Justice: Reflections on Cohen and Murphy." *Philosophy and Public Affairs* 29, no. 2 (2000): 137–69.

——. *Realizing Rawls*. Ithaca, N.Y.: Cornell University Press, 1989.

Pojman, Louis P. "Does Equality Trump Desert?" In *What Do We Deserve? A Reader on Justice and Desert*, edited by Louis P. Pojman and Owen McLeod, 283–97. New York: Oxford University Press, 1999.

Porter, J. *The Recovery of Virtue*. London: SPCK, 1994.

Qing, Dai, and Lawrence R. Sullivan. "The Three Gorges Dam and China's Energy Dilemma." *Journal of International Affairs* 53, no. 1 (Fall 1999): 56–57.

Rachels, James. *Can Ethics Provide Answers?* Lanham, Md.: Rowman & Littlefield, 1997.

——. *The Elements of Moral Philosophy*. 2nd ed. New York: McGraw-Hill, 1993.

Rajan, Raghuram, and Luigi Zingales. "Power in a Theory of the Firm." *Quarterly Journal of Economics* 113, no. 2 (1998): 387–432.

Rawls, John. *Justice as Fairness: A Restatement*, edited by Erin Kelly. Cambridge, Mass.: Harvard University Press, 2001.

——. *The Law of Peoples*. Cambridge, Mass.: Harvard University Press, 2001.

——. "Legal Obligation and the Duty of Fair Play." In *Law and Philosophy*, edited by Sidney Hook. New York: New York University Press, 1964.

——. *Political Liberalism*. New York: Columbia University Press, 1993.

——. "Political Liberalism: A Reply to Habermas." *Journal of Philosophy* 92, no. 3 (1995), 132–80.

——. *A Theory of Justice*, rev. ed. Cambridge, Mass.: Harvard University Press, 1999. First published 1971 by Oxford University Press.

——. "Two Concepts of Rules." *Philosophical Review* 64, no. 1 (1955): 3–32.

Raz, Joseph, ed. *Authority*. New York: New York University Press, 1990.

——. *The Morality of Freedom*. Oxford, UK: Clarendon Press, 1986.

Reder, M. W., "Chicago School." In *The New Palgrave Dictionary of Political Economy*, edited by John Eatwell, Peter Newman, and Murray Milgate. London: MacMillan, 1987.

Reed, Darryl. "Stakeholder Management Theory: A Critical Theory Perspective," *Business Ethics Quarterly* 9, no. 3 (1999): 453–83.

——. "Three Realms of Corporate Social Responsibility: Distinguishing Legitimacy, Morality, and Ethics," *Journal of Business Ethics* 21, no. 1 (1999): 23–53.

Rehg, William. *Insight and Solidarity: The Discourse Ethics of Jürgen Habermas*. Berkeley: University of California Press, 1994.

Richardson, Henry S. "Specifying Norms as a Way to Resolve Concrete Ethical Problems." *Philosophy and Public Affairs* 19 (1990): 279–310.

Riley, Patrick. *Will and Political Legitimacy: A Critical Exposition of Social Contract Theory in Hobbes, Locke, Rousseau, Kant, and Hegel*. Cambridge, Mass.: Harvard University Press, 1982.

Roe, Mark J. *Political Determinants of Corporate Governance: Political Context, Corporate Impact*. New York: Oxford University Press, 2003.

Roemer, John E. *Equality of Opportunity*. Cambridge, Mass.: Harvard University Press, 1998.

Rosenberg, Alexander. "On the Priority of Intellectual Property Rights, Especially in Biotechnology." *Politics, Philosophy & Economics* 3, no. 1 (2004): 77–95.

Rosenthal, Sandra, and Rogene Bucholz. "Toward New Directions in Business Ethics: Some Pragmatic Pathways." In *A Companion to Business Ethics*, edited by Robert Frederick, 112–27. Malden, Mass.: Blackwell, 1999.

Ross, W. D. *The Right and the Good*. Indianapolis, Ind.: Hackett, 1988.

Rowan, John R. "How Binding the Ties? Business Ethics as Integrative Social Contracts." *Business Ethics Quarterly* 11 (2001): 379–90.

Sagoff, Mark. "Do Non-Native Species Threaten the Environment?" *Journal of Agricultural and Environmental Ethics* 18 (2005): 215–36.

Sandel, Michael J. *Liberalism and the Limits of Justice*, 2nd ed. New York: Cambridge University Press, 1998.

Scanlon, Thomas. "Contractualism and Utilitarianism." In *Utilitarianism and Beyond*, edited by Amartya Sen and Bernard Williams, 103–28. New York: Cambridge University Press, 1982.

——. *What We Owe to Each Other*. Cambridge, Mass.: Harvard University Press, 1998.

Scheffler, Samuel. "Responsibility, Reactive Attitudes, and Liberalism in Philosophy and Politics." *Philosophy and Public Affairs* 21, no. 4 (Autumn 1992): 299–323.

Scherer, Andreas, and Guido Palazzo. "Toward a Political Conception of Corporate Social Responsibility: Business and Society Seen from a Habermasian Perspective." *Academy of Management Review* 32, no. 4 (2007): 1096–1120.

Scherer, Andreas, Guido Palazzo, and Dorothée Baumann. "Global Rules and Private Actors: Toward a New Role of the Transnational Corporation in Global Governance." *Business Ethics Quarterly* 16, no. 4 (2006): 505–32.

Schmidtz, David. "How to Deserve." *Political Theory* 30, no. 6 (December 2002): 774–99.

Schwartz, Judith. "Meaningful Work." *Ethics* 92, no. 4 (July 1982): 634–46.

Schweikart, David. "Should Rawls Be a Socialist? A Comparison of His Ideal Capitalism with Worker-Controlled Socialism." *Social Theory and Practice* 5, no. 1 (1978): 1–27.

Sen, Amartya. "East and West: The Reach of Reason." *New York Review of Books*, 20 July 2000, 33–38.

——. "Human Rights and Asian Values." In *Business Ethics in the Global Marketplace*, edited by Tibor Machan, 37–62. Stanford, Calif.: Hoover, 1999.

——. "Well-Being, Agency and Freedom: The Dewey Lectures 1984." *Journal of Philosophy* 82, no. 4 (April 1985): 169–221.

Sher, George. *Beyond Neutrality*. New York: Cambridge University Press, 1997.

——. *Desert*. Princeton, N.J.: Princeton University Press, 1987.

Shue, Henry. *Basic Rights: Subsistence, Affluence, and U.S. Foreign Policy*. 2nd ed. Princeton, N.J.: Princeton University Press, 1996.

Sidgwick, Henry. *The Methods of Ethics.* 7th ed. Indianapolis, Ind.: Hackett, 1981.

Skinner, Quentin. *Liberty before Liberalism.* New York: Cambridge University Press, 1998.

Slote, Michael. *Goods and Virtues.* Oxford, UK: Clarendon Press, 1983.

Smilansky, Saul. "Responsibility and Desert: Defending the Connection." *Mind* 105, no. 417 (January 1996): 157–63.

Smith, Adam. *The Wealth of Nations.* New York: Modern Library, 2000.

Smith, Jeffery. "Moral Markets and Moral Managers Revisited." *Journal of Business Ethics* 61 (2005): 129–41.

——. "A Précis of a Communicative Theory of the Firm." *Business Ethics: A European Review* 13, no. 4 (2004): 317–31.

Sollars, Gordon. "The Corporation as Actual Agreement." *Business Ethics Quarterly* 12, no. 3 (2002): 351–71.

Solomon, Robert. "Aristotle, Ethics and Business Organizations." *Organization Studies* 25, no. 6 (2004): 1021–43.

——. *A Better Way to Think about Business. How Personal Integrity Leads to Corporate Success.* New York: Oxford University Press, 1999.

——. "Business Ethics." In *A Companion to Ethics*, edited by Peter Singer, 354–65. Malden, Mass.: Blackwell, 1991.

——. "Business with Virtue: Maybe Next Year?" *Business Ethics Quarterly* 10, no. 1 (2000): 339–41.

——. "Corporate Roles, Personal Virtues: An Aristotelean Approach to Business Ethics." *Business Ethics Quarterly* 2, no. 3 (1992): 317–39.

——. *Ethics and Excellence: Cooperation and Integrity in Business.* New York: Oxford University Press, 1992.

——. *It's Good Business: Ethics and Free Enterprise for the New Millennium.* Lanham, Md.: Rowman & Littlefield, 1997.

——. "Victims of Circumstances? A Defense of Virtue Ethics in Business." *Business Ethics Quarterly* 13, no. 1 (2003): 43–62.

Soltan, Karol. *The Causal Theory of Justice.* Berkeley: University of California Press, 1987.

Sorrell, Tom. *Moral Theory and Anomaly.* Malden, Mass.: Blackwell, 2000.

Soule, Edward. "Managerial Moral Strategies: In Search of a Few Good Principles." *Academy of Management Review* 27 (2002): 114–24.

——. *Morality and Markets: The Ethics of Government Regulation.* Lanham, Md.: Rowman & Littlefield, 2003.

Suri, Manik. "A River in Peril: The Waters Rise at Three Gorges." *Harvard International Review* 25, no. 3 (Fall 2003): 10–11.

Swanton, C. *Virtue Ethics: A Pluralistic View.* New York: Oxford University Press, 2003.

Sweetman, David. *Paul Gauguin: A Complete Life.* London: Hodder and Stoughton, 1995.

Tan, Kok-Chor. "Justice and Personal Pursuits." *Journal of Philosophy* 101, no. 7 (2004): 331–62.

Taylor, Mark C. *Confidence Games: Money and Markets in a World without Redemption.* Chicago: University of Chicago Press, 2004.

Temkin, Larry. *Inequality*. New York: Oxford University Press, 1993.

Timmons, Mark. *Moral Theory: An Introduction*. Lanham, Md.: Rowman & Littlefield, 2002.

Treiman, Donald J., and Heidi I. Hartmann, eds. *Women, Work, and Wages: Equal Pay for Jobs of Equal Value*. Washington, D.C.: National Academy Press, 1981.

Van Oosterhout, J., Pursey M. A. R. Heugens, and Muel Kaptein. "The Internal Morality of Contracting: Advancing the Contractualist Endeavor in Business Ethics." *Academy of Management Review* 31, no. 3 (2006): 521–39.

Vargos Llosa, M. *The Way to Paradise*, translated by N. Wimmer. New York: Farrar, Straus & Giroux, 2003.

Walker, Margaret Urban. "Where Do Moral Theories Come From?" *Philosophical Forum* 26 (1995): 242–57.

Wall, Steven. "Perfectionism in Politics: A Defense." In *Contemporary Debates in Political Philosophy*, edited by John Christman and Thomas Christiano. New York: Blackwell, forthcoming.

Waluchow, Wil. "Pay Equity: Equal Value to Whom?" *Journal of Business Ethics* 7, no. 3 (March 1988): 185–89.

Walzer, Michael. *Spheres of Justice*. New York: Basic, 1983.

Wasserstrom, Richard. "A Defense of Programs of Preferential Treatment." *National Forum* 58, no. 1 (Winter 1978): 15–18.

Weaver, Gary. "Virtue in Organizations: Moral Agencies as a Foundation for Moral Agency." *Organization Studies* 27, no. 3 (2006): 341–68.

Webber, J. "Virtue, Character and Situation." *Journal of Moral Philosophy* 3, no. 2 (2006): 193–213.

Wempe, Ben. "In Defense of a Self-Disciplined, Domain-Specific Social Contract Theory of Business Ethics." *Business Ethics Quarterly* 15, no. 1 (2005): 113–35.

———. "On the Use of the Social Contract Model in Business Ethics." *Business Ethics: A European Review* 13, no. 4 (2004): 332–41.

Werhane, Patricia. *Adam Smith and His Legacy for Modern Capitalism*. New York: Oxford University Press, 1991.

———. *Moral Imagination and Management Decision-Making*. New York: Oxford University Press, 1999.

———. *Persons, Rights, and Corporations*. Englewood Cliffs, N.J.: Prentice Hall, 1985.

White, S. *The Civic Minimum: On the Rights and Obligations of Economic Citizenship*. New York: Oxford University Press, 2003.

Williams, Andrew. "Incentives, Inequality, and Publicity." *Philosophy and Public Affairs* 27, no. 3 (1998): 225–47.

Williams, Bernard. *Ethics and the Limits of Philosophy*. Cambridge, Mass.: Harvard University Press, 1985.

———. *Making Sense of Humanity and Other Philosophical Papers, 1982–1993*. New York: Cambridge University Press, 1995.

———. *Moral Luck*. New York: Cambridge University Press, 1981.

Williamson, Oliver E. *The Economic Institutions of Capitalism*. New York: Free Press, 1985.

———. "The Theory of the Firm as Governance Structure: From Choice to Contract." *Journal of Economic Perspectives* 16, no. 3 (2002): 171–95.

Wolff, Jonathan. "The Dilemma of Desert." In *Desert and Justice*, edited by Serena Olsaretti, 219–32. Oxford, UK: Clarendon Press, 2003.

Woodmansee, Martha. *The Author, Art, and the Market: Rereading the History of Aesthetics*. New York: Columbia University Press, 1994.

Young, Iris M. *Justice and the Politics of Difference*. Princeton, N.J.: Princeton University Press, 1990.

———. "Self-determination as Principle of Justice." *Philosophical Forum* 11 (Fall 1979): 30–46.

———. "Taking the Basic Structure Seriously." *Perspectives on Politics* 4, no. 1 (2006): 91–97.

Young, Robert. "Egalitarianism and Personal Desert." *Ethics* 102, no. 2 (January 1992): 319–41.

About the Contributors

Denis G. Arnold is the Surtman Distinguished Scholar in Business Ethics at the University of North Carolina, Charlotte. Previously he was associate professor in the Department of Philosophy and director of the Center for Applied and Professional Ethics at the University of Tennessee, Knoxville. His research focuses on ethical issues in international business and the pharmaceutical industry, as well as moral and political philosophy. He has published articles on topics such as sweatshops, human rights, coercion, and global capitalism that have appeared in *Business Ethics Quarterly*, *Journal of Business Ethics*, *American Philosophical Quarterly*, and *Human Rights Quarterly*, among other journals. He is the author of *The Ethics of Global Business* (2009, Blackwell) and coeditor of *Rising above Sweatshops: Innovative Approaches to Global Labor Challenges* (2003, Praeger) and *Ethical Theory and Business*, 8th ed. (forthcoming, Pearson-Prentice Hall). He received his PhD in 1997 from the University of Minnesota and is a past fellow of the National Endowment for the Humanities.

Norman E. Bowie is the Elmer L. Andersen Chair in Corporate Responsibility at the University of Minnesota's Carlson School of Management. His books include *Business Ethics: A Kantian Perspective* (1999), *Guide to Business Ethics* (edited; 2002), and *Management Ethics* (2005). His coedited text, *Ethical Theory and Business*, is in its eighth edition. Professor Bowie has published numerous articles in business ethics and political philosophy. He currently serves as associate editor of *Business Ethics Quarterly*. Professor Bowie has taught at the London Business School, has been a fellow in Harvard's Program in Ethics and the Professions, and is past executive director of the American Philosophical Association and past president of the Society for Business Ethics.

Mitchell R. Haney is assistant professor in the Department of Philosophy at the University of North Florida. He is also a senior fellow in the Blue-Cross/BlueShield of Florida Center for Ethics, Public Policy, and the Professions. In addition to numerous presentations in the United States and abroad, Professor Haney has published in the areas of epistemology, metaethics, and normative ethics, as well as business ethics. He received his PhD in moral philosophy from the University of Memphis.

Nien-hê Hsieh is currently associate professor in the Department of Legal Studies and Business Ethics at the Wharton School, University of Pennsylvania, with a secondary appointment in the Department of Philosophy. His research is in politics, ethics, and economics. He has published articles on topics such as Rawls's theory of justice, the moral responsibilities of multinational corporations, and incommensurable values; they have appeared in *Business Ethics Quarterly*, *Economics and Philosophy*, *Journal of Political Philosophy*, and *Philosophy and Public Affairs*, among other journals. Professor Hsieh has been a visiting research fellow at Australian National University, Oxford University, and Harvard University. He received his PhD in 2000 from Harvard University.

Alexei Marcoux is associate professor in the Graduate School of Business at Loyola University Chicago. He has published a series of respected articles on stakeholder theory in *Business Ethics Quarterly* and is now focusing his research on foundational questions in business ethics. His work in this area has appeared in the *Journal of Markets and Morality* and the *Journal of Private Enterprise* and has been presented at institutions such as Santa Clara University and the University of Illinois. Professor Marcoux has been a resident scholar at the Social Philosophy and Policy Center (2004) and Liberty Fund, Inc. (2008). He received his PhD in 2001 from Bowling Green State University.

Christopher Michaelson is assistant professor in the Opus College of Business at the University of St. Thomas (Minnesota) and a business advisor specializing in corporate responsibility and risk management with a global professional services firm. His recent publications explore meaningful work and business ethics through the work of such artists as Paul Gauguin, Philip Glass, Spike Lee, and Leo Tolstoy and in the context of such global threats as terrorism and climate change. Professor Michaelson received his PhD in 1997 from the University of Minnesota.

Geoff Moore is professor of business ethics in Durham Business School, Durham University, UK. His research includes work in the area of virtue theory and the Fair Trade movement. His papers have appeared in *Business Ethics Quarterly*, *Organizational Studies*, and *Journal of Business Ethics*. Professor Moore is a past chairman of the European Business Ethics Network (UK) and is on the editorial boards of *Business Ethics Quarterly*, *Journal of Business Ethics*, and *Business Ethics: A European Review.*

Jeffrey Moriarty is assistant professor in the Department of Philosophy at Bowling Green State University. His research interests lie at the intersection of political philosophy and business ethics. He is especially interested in questions of distributive justice as they arise in state and organizational contexts. Professor Moriarty's publications on these topics have appeared in journals such as *Business Ethics Quarterly*, *Journal of Business Ethics*, *Noûs*, and *Utilitas*. He received his PhD in 2002 from Rutgers University.

Jeffery Smith is associate professor and director of the Banta Center for Business, Ethics, and Society at the University of Redlands. His broad research interests lie at the intersection of moral and political philosophy with management. His work has focused on communicative ethics, the role of principles in moral judgment, and the relationship of market norms to other moral values. His articles have appeared in the *Journal of Business Ethics*; *Business Ethics: A European Review*; *Southern Journal of Philosophy; Business Ethics Quarterly*; and other journals. In 2008 he served as visiting professor in the Department of Philosophy at the Universiteit van Tilburg. He received his PhD from the University of Minnesota.

Ben Wempe is associate professor in the Business and Society Program at Erasmus University in Rotterdam. He completed his PhD in political theory at the University of Leiden after studying at the European University Institute in Florence. His publications in the areas of freedom and contractarian thought have appeared in *Business Ethics Quarterly*, *Journal of Business Ethics*, and *Organization Studies*. His book titled *T. H. Green's Theory of Positive Freedom* was published in 2004. He served as president of the International Association of Business and Society in 2008–2009.